International Business Mergers and Acquisitions in Japan

Ralf Bebenroth

International Business Mergers and Acquisitions in Japan

Springer

Ralf Bebenroth
Kobe University
Research Institute for Economics
& Business Administration (RIEB)
Kobe, Hyogo
Japan

ISBN 978-4-431-54988-8 ISBN 978-4-431-54989-5 (eBook)
DOI 10.1007/978-4-431-54989-5

Library of Congress Control Number: 2015934139

Springer Tokyo Heidelberg New York Dordrecht London

Printed on acid-free paper

Springer is part of Springer Science+Business Media (www.springer.com)

Preface

This book is about mergers and acquisitions (M&A) in Japan and contains 15 chapters, which can be split into three major parts. First, international business topics; second, M&A; and third, human resources in M&A processes. Most of the chapters have been developed steadily over the years while teaching the topic of mergers and acquisitions. Not only did I teach this subject at Kobe University, my home university, but also at Konan University for 8 consecutive years and at Ritsumeikan University for 4 consecutive years. I was also a guest lecturer at several other Japanese and foreign universities such as Doshisha, Tuebingen, Hamburg, and Kassel universities.

This book is written for everyone interested in M&A and Japan, especially for students. The targeted audience is Japan interested business students at the master's level. English-speaking Japanese students should also find this book useful. Recently, there has been an increase in English-speaking business classes at Japanese universities. It is my hope that some M&A classes can be created in which this book serves as the basis for the curriculum.

Several people helped me to successfully prepare and finish the book. I want to express my gratitude to Prof. Shinobe Muramatsu (Emeritus Professor at Seikei University, Tokyo) who touched me with his kindness for over 13 years. He is not only passionate about M&A but also has supported me in my research over the years. I would also like to thank William Wainwright, one of my previous students at Konan University, for a very careful proofreading. I would also like to thank Lara Makowsky, my research assistant and master's student in the SESAMI program at Kobe University, who amended some of my English sentences, and Nakahara Sho, a Ph.D. candidate at the graduate school of business at Kobe University, for finding literature and correcting the spelling of some of the translated Japanese literature. I would also like to thank my friend Ian Mackenzie for correcting one chapter and Keith Jackson for giving me guidance in the early stages of the book.

This book is dedicated to my wife, Tomoko, and our daughter, Aiko chan. Without their patience, support, and encouragement this book would not have existed.

The author hopes that this book will find its intended readers.

Kobe, November 11, 2014 Ralf Bebenroth

Contents

About the Author

Ralf Bebenroth was born and raised in Kassel, Germany. After graduating from compulsory high school he completed a three-year internship (*Ausbildung*) as a locksmith. After that experience, he returned to school with aspirations for business school. Bebenroth enrolled in the program of business administration at the University of Kassel and received his Ph.D. in March 2001.

From April 2001 to March 2003 he was awarded a postdoctoral fellowship by DAAD (*Monkasho*) at the Tokyo Institute of Technology and conducted research about the integration period of mergers and acquisitions. From July 2003 to May 2005 he was again awarded a two-year post-doctoral fellowship, this time by the Humboldt Foundation (JSPS) to research corporate governance issues at the Osaka University of Economics.

In May 2005 Bebenroth became an associate professor at Kobe University in the Institute for Economics and Business Administration. He taught all classes at the faculty in Japanese for the next 5 consecutive years. In 2009 he moved to a tenured position as associate professor at Kobe University and from September 2012 he was appointed as a full professor. His primary interest is in cross-border issues of mergers and acquisitions.

Chapter 1
Introduction

Abstract This book deals with international business, in particular the Japanese mergers and acquisitions market. The main objective of the book is to investigate the structure of Japanese firms and the recent changes in a globalized M&A market. The whole book is divided into 15 chapters. The book starts with general issues of trade (Chaps. 2 and 3) and distribution issues (Chaps. 4 and 5). Chapters 6 to 11 deal with M&A and relevant issues for investments. The last four Chaps. (12 to 15) deal with the human side of things. Chapter 12, specifically, deals with a framework of organizational identification while Chap. 13 is an empirical piece. Chapter 14 discusses culture, and Chap. 15 discusses human resources, especially those who are expatriates in Japan.

This book deals with international business, in particular the Japanese mergers and acquisitions market. It will be shown how business in Japan has recently become more international. In this vein, to Japan as an island nation, international business (IB) is an important issue. About 100 years ago, the Japanese emperor himself founded three universities for learning how to conduct business and trade with foreigners. One of those universities is Kobe University, where this book was written. Since the 1980s, the economic strength of Japanese exports has been apparent. However, Japan has the image of being relatively closed to firms coming into the country to conduct business. Therefore, this book looks at the inner structures of the Japanese business system.

The Chap. 2 discusses foreign direct investment (FDI) in terms of Japan. Capital flows will be split into outflows and inflows. Outflows occur when Japanese buy foreign stock or invest money to join or even establish a subsidiary in another country. Inflows occur when foreigners buy Japanese stocks or when foreigners invest in a Japanese firm via FDI. That means a foreign firm either establishes a greenfield or takes over a Japanese firm. Another way of FDI inflow is by forming joint ventures, which frequently takes place in Japan. As Eleanor Westney stated: "No discussion of Japan and the IB field would be complete without some attention to Japan as a host country for FDI" (2009, p. 638). This book will be taking care of these suggestions.

R. Bebenroth, *International Business Mergers and Acquisitions in Japan*,
DOI 10.1007/978-4-431-54989-5_1

The third chapter deals with imports, exports, and foreign firms' investment in Japan especially on the micro level. Most foreign FDI is in the Tokyo area while the Kansai area is the second most popular destination. Therefore, instead of focusing on just investments in the Kanto area, investments in the Kansai area will also be highlighted. In addition, foreign-affiliated firms doing business in Japan will be presented using JETRO surveys. At the end of Chap. 3, some examples of success stories of foreign-affiliated firms located mainly in the Kansai region will be given.

The fourth chapter aims to provide insight into the Japanese distribution system and in its recent developments in the retail market. A previous version of the fourth chapter was published under Bebenroth (2011). Historically, Westerners used to criticize the Japanese market as being a closed system with high barriers to entry. Recent changes to the distribution system and retail market will be shown as well as some success stories of foreign apparel makers in Japan.

Complexities in the Japanese distribution system will be discussed in Chap. 5. This empirical chapter examines how institutional barriers to entry as well as channel adjustments of foreign firms affect their market involvement in Japan. A similar publication appeared as Bebenroth et al. (2014). It will be shown that investments in greater "Japanese market accessibility" and a higher "quality business network relationship" help firms to become more successful in the Japanese market.

The following chapters, starting with Chap. 6, focus specifically on M&A. Chapter 6 is about "setting the stage for M&A" and focuses on M&A in general. Developments of the shareholder structures and theories that explain why M&A occurs will be discussed.

Chapter 7 focuses primarily on Japanese M&A, stating developments as well as examples of acquisitions. This chapter also discusses financially driven institutional investors by contrasting them with strategically driven bidder firms. Financially driven investors undertake their purchases merely for financial reasons. The first example presented of a strategic takeover is the acquisition of Nycomed by the Japanese pharmaceutical maker Takeda. The second example discusses Daikin's acquisition of Goodman, an air-conditioning firm from the USA.

Chapter 8 focuses on a comparison between foreign bidders and Japanese bidders aiming to take over Japanese firms. This empirically oriented chapter has been published in a similar fashion in Bebenroth (2010).

Chapter 9 focuses on unfriendly takeovers. Based on theories that explain unfriendly acquisitions, the developments of Japanese unfriendly takeovers will be presented. This chapter also gives two examples. The first is Panasonic's acquisition of Sanyo and the second is Steel Partner's unsuccessful takeover of Noritz Kitchen, a Kobe-based firm. The last part of Chap. 9 discusses defense measures. These measures are known in M&A literature as poison pills, measures that can be taken by a potential target firm to prevent being taken over. These poison pills have been especially popular in Japan recently.

Chapter 10 deals with valuation of target firms and market concentration. It will be shown how a target firm's price can be estimated. The second part of the chapter discusses market concentration. Especially in bigger acquisitions, a firm might become too strong compared with its competitors and restrains competition. In this case, the Fair Trade Commission would prohibit the deal.

Chapter 11 is an empirical chapter that deals primarily with institutional investors. Equity stake purchases by institutional investors are phenomena that have become increasingly common in Japan. There is an investigation of how the post-acquisition performance of target firms differs depending on whether the deal is domestic or cross-border and whether it is friendly or unfriendly. A previous version of this chapter was published in Bebenroth and Kshetri (2013). Two contrasting concepts are applied: the arms-length principle and the geographic proximity theory. Results partly confirm that unfriendly Japanese-equity-stake-purchased firms performed better right after the deal. Also, the performance was significantly higher for firms that were equity-stake purchased by foreign institutional investors as compared with domestic investors. Against better theoretical arguments, the number of employees after the purchase decreased significantly for friendly attempts but increased for cross-border and unfriendly ones.

Chapter 12 proposes a theoretical framework of organizational identification of target employees in cross-border M&A. Three areas will be discussed: communication, training, and consulting. Against arguments from the literature that target employees will automatically identify less with the new firm, it will be shown using Japan as an example that this is not automatically true. Whether or not employees of a target firm identify less with their new firm depends on certain characteristics. It matters, for example, whether employees are in regularly employed positions or not. Non-regular employees might even see some advantages in their organizational identification with a strategically driven foreign-bidder firm. Younger regular employees might see an acquisition also as a chance for them to be promoted. The new firm might be able to more effectively use their talents after becoming bigger and more international.

Chapter 13 is an empirical piece and sheds light on the perception of Japanese target firm employees after being taken over by a German firm. How target firm employees' perceptions of procedural justice and their cultural intelligence influenced job satisfaction and organizational identification was tested. It was found that the perceived procedural justice leads to higher levels of job satisfaction. Also, more fairly treated employees show a better organizational identification. Finally, fair treatment matters more to job satisfaction when employees' cultural sensitivity is higher.

The last two Chaps. (14 and 15) deal with culture. Chapter 14 discusses differences in national cultures in order to gain an understanding of their impacts. When managers do not understand cultural differences, especially in the case of the Japanese culture, it may have a disastrous impact. Therefore, culture is defined using the seven dimensions of the most influential study undertaken by Hofstede and are reported and interpreted in the case of Japan. In addition, the GLOBE project and the cultural dimensions by Trompenaars are discussed.

Chapter 15 examines firms and their human resources and focuses especially on the management by expatriates. Questions raised are, "Should headquarters send its 'own' expatriates to a foreign-based subsidiary?" or "Is it better to rely on local executives?" Expatriation issues are discussed all over the world. For Japan, however, expatriates have to be discussed in a special light due to the fact that the management style of the firms in Japan is very different to that of Western countries. Chapter 15 focuses especially on the Japanese human resource context. For this, expatriation is described in more detail and contrasted against other alternatives.

References

Bebenroth R (2010) Inbound M & A to Japan: cherry picking versus rescue mission? Kobe Econ Bus Rev 54:1–16

Bebenroth R (2011) Ryūtsū kakumei: the Japanese distribution revolution. In: Mann A (ed) Herausforderungen der internationalen marktorientierten Unternehmensführung. Gabler Verlag, pp 525–536

Bebenroth R, Kshetri N (2013) Post-acquisition performance of Japanese firms: domestic vs. cross-border equity stake purchases. J Knowl Glob 6(1):1–22

Bebenroth R, Kshetri N, Huenerberg R (2014) Foreign firms' access to the Japanese market. Eur J Int Manag 8(1):1–19

Westney E (2009) Japan. In: Rugman AM (ed) The Oxford International Business. 2nd edn. Oxford University Press

Part I
Trade and Distribution

Chapter 2
Japan and Foreign Direct Investment

Abstract This chapter covers the historical economic developments of Japan and discusses recent FDI investment flows. It will be shown that Japan has a relatively low inward, but a high outward FDI. Furthermore, some data from World Investment Report about M&A will be presented. Finally, trade agreements are shortly discussed.

2.1 Introduction

The Japanese government, like any other government considers the export of products and services as a very helpful tool as it brings a money inflow into the country. In accordance to governmental initiatives, export supports an increased economic growth of a country and leads to an increase in productivity. In addition, there is a higher diversification and export supports the pace of innovation, which leads to an improved survival prospect of firms. Furthermore, employment opportunities and salaries of the employees may increase.

Recently, the Japanese government pays also increased attention; not only to exports but also to higher inward foreign direct investment (inward FDI). All country governments in the world highly appreciate potential economic benefits through inward FDI. The reason for this is that inward FDI leads to many positive economic effects for local firms as well as to consumers. Consumers enjoy lower prices and inward FDI leads to more job-creation in the local economy (Fleming and Johnson 2008). Also, Japanese officials highly appreciate foreign direct investment coming to Japan; therefore, the Japanese government has launched a number of political measures to promote inward FDI. Former Prime Minister Junichiro Koizumi promised several years ago in his general policy speech to the Diet in 2003 to double the cumulative amount of inward FDI until 2008 (Paprzycki and Fukao 2005). Even if the program failed in absolute terms, an increase of FDI to Japan was visible. The largest part of this increase in inward FDI has been realized through M&As (Schaede 2008, p. 117). However, the inward FDI to Japan by total numbers is still low. Japan had only 5 % inward FDI stock compared to the USA in 2012 and a relatively low inward FDI compared to other leading world economies (Table 2.1).

R. Bebenroth, *International Business Mergers and Acquisitions in Japan*,
DOI 10.1007/978-4-431-54989-5_2

Table 2.1 Inward FDI into Japan. (Source: JETRO (2014)

Year	Amount ($ mil.)	Year	Amount ($ mil.)
1983	416	1999	12,308
1984	−10	2000	8226
1985	642	2001	6191
1986	226	2002	9089
1987	1165	2003	6238
1988	−485	2004	7808
1989	−1054	2005	3223
1990	1753	2006	−6789
1991	1368	2007	22,181
1992	2728	2008	24,550
1993	86	2009	11,839
1994	888	2010	−1359
1995	40	2011	−1702
1996	208	2012	1761
1997	3199	2013	2358
1998	3269		

This led the Ministry of Economy, Trade and Industry (METI) to propose amendments back in the year 2007 and several changes were implemented. For example, Japanese regulations were harmonized with other leading countries in order to improve inward FDI to Japan. In spite of relatively small Japanese inward FDI figures, recently the number of inbound M&A transactions in Japan has increased.

The first part of this chapter shows the history of inward FDI in Japan, examining how attractive the country was (and still is) in receiving FDI. The second part discusses the outflow of Japanese FDI in contrast to other countries. The third part discusses trade agreements and then the groundwork for M&A is to be laid out.

2.2 History of Inward FDI to Japan

Records indicate that Chinese immigrants from an area called Qin introduced a wide variety of new techniques to the Japanese archipelago such as weaving and rice cultivation at a time between 221–207 B.C. (Qin dynasty) and 206 B.C.–220 A.D. (Han dynasty) (Burns 2000). These Chinese cultural influences were naturally filtered through Korea. Between the fifth and tenth centuries A.D., the Sino–Japanese relationship are said to have blossomed. Economic ties expanded, bringing Chinese influence to a broad spectrum of spheres, naturally also economic ones (Burns 2000).

Sui dynasty (581–618 A.D.) and Tang dynasty (618–907 A.D.) served as models for Japan. Most significant among these were the introduction of Buddhism and Confucianism. The adaptation of the Chinese writing system, and the proliferation of Chinese arts and crafts implemented Chinese influence. Under Japan's Yamato period (300–710 A.D.), Prince Shotoku (574–622 A.D.) propagated Buddhism, while another important Japanese figure at that time, Nakatomi-no-Kamatari (614–669 A.D.), instituted the Taika Reforms. In this, Chinese political institutions and policies were adopted, as well as tax and land policies, including nationalization and equalization of landholdings. Most significantly, China's example inspired Japan to establish a fixed capital city, first at Nara in 710 A.D., and later at Kyoto in 794 A.D (Bruns 2000). In that, the streets of both cities, Nara and Kyoto were built in a chess board style based on the previous ancient capital city of Xian in China (Matsubara 1987). Evidence is also found that already at these times neighboring Asian countries had connected their businesses of ceramics and silk production with the Japanese archipelago (Matsubara 1987).

Years later in early 1600s, the Ieyasu Shogunate managed to establish trade agreements with the Korean Peninsula as well as to other Asian countries; although an agreement with China could not be fixed. This enabled Portuguese firms to control the entire Japanese silk trade with China. Therefore, if a Japanese firm wanted to buy silk from a Chinese firm, they would need to go through a Portuguese intermediary in Macao. Because Japanese firms were not allowed to directly trade with China at that time, intermediary traders made a high profits (Matsubara 1987).

Operations of foreign businesses of the western world in Japan dates back to the sixteenth century, when traders from the Netherlands, Portugal and England established connection points for their East Asian trading network (Boxer 1968; Weinstein 1996). These trade connections were abolished by the Ieyasu Shogunate in the early seventeenth century. Japanese traders with close contacts and shipments to most Asian countries reported to the Shogunate what was happening, for example to the natives at Macao. First, Portuguese catholic "patres" converted the natives at Macao to their belief system by teaching them Christianity, but then as a second wave the Portuguese military came to conquer Macao to establish a Portuguese colony (Matsubara 1987). As a result, at the beginning of the seventeenth century the military leaders of Japan, the Shogunate, decided to close the country off from the foreign world. All Christian padres were banished from the Japanese archipelago and even the converted Japanese believers were persecuted by the Japanese Shogunate. For the next 250 years, no foreigners were able to access the Japanese islands, nor were Japanese permitted to stay abroad. Those going abroad had to repatriate themselves to Japan within 2 years, those who failed to return within 2 years were punished by death. Only a small settlement of Dutch traders was allowed to conduct trade with Japan. This settlement called "Dejima" was placed on a manmade island in front of Nagasaki, on the southern Island of Kyushu (Matsubara 1987).

The arrival of Commodore Perry in 1854 with his "black ships" ("kuro fune") brought the subsequent economic re-opening of trade with Japan. Western foreign firms established bases at by then open ports for foreigners e.g. at Nagasaki, Kobe, Yokohama, Hakodate. In this, countries showed different preferences for their port of entry. Chinese firms predominantly entered Japan through Nagasaki on the southern island of Kyushu. Russian firms arrived in the northern island of Hokkaido, at the port of Hakodate. US and European firms arrived mainly at the two remaining open ports. While US firms mainly entered Japan at the eastern part of the peninsula at the port of Yokohama, close to Tokyo, European firms arrived at Kobe port, which is located in the Kansai region. In the heart of Kobe, in the "old settlement", Western firms undertook business. Even today, the city of Kobe is still European flavored with many European style coffee houses and bakeries.

It is to mention that in the years around the eighteenth century every Asian country dealing with the West was forced to accept Western treaties. For Example, Japanese firms dealing with foreign firms were forced to apply European or US country laws in a case of a dispute, giving Japanese firms disadvantages. That led to the so called "unequal treaties" ("ansei keiyaku"). Potential business related problems with foreigners were dealt with using foreign law, instead of applying Japanese law (Auslin 2004). Furthermore, an advantage given to one foreign firm was—upon request—transferable to any other country`s firm. Firms also received a standard low tariff rate of 5 % for all imported goods, whereas Japanese firms had to pay much higher tariffs when exporting their products to Western countries (Matsubara 1987). This situation continued until the end of the nineteenth century, when Japanese firms finally regained full control of their trade activities with the outside world (Westney 2009).

Before the opening of Japan in 1854, some Japanese families had already managed to form strong ties and build their own business empires, resulting in only a few firms ruling entire industries (Morikawa 1992). These conglomerates, known as Zaibatsu, became a famous buzzword (Morikawa 1992). These family controlled businesses were known as financial clique firms. Zaibatsu were not common to the Western world until World War I, even though they existed in Japan from the nineteenth century. By definition, Zaibatsu are large family controlled firms, vertical in structure. These Zaibatsu covered all major industries such as mining, steel, trade and banking. Just a handful of these Zaibatsu controlled large parts of the whole country.

The "big four Zaibatsu" consisted of Mitsui (the biggest), Sumitomo, Mitsubishi and Yasuda. These four Zaibatsu controlled more than half of the whole Japanese industry at that time. In the aftermath of the Second World War, Western occupational forces destroyed the Zaibatsu structure by dividing them into separate firms in order to prevent the reemergence of a strong Japanese war industry. The biggest Zaibatsu Mitsui, for example was split in more than 100 independent firms (Westney 2009).

Despite the dominance of Zaibatsu firms, foreign firms managed to exist in Japan. There is evidence that in the prewar era, 59 foreign affiliated firms were located and successfully operated their business in Japan. Out of them, 13 firms were wholly owned and managed by foreigners and 36 were run as a joint venture managed by Japanese (Yamamura 1986; Westney 2009).

After eliminating the unequal treaties, Japanese authorities set heavy FDI inward controls on foreign firms dealing with Japan. One of the few ways for foreign firms to enter Japan before the 1960s was to set up a "yen" company, which was not allowed to repatriate their profits out of the country (Westney 2009).

The 1960 GATT negotiations let to a removal of these investment restrictions set by the Japanese government. The easier access to the Japanese market through not only FDI, but also by acquisitions was appreciated by western firms. In contrast, several Japanese firms saw this as a threat and joined into cross-shareholdings, in which firms would interchangeably hold each other's shares. This was seen as the beginning of protection against takeovers and interestingly, happened to become the so called "first Japanese merger wave", where firms like Nippon Steel were created (Muramatsu 2007).

In the years after World War II, the Japanese economy grew at a high rate. In these economic boom years, Japan was known as a strong exporting country. It was also the time where Japan catapulted into the second biggest economy. Other countries were interested to learn from the Japanese miracle, e.g. about the concept of lifetime employment, or the closely knit groups, called keiretsu. Japan became economically so dominant that other countries, especially the US, worried about the health of their own firms. 1985 under the Plaza Agreement, the strong dollar was balanced through intervention by advanced industrialized nations. This led to a strengthened yen what made Japanese exports more difficult. Put different, the Plaza Agreement led to a sharp appreciation of the yen to the US dollar. From Sept. 1985 to 1988, the value of the yen jumped from 260 to 125 yen per dollar (Adams and Gangnes 1996). This enormous price disadvantage caused difficulties for Japanese firms to export their products not only to the US but also to any other foreign country as the exchange currency was always handled in US dollars. Japanese firms experienced a high pressure what challenged once more life time employment (Moriguchi and Ono 2006). However, the Japanese economy bottomed up by the end of 1986 and saw a quick recovery (to the surprise not only of Japanese citizens). This economic recovery was stabilized by a low interest rate policy of the Bank of Japan to stabilize the economy. These low interest rates led firms to aggressively invest in land and in the stock markets. This development was encouraged by the appreciation of land and of stock prices. This upward spiral ended in 1989 with the so-called bubble economy (Noguchi 1994).

Outsiders saw the Japanese industry as a highly connected establishment. The term "keiretsu," which means to have interconnected firms, became a famous catchphrase. One of the ways that these firms connected themselves was (and still is today) the so called "shacho kai" in which the leaders of all connected firms meet once a month to discuss relevant issues and ideas. Keiretsu structures of Japanese firms were the study object of many researchers worldwide in the late 80s. Toyota for example was and still is famous for having a vertical Keiretsu structure, meaning there were only a few direct suppliers. These suppliers have other suppliers (2nd rank suppliers for Toyota), which again get supplied by 3rd rank suppliers. Even today this gives Japanese automobile firms advantages against US and European makers because the 2nd and 3rd tier suppliers do not belong to any union. That is to say, Japanese unions are not industry unions, but merely company unions which have different roles than their Western counterparts. Unions try to work out the best for the firm but also for the regular employees as well. Union members often work closely together with the top management, many of them even share the same office (with the top managers). Also a common way for young and promising talents to become a top manager at the firm is to start their career at the (company) unions. Even though unions are not independent of managers, they actively support their employee's interests. Employees at supplier firms, in particular at the 3rd rank have worse income conditions. Under this structure Japanese car makers can better adjust to a changing market because of a higher flexibility in times of crisis, or at economic recessions. As a result, Toyota for example saves money and is more flexible in its strategic movements to successfully compete on a worldwide competitive automobile market.

The difficulty of entering the Japanese market was pronounced repeatedly by foreign firms even at an early stage. In the 1980s, Japan lowered its formal restrictions on FDI inflow to boost new investments to the country. Nevertheless, only a very limited number of firms found its way to Japan. Since then, Japanese argue widely that the lowering of formal barriers to inward FDI as well as formal restrictions on imports and inward investment were more favorable to foreign investment (than in the past). Some examples of successful Japan-based foreign firms already existed in the 1980s. IBM-Japan for example, historically with strong local networks was always a financially successful operating subsidiary. Some other Japan-based foreign affiliates were considered to be the most profitable firms in Japan at that time, especially after the yen appreciation of the mid 1980s (Christopher 1986).

In spite of the lowering of formal restrictions, very few foreign firms came to Japan to set up a business. The list for complains was (and still today is) long. One of these complaints was that foreign firms perceived a successful entry into Japan as very difficult, not because of formal restrictions by law, but, because of informal hindrances caused by other Japanese firms, differences in thought, and even because of the behavior of Japanese people themselves. For example, even though a foreign firm may offer more advanced technology, they still may not be able to compete with a Japanese firm. The reason is that a Japanese firm may have more confidence in another Japanese firm. In other words, even if foreign firms outperform Japanese ones in the technical level, Japanese firms can count on advantages in service, to be close to the customer. That means foreign firms in Japan have to adjust to the Japanese market to be successful in doing business (Bebenroth et al. 2014; Mason 1992).

2.3 Competition for FDI

The modern economy is built on the transfer and exchange of ideas at unprecedented speed. FDI can facilitate this process. Positive effects of FDI are often articulated and it is unquestionable that the market for FDI is competitive worldwide. This also includes inward FDI. Every nation attempts to attract advanced foreign technologies to transfer them to their own firms. FDI in terms of technology diffusion can lead to direct or indirect positive spillover effects. A direct effect for example, could be that foreign firms transfer to Japan and simply absorb (Japanese) employees to work at their affiliates. This would in turn cause more foreigners to come to Japan and spend their incomes in Japan. This, however, is considered as rather of lower importance for many countries' governments. More importantly are the indirect effects of inward FDI (Aitken and Harrison 1999). In other words, the spillover effect may come in the form of higher qualified labor. Besides the direct effect that foreign firms hire Japanese employees, they can indirectly help them in getting a higher qualification in their job. Japanese employees may improve their technological knowledge and may even start their own business to connect foreign firms to Japan. That means, indirect effects can help to internationalize Japan's economy. Without an internationalized economy, there is worry that an increased number of employees need to get subsidized by social welfare, or on the job. Some countries are reported to subsidize their own employees in high tech area with more than US$ 250.000 per year (Blomstroem and Kokko 2003).

It should be noted however, that FDI can also have negative effects on domestic firms (Dunning 1994). For example, FDI could negatively influence domestic producers so that production calms down and operations shut down. It is also possible that the increased competition through a higher inward foreign FDI could crowd out domestic operations. In the worst-case scenario, international competition could completely eliminate the existence of domestic firms. Hence, FDI can also lead to a negative growth by taking out domestic competitors.

2.4 Inward FDI to Japan

FDI activities to Japan were tightly controlled until the 1970s. Since then, almost all Japanese industries were heavily deregulated to open up for an increased inward FDI. The Japanese government is trying to attract inward FDI by protecting property rights and giving investors' security that their technology will not be copied or stolen by domestic firms (Belderbos et al. 2006).

Table 2.1 depicts the inward FDI to Japan on a yearly basis. The amount of FDI to Japan (compared to the year before) was quite low in the years from 1983 until 1996. The only exceptional time period for a higher inward FDI was right after the Japanese bubble economy burst from 1990 to 1992. In these 3 years, a higher inward FDI was absorbed. There are many reasons that the selloff of foreign firms and equity led to a high inbound financial stream. It could be that foreign firms expected Japan to recover quickly and therefore wanted to participate in this development.

From the year of 1998, Japan received more inward FDI with a first peak in 1999 at about $ 12.3 billion. It is clearly visible that the inbound FDI to Japan was negative in 2006 but positive in 2007 and 2008 with US$ 22.1 Billion and US$ 24.5 Billion respectively. From 2007 onwards, Japan has received a steadily increasing amount of FDI until 2009 with a sharp decrease. In the last 2 years of observation, Japan receives $ 1.7 and US$ 2.3 billion respectively.

Table 2.2 depicts the stock of inward FDI coming to Japan. In the year 2012, inward FDI stock was worth only US$ 205 billion, only about 5 % of the level seen

Table 2.2 Inward FDI Stock for years of 1990, 2000 and 2012. (Source: World Investment Report 2013, Annex Table 2.3, (in billion US $ dollars))

FDI inward stocks			
Region/economy	1990	2000	2012
Japan	9	50	205
United States	539	2783	3931
Germany	111	271	716
France	97	390	1094
UK	203	438	1321

in the US. To compare FDI stock in time, there is an increase visible, however. The inward FDI to Japan increased almost fivefold from 1990 to 2000, jumping from about $ 9 billion to about $ 50 billion. Finally, in the year 2012, inward FDI in Japan was worth about US$ 205 billion. However, in contrast to Japan, other countries have a higher inward FDI Stock at all three time periods. In other words, compared to other European countries or to the U.S., Japan receives comparably low inward FDI. The U.S. and the UK receive the largest volumes of FDI.

When looking at yearly changes of inward FDI to Japan, it is visible that the highest inflow was in the 2 years before the Lehman shock, totaling roughly US $ 22 Billion in 2007 and US $ 24.5 Billion in 2008 (Fig. 2.1). As a side note, even though these were the highest volumes of investment ever received it was still far less than that received by the U.S. and the U.K at the same time.

After the financial crises in 2008, Japan experienced a sharp decrease in FDI inflow to the point of negative US$ 1.3 billion in 2010, but has since recovered.

When looking specifically where the investment comes from, it is clearly visible that in both 2007 and 2008, US investments made up the biggest part of FDI inflow to Japan. The sharp decrease in 2010 was caused by FDI from Central and South America. Finally, in the year 2012, European FDI inflow was negative while Asian FDI inflow was positive (Fig. 2.1).

It should be mentioned that one could interpret the information in different ways. Paprzycki and Fukao (2005) for example report that volume of investment differs by industry. According to their study, inbound FDI to Japan is in several areas on par with that of the USA. Applying their figures, inward FDI in the automobile and machinery industry, for example, is high while there is hardly any investment in other industries. Therefore, of a complete lack of investment at some industries, the FDI to Japan is on the whole rather low.

2.4.1 Attractiveness of Japan as An Investment Location

One way of looking at a country's FDI attractiveness is by means of its received investment. Figure 2.2 shows the top 20 countries, which received the highest FDI inflow. USA received the highest FDI investment followed by China and Brazil. In contrast to these countries, France, Indonesia and Sweden, for example, have received a much lower FDI. Japan doesn't even make the list of the top host economies for FDI in 2012 (World Investment Report 2013).

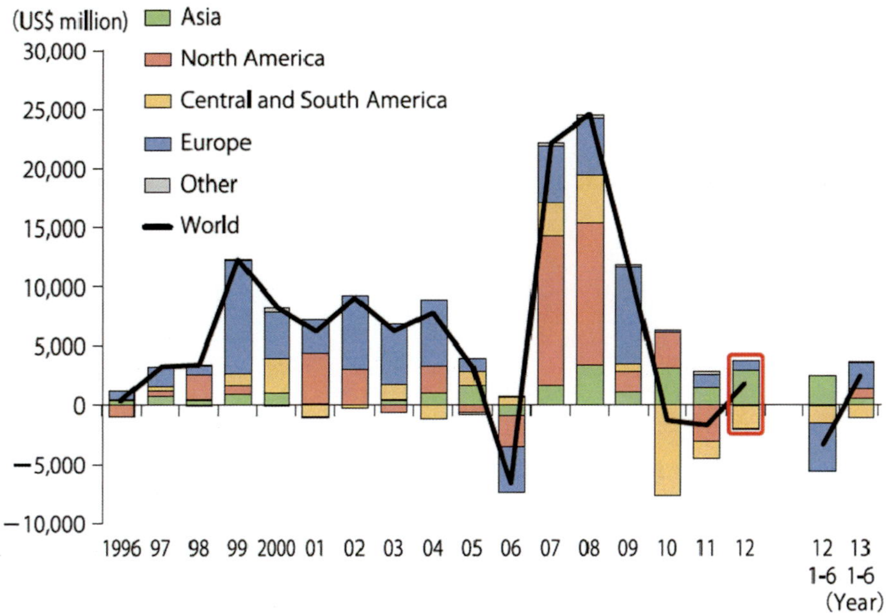

Fig. 2.1 Changes in Japan's Inward FDI by Region. Jetro (2013) Global Trade and Investment Report,. Revitalizing Japan through global business, p. 4. https://www.jetro.go.jp/en/reports/white_paper/trade_invest_2013.pdf, accessed on Febr. 24th 2014. (Note: The yen-based value is converted to dollars by quarter, using the average quarterly Bank of Japan interbank rate, and then the annual total is calculated. Source: Balance of payment statistics, Ministry of Finance, Bank of Japan)

Fig. 2.2 Top host economies for FDI in 2012 (billions of dollars). (Source: World Investment Report 2013, p. XIV)

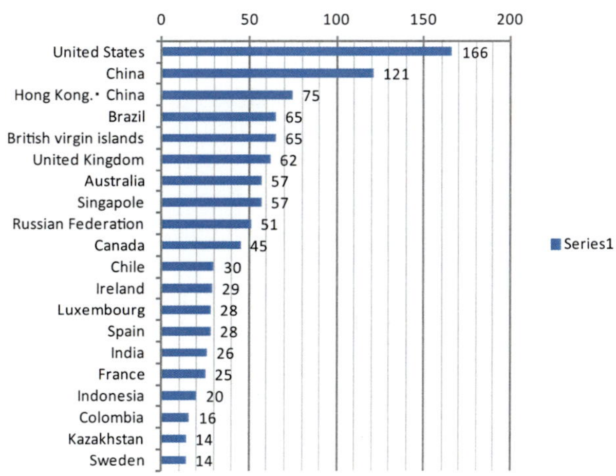

Table 2.3 Number of inward cross-border M&A, 2005–2011. (Source: World Investment Report 2013, p. 221 (in %))

	2005	2006	2007	2008	2009	2010	2011	2012
World	100	100	100	100	100	100	100	100
Developed Economies	76	75	74	72	69	67	45	84
European Union	42	41	39	38	32	33	28	40
France	4	4	3	3	2	3	2	4
Germany	7	7	6	5	4	3	3	2
United Kingdom	10	9	10	10	7	9	6	11
United States	19	18	18	17	17	16	11	21
Japan	1	1	2	2	2	2	1	1

2.4.2 *Japanese Inward M&A*

To compare several countries' cross border inward M&A, Japan receives rather low scores (World Investment Report 2013). For the years from 2005 till the end of 2012, Japanese inward cross border activities remain very scarce. According to UNCTAD data, Japan absorbed little over 100 acquisitions from the years starting in 2007. In contrast to Japan, the U.S. market absorbed about 1000 inward M&A a year until the beginning of the Lehman shock.

In the second year after the Lehman shock in 2010 (especially), the number of inward M&A to the US went down to around 700 to 900 cases a year, respectively. Even some European countries like France and Germany are absorbing more inward cross border M&As than Japan. In the fiscal year of 2012, both countries had a higher M&A inflow than Japan. France, for example, which has a much lower GDP, reported about 4 % M&A cases and Germany was around 2 % inward M&A cases.

To demonstrate the gap between Japan and other developed countries in percentage terms, Japan has an inward cross border activity of only 1 to 2 %. The United States was around 16–19 % until 2010 and again to a volume of about 21 % for the year of 2012 (Table 2.3).

It is to state that also so called Greenfield investments exists. It happens when firms settle down their businesses at other countries without any help of locals that means to establish a business "on the green field". This kind of investment hardly exists in Japan, however (Fukutani and Dobashi 2008, pp. 61–62).

2.5 Outward FDI from Japan

In the year 2012, the worldwide outward FDI from all developed countries rose to a level of $ 1.5 trillion (World Investment Report 2013, p. 32). All three major developed-economies namely the European Union (EU), North America and Japan increased their FDI investments and, therefore, contributed to this stimulation. However, each economy had different driving factors. The United States was driven

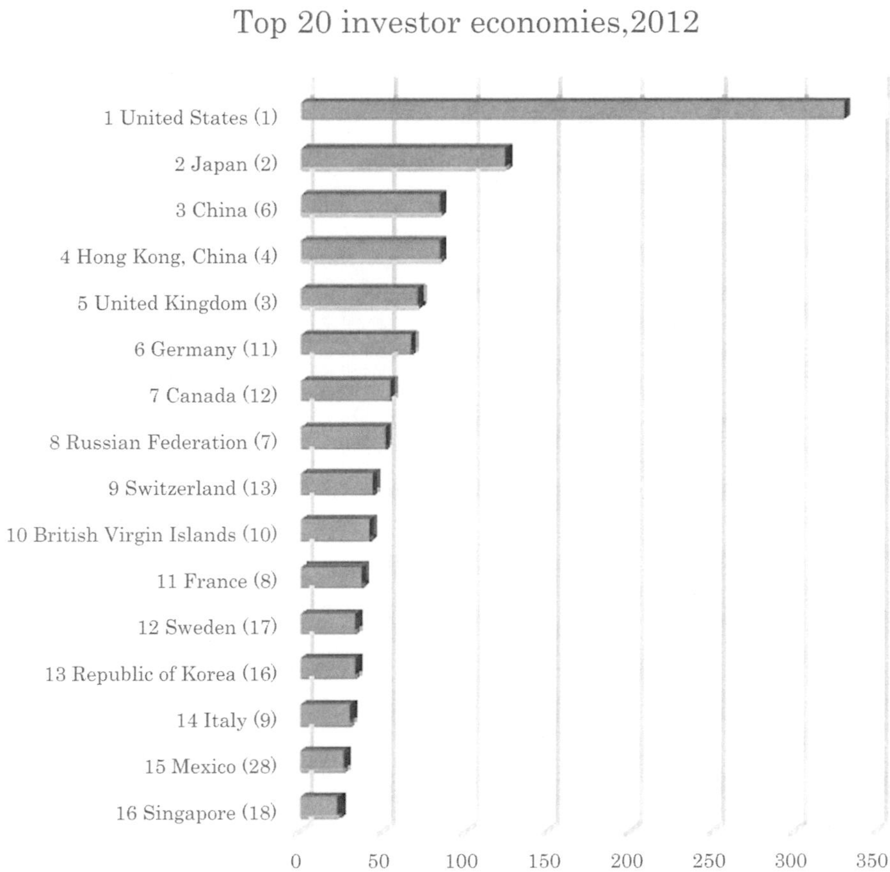

Fig. 2.3 Outflow FDI of several industrialized countries. (Source: World Investment Report 2013, p. 6)

by a record level of reinvested earnings (82 % of total FDI outflows). That means, US MNCs were driven to invest abroad by spending their cash reserves. The rise of outward FDI from the EU, in contrast, was driven by cross-border M&As. That means, in Europe FDI increased because investments in foreign targets accelerated. According to World Investment Report, Japanese firms used the advantage of an appreciating yen, which improved their purchasing power by overtaking foreign firms at other countries. All these circumstances resulted in a doubling of outward FDI in 2011 (World Investment Report 2012, p. XIV) with net M&A purchases in North America and Europe, rising 132 % compared to the year before.

In the year 2012, there was a decreasing cross border M&A market. Also, in 2012, there was a visible shift of M&A to transition economies (World Investment Report 2013, p. X). Considering the outward FDI figures of 2012, the USA is the biggest investor with $ 323 billion. Japan is (also in 2012) the second strongest investor after the US with around US$ 123 billion. China and Hong Kong came third and fourth with each around US$ 84 billion of FDI investment (Fig. 2.3).

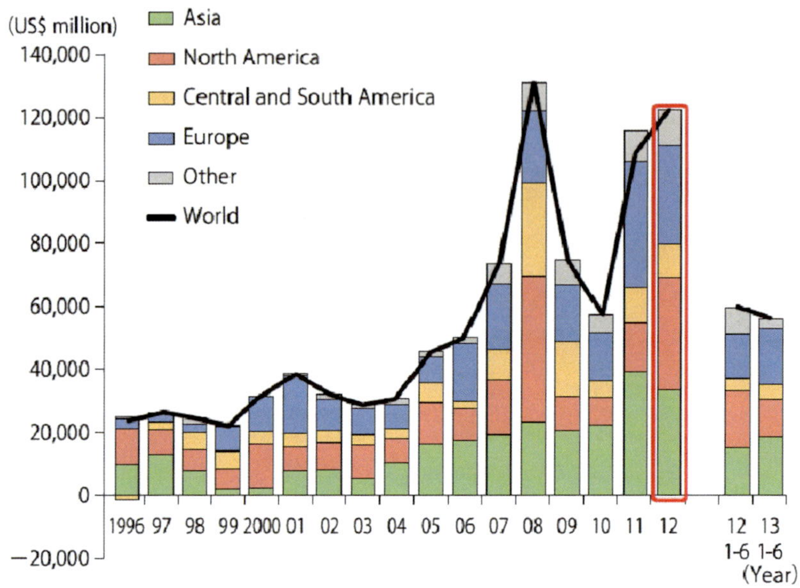

Fig. 2.4 Changes in Japan's outward FDI by region. Jetro (2013) Global Trade and Investment Report. Revitalizing Japan through global business, p. 4. https://www.jetro.go.jp/en/reports/white_paper/trade_invest_2013.pdf, accessed on Febr. 24th 2014. (Note: (1) The yen-based value is converted to dollars by quarter, using the average quarterly Bank of Japan interbank rate, and then the annual total is calculated. (2) Figures for Jan–June 2013 are preliminary. Source: Balance of payment statistics, Ministry of Finance, Bank of Japan)

The most recent figures for Japanese outward FDI are positive. According to World Investment Report of 2012, Japan gains ground again as an investor in the Asian region. That is partly seen as the result of the significant appreciation of the Japanese yen in 2011 and 2012. Hence, Japanese MNCs strengthened their efforts in investing abroad (see also section A.7 of World Investment Report 2012). For undertaking relocation of production plants, Japanese firms chose especially low-cost production locations in South-East Asia. In addition, this came along with the advantage of being close to emerging markets where products are to be sold. In other words, not only does relocating provide a cost advantage for producers it provides the added advantage of being close to emerging markets. Attracted by low labor costs and good growth opportunities, Japanese companies invested heavily in China in 2011. In 2010, the Japanese FDI to China was already at US$ 4 billion (or 4 % of total inflow to China). It went up in 2012 to US$ 6 billion (or 9 % of total inflow). Also countries like Vietnam absorbed $ 1.8 billion Japanese FDI in 2011 (Fig. 2.4).

2.6 Trade Agreements

International Investment Agreements are increasing in popularity worldwide. Already in the year of 2011, there were 47 international investment agreements (IIAs) signed worldwide (World Investment Report 2012, p. 84).

In these, bilateral pacts, regional blocs are created. By the end of 2011, International Investment Agreements dominate regional development of countries and act as forces to enhance dependences on regions. In quantitative terms, bilateral agreements still dominate international investment policies for most countries. However, in terms of economic significance, there has been a gradual, but visible, shift towards increased regionalism. This trend is illustrated by several developments in Asia, but also in Europe and North America.

For Japan, the Trans-Pacific Partnership (TPP) Agreement is of special interest. It will have a great impact for Japan, positive for e.g. car part manufacturers and negative for Japanese farmers (Toda 2014, pp. 1–2). However, until know the Japanese delegation still struggles with the US about Japanese environmental protection of farming and meat products. US President Obama left Tokyo in May 2014 without a positive result, however, it is very possible that Japan will join this important trade agreement. Currently, there are the following 12 negotiating countries at the TPP: US, Japan, Australia, Peru, Malaysia, Vietnam, New Zealand, Chile, Singapore, Canada, Mexico, and Brunei. The agreement is expected to establish a free trade area with high standards for investment liberalization and protection. The combined economic weight of all 12 countries signed amounts to 35 % of global gross domestic product (World Investment Report 2012, p. 85).

Moreover, China, Japan and the Republic of Korea signed a trilateral investment agreement in 2012 with an economic weight not far from that of the North American Free Trade Agreement (World Investment Report 2012, p. 84).

2.7 Conclusion

Like many other countries' governments, recently the Japanese government has appreciated higher inward FDI investment. The competition for FDI is fierce all over the world. For several decades, Japan had a high outward FDI but a relatively low inward FDI. Still in 2011 World Investment Report stated: "Japan is the only country having more than US$ 100 billion in outward FDI stock but only under US$ 1 billion inward FDI stock" (World Investment Report 2012, p. 60). Even if this low inward FDI increased fourfold, the level of inward FDI to Japan is still low. That means, even if Japanese authorities lowered investment restrictions for FDI, only a few foreign firms would invest in Japan.

In contrast to Japan, Western countries, especially the United States are more successful in attracting FDI investments. In recent years, inward FDI to Japan slowed down due to the Lehman Shock (in 2008) but has recovered since then.

The data for Japan show a clear unbalance of relatively low inward FDI and relatively high outward FDI investment. Also, exports from Japan have decreased due to Japanese firms shifting their production to other countries, especially to emerging Asian countries. That means they produce abroad. The world investment report data shows that Japan absorbs a relatively low FDI compared to other major European players or to the USA.

Questions

1. Which century did Japanese archipelago receive strong economic foreign influences?
2. Which influences from ancient history are still visible today in Japanese cities?
3. What was a Zaibatsu?
4. What undertook Japanese firms after GATT negotiations and an opening of markets in order not to fear to get taken over by foreign firms?
5. How much inward FDI stock hold Japan in 2012 compared to the USA?
6. How much differs inward FDI investment into Japan against European countries like France and GB?
7. What makes Japan unattractive to invest in?
8. How is the inbound Cross border M&A activity to Japan compared to the US, UK or to Germany?
9. How strongly do Japanese firms invest abroad in recent years?
10. What are reasons behind the high foreign FDI of Japanese firms?

Answers

1. Japanese archipelago received strong economic influences at around the seventh century mainly from today China.
2. Structures of cities like Nara or Kyoto stemming from previous Chinese Capital Xian are still visible, which were built in a chess format.
3. A Zaibatsu was called a "financial clique", a powerful alignment of Japanese family firms, which controlled a big part of the business at the country. Zaibatsu were destroyed by American laws. That means previous Zaibatsu firms were divided in separate firms.
4. Many Japanese firms went into a cross shareholding system. Holding each other's shares prevented Japanese firms to become a target of any foreign investors.
5. Japan hold about US $ 205 Billion (or 5% of the inward FDI stock compared to the USA) in the year 2012.
6. Much less inward FDI goes to Japan than to other European countries like France and GB. The USA receives the highest inward FDI worldwide.

7. Non-tariff-barriers. Language problems, high labor costs, high costs of market entry and a fierce competition to local Japanese firms.
8. Cross border activity to Japan is lower than at the USA, UK or at Germany.
9. Japanese firms spent around US$ 120 billion (in 2012) as outward FDI. Japan is worldwide the second biggest outward FDI investor, only behind the USA.
10. Reasons behind this strong Japanese outward FDI is that Japanese firms become more globalized. Some firms have a higher turnover abroad than at home. They need to be at the foreign markets to successfully compete against other competitors. Also the strong yen was a good opportunity for some firms to invest by FDI at other countries.

References

Adams FG, Gangnes B (1996) Japan's persistent trade surplus. Policies for adjustment. Jpn World Econ 8:309–333.

Aitken BJ, Harrison AE (1999) Do domestic firms benefit from direct foreign investment? Evidence from Venezuela. Am Econ Rev 89(3):605–618

Auslin MR (2004) Negotiating with imperialism. Harvard University Press, Cambridge

Bebenroth R, Kshetri N, Huenerberg R (2014) Foreign firms' access to the Japanese market. Eur J Int Manage 8(1):1–19

Belderbos R, Fukao K, Kwon HU (2006) Intellectual property rights protection and the location of research and development activities by multinational firms. ICSEAD Kita Kyushu, Working Paper, 2006–2002

Blomstroem M, Kokko A (2003) The economics of foreign direct investment incentives. Stockholm School of Economics. Working Paper. (1) No. 168

Boxer C (1968) Jan Compagnie in Japan 1600–1807: an essay on the cultural, artistic and scientific influence exercised by the hollanders in japan from the seventeenth to the nineteenth century. Oxford University Press, New York

Burns KG (2000) China and Japan: economic partnership to political ends. In: Krepon K, Gangne C (eds) Economic cooperation and regional security. Henry L. Stimson Center, Washington, pp 32. http://pdf.thepdfportal.com/PDFFiles/132895.pdf. Accessed 7 April 2014

Christopher C (1986) Second to none. Charles Tuttle, Tokyo

Dunning JH (1994) Multinational enterprises and the globalization of innovatory capacity. Res Policy 23(1):67–88

Fleming G, Johnson RS (2008) How countries are impacted by mergers and acquisitions: a theoretical approach. Va Econ J 13:33–40

Fukutani N, Dobashi M (2008) M & A tekitaiteki baishuu bouei kanzen manyuaru (Full manual against unfriendly acquisitions). Chuuo Keizai Sha, Tokyo

Jetro (2013) Global trade and investment report. Revitalizing Japan through global business, p 4. https://www.jetro.go.jp/en/reports/white_paper/trade_invest_2013.pdf. Accessed 24 Feb 2014

Mason M (1992) American multinationals in Japan: the political economy of Japanese capital controls 1899–1980. Harvard University Press, Cambridge

Matsubara H (1987) Weg zu Japan—West—Oestliche Erfahrungen. Albrecht Publishing House, Hamburg

Moriguchi C, Ono H (2006) Japanese lifetime employment: a century's perspective. In: Blomstroem M, La Croix S (eds) Institutional change in Japan. European Institute of Japanese Studies, East Asian Economics and Business Series, Routledge, Abington, pp 152–176

Morikawa H (1992) The rise and fall of family enterprise groups in Japan. University of Tokyo Press, Tokyo
Muramatsu S (2007) M & A in Japan—past and present. In: Bebenroth R (ed) In the wave of M & A: Europe and Japan. Iudicium, Germany, pp 70–93
Noguchi Y (1994) Bubble no Keizaigaku (Economics of the bubble). Nihon Keizai Shimbunsha, Tokyo
Paprzycki R, Fukao K (2005) The extent and history of foreign direct investment in Japan. April 2005, Discussion Paper Series No. 84. http://hi-stat.ier.hit-u.ac.jp/research/discussion/2005/pdf/D05-84.pdf. Accessed 3 May 2013
Schaede U (2008) Choose and focus. Cornell University Press, New York
Toda R (2014) Nogyou hatten ni muketa boki no yakuwari, [Ratio of Environmental Development Account]. Chuuo Keizai Sha, Tokyo
Weinstein D (1996) Structural impediments to Investment in Japan: what have we learned over the last 450 years? In: Yoshitomi M, Edward MG (eds) Foreign direct investment in Japan. Edward Elgar, Cheltenham
Westney E (2009) Japan. In: Rugman AM (ed) International business, 2nd edn. Oxford University Press, Oxford
World Investment Report (2012) http://www.unctad-docs.org/files/UNCTAD-WIR2012-Full-en.pdf. Accessed 24 March 2014
World Investment Report (2013) Global value chains: investment and trade for development. http://unctad.org/en/PublicationsLibrary/wir2013_en.pdf. Accessed 24 Feb 2014
Yamamura K (1986) Japan's deus ex machina: western technology in the 1920's. J Jpn Stud 12(1):65–94

Chapter 3
Imports, Exports and Foreign Businesses in Japan

Abstract This chapter discusses imports, exports, and foreign firms' investments in Japan. Imports to Japan total to about US$ 812 billion and exports from Japan total to about US$ 697 billion in the year of 2013.

Japan consists of two economically vivid areas, Kanto consisting of Tokyo, Saitama, Kawasaki and Yokohama; and the Kansai area consisting of Osaka, Kyoto and Kobe. Both areas are discussed separately. It will be shown that Chinese trade has a bigger impact on Kansai than on Kanto area.

In the next part, information about foreign affiliated firms doing business in Japan will be demonstrated by expanding on Japanese External Trade Organization data. Kansai will also be discussed separately here. At the end of the chapter, some examples of success stories will be given of foreign affiliated firms located in the Kansai region.

3.1 Introduction

The Japanese economy stagnated after the burst of the bubble economy for many years (Chap. 2). However, recently under the Liberal Democratic Party and the administration of Prime Minister Shinzo Abe there have been some signs of an economic recovery (Urata 2014). These developments are visible when looking at the imports to Japan and exports from Japan, which have both increased in recent years.

A stronger Japan is closely connected to more trade to and from Japan. From 2012, the reelected Prime Minister launched his economic recovery plan called "Abenomics," a strategy that consists of "three arrows". These three arrows refer to, aggressive monetary easing, flexible public spending, and a growth strategy to spark private investments. Recently, a three-action program plan titled the "Japan Revitalization Strategy" which is meant to increase imports and exports was announced. Therefore, Japanese imports and exports will be investigated in this chapter. This chapter also sheds light on foreign firms in Japan.

R. Bebenroth, *International Business Mergers and Acquisitions in Japan*,
DOI 10.1007/978-4-431-54989-5_3

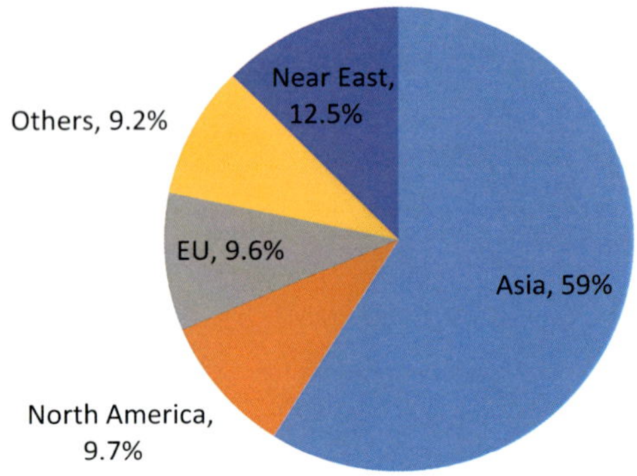

Fig. 3.1 Japanese imports, classified by geographical origin (2013). (Source: Japan Tax Office. Download at: http://www.customs.go.jp/toukei/suii/html/data/y5.pdf, May 22nd 2014 (converted from 100 yen to $ 1 U.S. dollar))

3.2 Imports and Exports

3.2.1 Japanese Imports

Japan imports totaled to about $ 812 billion U.S. (81,242 billion yen; Fig. 3.1) in the year of 2013. Out of that, Asian imports to Japan count for about 59 %. Imports from other countries consist mostly of oil from the Middle Eastern countries (12.5 %). This steep increase compared to the previous years is a result of the closing down of atomic power plants following Great East Japan Earthquake disaster in 2011. Also Hosoe finds empirical support that due to the loss of nuclear power supply after Fukushima disaster, more fossil fuels were imported to Japan (Hosoe 2014). The Fukushima power plant accident also had a disastrous impacts on domestic manufacturing industries, which have resulted in higher costs. For example, when Kobe Steel exported steel products, it was necessary to certify that their steel was not contaminated with radiation.

US imports from Japan count for about 9.7 % and imports from the EU count for about of 9.6 % (Fig. 3.1).

3.2.2 Japanese Exports

Against US$ 812 billion of imports, Japanese firms exported about US$ 697 billion in the year 2013 (Fig. 3.2). Of this, exports to Asia counted for 38.1 % of the total. This means that Asia is the most important destination for Japanese firms.

It is prudent to mention that exporting is sometimes replaced by another trend of foreign direct investment (FDI) where firms accelerate offshoring their activities to Asia, and especially to China. This development is mostly driven by the Asian market attraction for Japanese firms.

Japanese exports to the US (in this included is Kansai area) count for about 28.5 %. This means that the US market for exports is much higher than the Japanese market for US imports.

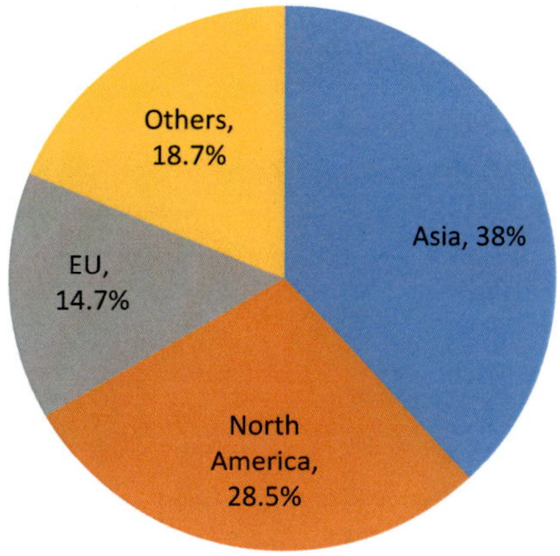

Fig. 3.2 Japanese exports, classified by geographical destination (2013). (Source: Japan Tax Office. Download at: http://www.customs.go.jp/toukei/suii/html/data/y4.pdf, May 22nd 2014 (converted from 100 yen to $ 1 U.S. dollar))

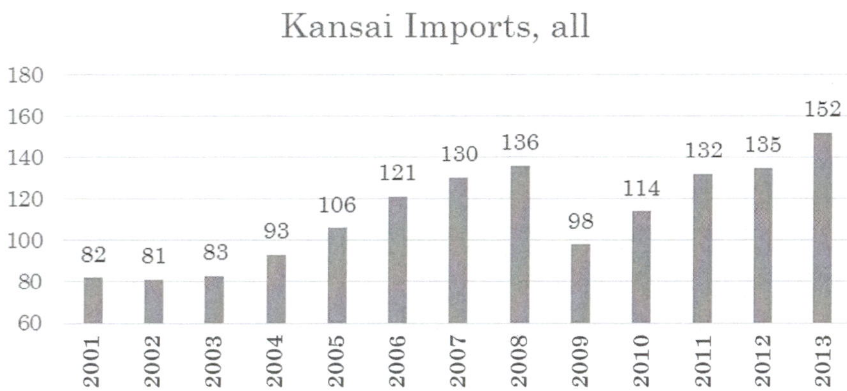

Fig. 3.3 Timely Development of Kansai Imports. (Source: Kinki En: Boeki Gaikyou (General Outlook of Exports from Kansai Area Japan). Osaka Finance Office 2014, p. 2)

To compare exports to imports, it is to state that the volume of imports is higher than that of exports. Imports are relatively high from Asia and the Middle East. Finally, recently Asia has become a more popular destination for Japanese exports (38 %) and Europe and the US consumes more Japanese products than they sell to Japan.

3.2.3 Kansai Imports

The development of imports to Kansai area in Western Japan are presented in Fig. 3.3. The amount of imports to Kansai region is merely $ 152 U.S. billion (15,242 billion yen) much lower than that of Japan as a whole. Kansai receives merely 18.8 % of the total share of import to Japan. However, imports to Kansai have increased over the years, From $ 82 US billion in 2001 to $ 152 US billion

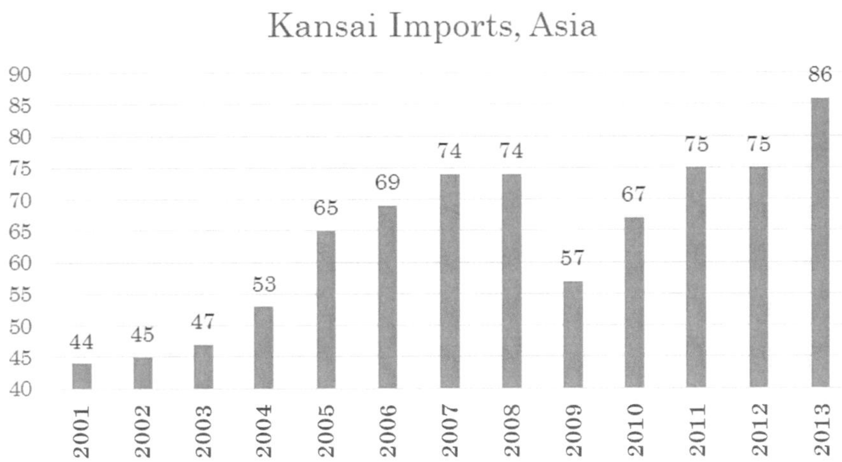

Fig. 3.4 Timely development of Kansai Imports from Asia. (Source: Kinki En: Boeki Gaikyou (General Outlook of Exports from Kansai Area Japan). Osaka Finance Office 2014, p. 3)

in 2013. It is also visible that imports to Kansai steadily increased until the year of 2008, the year of the Lehman Brothers shock, when the American trading house went bankrupt. This shock also reduced imports to Kansai down to $ 98 US billion dollars. However, starting in 2009, imports began to increase again and reached record levels in 2013, an increase of 12.7% compared to the year before (Fig. 3.3).

When imports are divided into three geographical regions, it is clearly visible that trade in Kansai trade is dominated by Asian firms. In 2013, Kansai imports received from Asia totaled at US$ 86 billion, imports from Chinese firms made up US$ 49 billion. In contrast, Kansai imports from the US were merely US$ 15.9 billion and $ 18.5 billion from the EU. Already in 2001 Kansai received about half of its imports from Asian countries. That means that out of $ 82 US billion dollars of imports more than half ($ 44 US billion dollars) came from Asia. This rate increased to more than 55% of imports in 2013. Asian imports show a similar pattern to imports as a whole, decreasing in 2008 but recovering strongly right after (Fig. 3.4).

3.2.4 *Kansai Exports*

Looking at the exports from Kansai region one can see a similar pattern to the growth of imports but on a larger scale. Exports from Kansai totaled to $ 146 billion U.S. dollars (14,678 billion yen) in the year 2013. Similar to imports, exports were also negatively impacted by the Lehman Shock, falling to US$ 123 billion in 2009. After the year of 2009, an increase is again visible (Fig. 3.5).

Asia is the predominant location of Kansai exports, with US$ 99 billion' worth of exports going to Asia in 2013. Again China received the largest share of Kansai

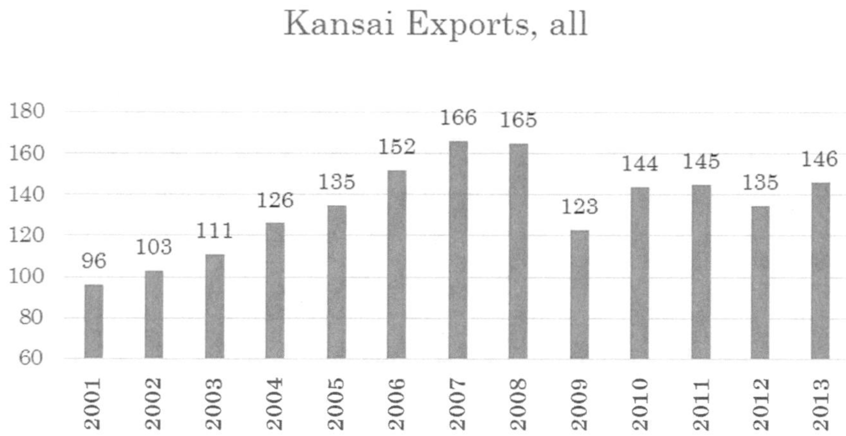

Fig. 3.5 Timely development of Kansai exports. (Source: Kinki En: Boeki Gaikyou (General Outlook of Exports from Kansai Area Japan). Osaka Finance Office 2014, p. 2)

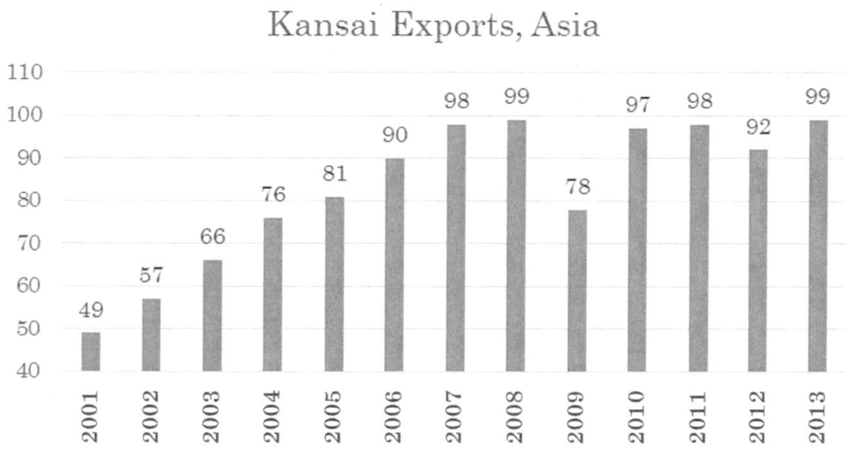

Fig. 3.6 Timely development of Kansai exports to Asia. (Source: Kinki En: Boeki Gaikyou (General Outlook of Exports from Kansai Area Japan). Osaka Finance Office 2014, p. 3)

exports, total to US$ 34 billion. In the same year, Kansai firms exported merely US$ 17 billion to the US and US$ 14 billion to the EU. This means that firms from Kanto region have much closer business relationships with US firms while firms from Kansai region have closer relationships to Asia.

When looking at the development of exports over time, Kansai firms increase there exports on a steady basis between 2001 and 2008, after sharply decreasing in 2009, exports again increase. In 2010 exports increased to $ 97 US billion. This means that Kansai firms almost fully recovered from the situation immediately after the Lehman Shock (Fig. 3.6).

3.3 Example of Car Manufacturers and Their Exports

To illustrate the streams of exports, imports, and trade an industry example is used. When looking at the last 20 years of the automobile industry one can see the following pattern. In 1993 Japan's car production stood at 11 million cars; however that number decreased to around 10 million units in 2000. Since then car production has again increased to 11.6 million units in 2008. In 2009, at the time of the Lehman Shock, that number decreased sharply to 8 million units; however, since then, car production has bounced back and totaled 9.6 million units in 2013 (Fig. 3.7).

Table 3.1 shows that car production in Japan has been relatively stable. However, it is also important to look at the worldwide production of Japanese cars including those produced in other countries. For simplicity, we will look only at the number of cars produced by Japanese automotive manufacturers in 2013. It is clearly visible that all Japanese makers shifted most of their production overseas. Toyota, for example, produced 8.94 million cars in 2013, but only 3.37 million were produced in Japan and out of this number, 1.85 million units were shipped overseas. Nissan Motors, the second biggest car manufacturer in Japan, shows a similar pattern. In 2013, Nissan Motors produced more than 5 million cars in total, but only 1 million units were produced in Japan. Out of the one million produced cars, almost half were exported to other countries. See Table 3.1:

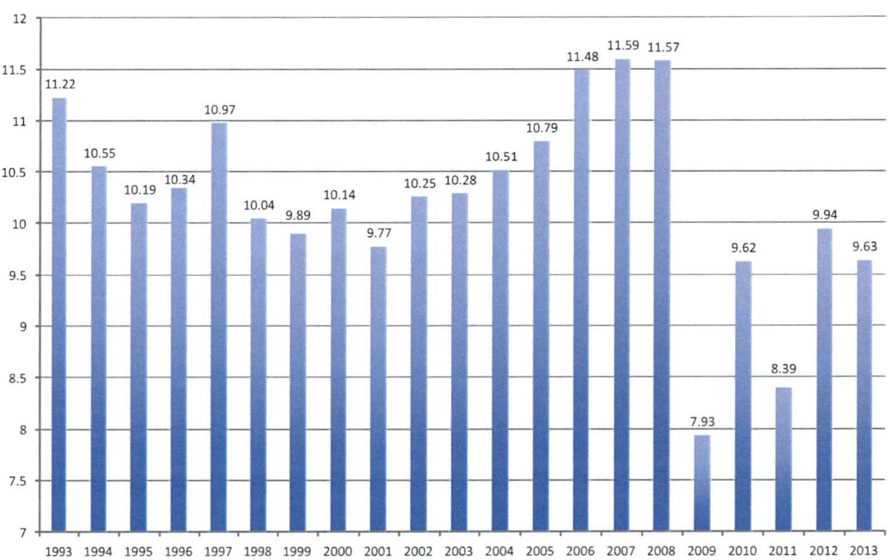

Fig. 3.7 Timely development of Japanese firms' car production. (Source: (JAMA 2014) Japan Automobile Manufacturers Association. Internet: http://jamaserv.jama.or.jp/newdb/index.html. Accessed 23 May 2014 (year 1993 to 2013))

Table 3.1 Japanese automobile industry: export (in million units). (Source: Enyasu de mo kaigai shifuto (Transfer of car manufacturing plants in spite of a weak yen). Asahi Shinbun April 24th 2014, p. 8)

	Total production	Domestically produced	Exports from Japan
Toyota	8.94	3.37	1.85
Nissan	5.07	1	0.54
Honda	4.4	0.93	0.09
Suzuki	2.85	0.99	0.15
Matsuda	1.26	0.97	0.79
Mitsubishi	1.26	0.63	0.34
Daihatsu	1.1	0.8	0.008
Fujitsu	0.81	0.64	0.49

3.4 Foreign Affiliated Firms in Japan

3.4.1 Foreign Affiliated Firms in Overall Japan

Foreign affiliated firms in Japan are owned by non-Japanese. These firms could be established in Japan as subsidiaries, joint ventures, or as representation offices to observe recent developments at the Japanese market. 37.8 % of all registered foreign affiliated firms in Japan come from the United States followed by European firms which represented 41.9 % and Asian firms with 16.5 %. This means that though even trade relationships with Asia are very strong, very few Asian firms operate in Japan (Fig. 3.8).

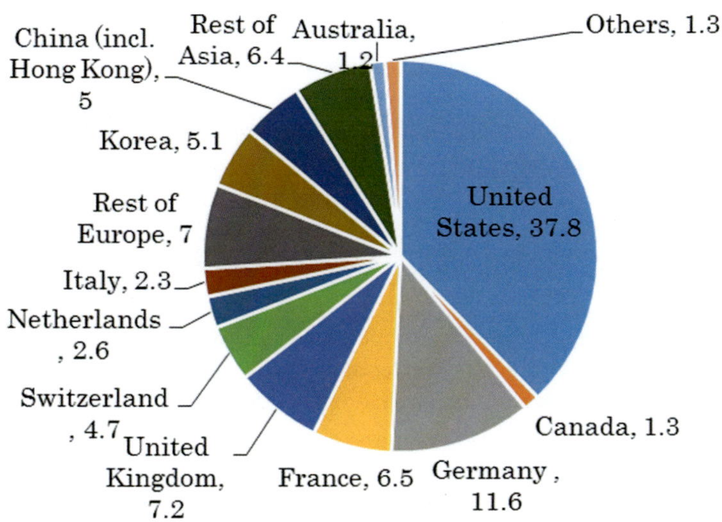

Fig. 3.8 Foreign affiliated firms in Japan. Gaishi kei kigyo soran 2013. p. 147

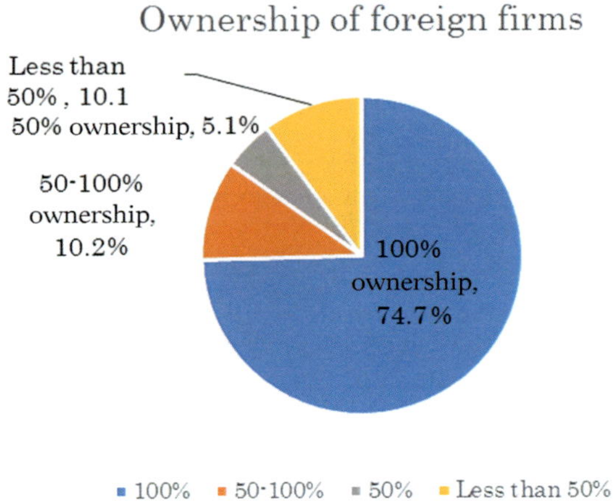

Fig. 3.9 Ownership share of foreign affiliate firms in Japan. Numbers: 100 %, 74.7; 50–100 %, 10.2; 50 %, 5.1; Less than 50 %, 10.1. Gaishi kei kigyo soran, 2013, p. 147

There is evidence that the intensity of foreign headquarters' commitment towards a subsidiary depends on the degree of ownership of those subsidiaries (Bebenroth et al. 2008). Therefore, the next chart shows how strongly involved foreign affiliated firms are in their Japanese investments. It can be seen that more than 70 % of foreign affiliated firms have 100 % ownership of their Japan based affiliated firm. Put differently, only 11.1 % of the foreign affiliated firms had less than 50 % of ownership of their Japan based subsidiaries. This tendency shows clearly that the majority of the foreign firms in Japan have a rather big stake in their investment (Fig. 3.9).

Another factor of commitment is the endurance of a foreign investor in the country. Investors with many years of experience in Japan should have a higher commitment than those who just entered the Japanese market. The next graph shows the time of entrance to the Japanese market. It is clearly visible that a third of all Japan based foreign affiliates arrived before the year of 1985, that means more than 30 % of the foreign affiliated firms have been in Japan for more than 30 years. There are only around 15 % of the firms that are classified as very young, meaning they started business in Japan after 2006 (Fig. 3.10).

3.4.2 Foreign Firms in Japan, Especially in Kansai Area

The number of foreign affiliated firms operating in Japan for the year of 2012 was 3086. Out of them, 2331 are headquartered at Tokyo and 227 are headquarterd in Kanagawa, near Tokyo. Kansai is home to only 225 Japan offices (Fig. 3.11, Gaishikei kigyo soran 2013, p. 164).

Previously, Kansai's businesses consisted primarily of small and medium sized firms and had a reputation as a production site. However, there are signs that policies of several Kansai based firms have shifted. Kansai based firms are moving into new areas of development, for example environmental friendly solutions and life science technologies (Kankeiren 2010, p. 10).

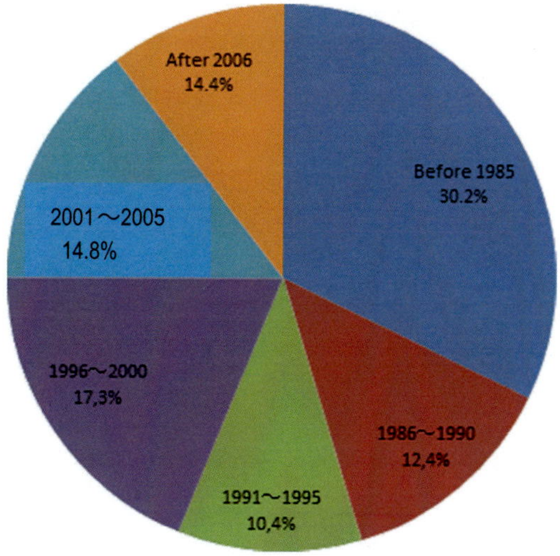

Fig. 3.10 Time of entrance into Japan. (Source: Gaishikei kigyo soran 2013, p. 147)

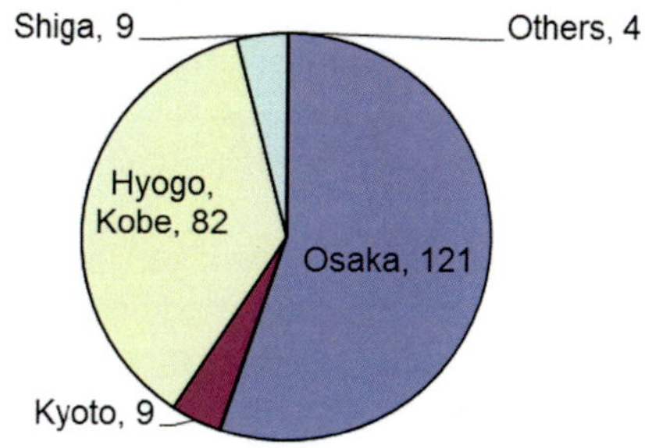

Fig. 3.11 Foreign affiliated firms headquartered at Kansai area. (Source: Gaishikei kigyou soran 2013, p. 164)

The majority of foreign affiliated firms in Kansai area are located in Osaka (121 firms). Next comes Kobe, which is the capital city of Hyogo prefecture (82 firms). Some other firms are settled in Shiga prefecture (9 firms) and Kyoto (9 firms) (Fig. 3.11).

Next, we will look at the origin foreign affiliated firms headquartered in Kansai (Fig. 3.12). The majority of firms are from Europe (44.1 %). Only 31.7 % are from the U.S. and around 21.1 are from Asia. Only 3.1 % of the firms are from the rest of the world.

There is a historic reason that Kansai area is dominated by European firms. After Japan's opening in the 1850s, Kobe port became the preferred harbor for European ships (see Chap. 2). US American ships preferred Yokohama port, close to Tokyo. Russian ships entered the north at Hakodate port in Hokkaido. Finally, Chinese ships entered the southern island of Kyushu at the port of Nagasaki. Even today, some European firms prefer to stay in Kansai in contrast to their US counterparts, which prefer to stay at Kanto area.

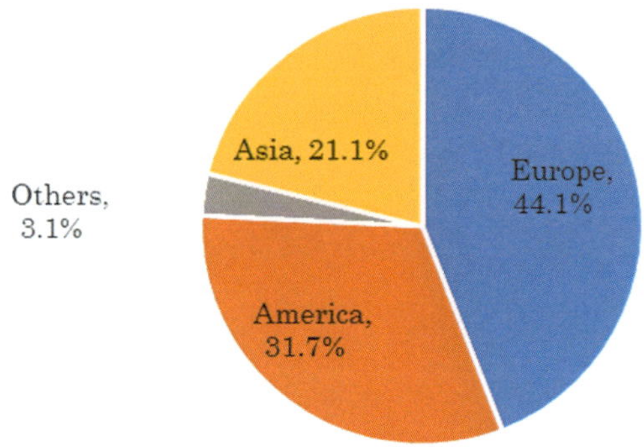

Fig. 3.12 Origin of foreign affiliated firms at Kansai. (Source: Toyo Keizai Foreign Affiliated Companies in Japan (from year 2011), Kansai Kokusai jouhou, 2011, http://www.kansai.meti.go.jp/2kokusai/file2011/New/Chap. 2_2011_.pdf)

3.4.3 Examples of Foreign Firms in Japan

Some examples of foreign firms in the Kansai area are discussed in the following so called "success stories". As seen above, many foreign affiliated firms have a long history in Japan having been there for many years. Nestlé K.K. which is located in Kobe is one example. The beverage and food company Nestlé, founded in 1867 in Switzerland opened its first Japan office in 1913. A Jetro prospect puts it this way: "Nestlé has permeated Japanese life to such an extent that scarcely a day goes by without seeing Nestlé products" (Invest Japan 2005, p. 16). Under the slogan "Good Food, Good Life," Nestlé Group worldwide has one of its biggest subsidiaries located in Japan.

Another example, the large US consumer products company Procter & Gamble (P&G) has a reputation as one of the world's best marketers. With its 80-plus major brands, P&G generates more than $ 37 billion in annual revenues worldwide. P&G's Asian headquarters for many years was located on Rokko Island (Kobe) before it moved to Singapore (Kobayashi 2013, p. 165). However, P&G's Japan headquarters is still located in Kobe and is actively competing against its Japanese rivals such as Kao. P&G's business is considered to be a success story in Japan (Pfoertsch 2010).

There are also successful Indian and Chinese firms as well. One Indian firm operating in Japan is Infosys. Infosys Limited is a Bangalore based global leader IT consulting firm. The firm established its first Japanese office in Tokyo in 1997. With approximately 250 employees, the Tokyo office serves as a base for the Asia Pacific region. In June 2012, Infosys opened a second office in Nagoya (Jetro 2012). This development shows that the Indian affiliate should also in the near future be able to participate in the Japanese market.

The Chinese firm Biotechnology Genome Institute (BGI) Japan K.K, a biological science research institute, is also a successful firm located in the Kansai area. BGI is one of the worldwide largest biological science research institutes, and established its first Japanese branch, BGI Japan K.K., in Kobe in September 2011. BGI Group is a key player in biotechnology and is involved in many important research projects such as the 1000 Genome Project and the International Cancer

Genome Project (Jetro 2011). Also, BGI Group is known to be the first research team to decode the genome sequence for the SARS virus in the year 2003.

The Chinese firm had several reasons for opening an office in Japan. BGI Japan Director Mr. Liu, commented that one of these reasons was that: "BGI has an advantage in collaborating in genome analysis and biological sciences, and since Japan has one of the best biological science researches in the world, we can expect further expansion of our services. Up to now, we have been developing our businesses in Japan from our bases in China; however, by being physically closer, further development with BGI and Japan's biological science sector can be expected" (Jetro 2011, p. 2)

3.4.4 Changes Caused Through Foreign Firms?

It was shown that Japan relies heavily on exports and imports to and from foreign countries. It was also shown that there are an increasing number of foreign affiliated firms in Japan. It can be assumed that Japanese firms have become more international. Internationally acquired Japanese firms may also change in their behavior because of the pressure of the foreign firms' management.

However, on average, there is remarkably little evidence of radical change in Japanese economic institutions despite the long period of stagnation between 1989 and 2002, this also includes employment relations. Evidence of a Confucian legacy can be found in gender relations, specifically between men and women, with the latter's role being predominantly weaker (Sekiguchi 2010). As we will discuss starting in Chap. 6, there is a big market for mergers and acquisitions in Japan, this development can challenge the existing institutional patterns of Japanese firms. For example that women are traditionally excluded from the core memberships of Japanese firms. By comparing five Japanese firms taken over by foreign firms, Olcott and Oliver examined the impact of foreign ownership on the role of women in the Japanese workplace (2014). Their finding is; however, that even prospects for women improved at foreign-acquired firms; however, it was not necessarily accompanied by a change in attitudes towards gender. They find that while a takeover causes some changes in a target firm, a wider societal shift would be required to significantly alter the behavior of the firms, in this case, to put women in better positions according to their abilities at foreign affiliated firms located in Japan (Olcott and Oliver 2014).

3.5 Conclusion

This chapter discussed imports, exports and foreign firms' investments in Japan. Regarding exports and imports in 2013, Japan imported ($ 812 US billion dollars) more than it exported ($ 697 US billion dollars). This relatively high volume of imports is caused by an increase of oil exports due to the shutting down of Japan's nuclear power plans following the Great East Japan Earthquake disaster in 2011.

Besides the trade with Japan as a whole, imports and exports for the Kansai area were also discussed separately. It was shown that firms from Kansai area have stronger economic relationships with firms from Asia. Kansai firms' exports to Asia totaled $ 99 billion dollars (out of $ 146 US billion dollars), while imports totaled US$ 86 billion (out of $ 152 US billion dollars). Finally, the chapter ended with some foreign success stories in Kansai region.

Questions

1. How much does Japan import and export in US dollars?
2. How many foreign affiliated firms are operating in Japan (in 2012)?
3. From which parts of the world do these foreign affiliated firms come from?
4. How has the Japanese Automobile market developed in terms of domestic production and their export to the world?
5. Recently, which geographic region has become more important for Japanese car makers?
6. How many foreign affiliates are headquartered in the Kanto region in contrast to the Kansai region?
7. How strong are European firms at Kansai?
8. How has the Kansai attractiveness changed recently?
9. With which geographical region does Kansai have strong relationships?
10. Recall at least two foreign success stories which are located in the Kansai region?

Answers

1. (At the year 2013 figures) Japan had around 812 US billion dollars of imports and around 697 US billion dollars of exports.
2. Around 3086 foreign affiliated firms existed in Japan in the year 2012.
3. Nearly 40% all foreign affiliated firms come from the USA. Second biggest investor is Germany with more than 370 firms. Then UK and France come as investors with around 200 foreign affiliated firms. Recently, Chinese firms come more often to Japan, participating at Japanese firms.
4. Japanese automobile production lost momentum after 2008 at the Lehmann Shock. However, Japanese manufacturer produce recently (only in their home country) again up to 10 Mio cars, exporting almost 5 million units.
5. An increasingly important destination for Japanese car makers is nowadays Asia, in front with China.
6. Kanto region hosts about 87 % of all foreign firms' headquarters in Japan, while Kansai only hosts 7 %.

7. European firms are still dominating at the Kansai region.
8. Recently, Chinese firms get stronger in presence at Kansai region some Chinese firms resulted from acquisition with Jap. target firms.
9. Kansai region has a strong connection to Asian region.
10. Nestle or Procter and Gamble (P&G)

References

Bebenroth R, Li D, Sekiguchi T (2008) Executive staffing practice patterns in foreign MNC affiliates based in Japan. Asian Business and Management. Palgrave, pp 381–402

Gaishikei Kigyou Souran (2013) Toyo Keizai. Tokyo

Hosoe N (2014) Japanese manufacturing facing post-Fukushima power crisis: a dynamic computable general equilibrium analysis with foreign direct investment. Applied Economics 46(17):2010–2020.

JAMA (2014) Japan automobile manufacturers association. Internet: http://jamaserv.jama.or.jp/newdb/index.html. Accessed 23 May 2014

Jetro (2005) Japan invest. Nestle. http://www.jetro.go.jp/en/invest/reports/newsletter/pdf/ij_05.pdf. Accessed 11 July 2013

Jetro (2011) Japan invest. Chinese genomic research institute BGI, sets their first Japan base in Kobe. March. http://www.jetro.go.jp/en/invest/success_stories/pdf/1203_bgi_new.pdf. Accessed 11 July 2013

Jetro (2012) Japan invest. Infosys Limit http://www.jetro.go.jp/en/invest/success_stories/pdf/infosys.pdf. Accessed 11 July 2013

Kankeiren (2010) Kansai's new development. An introduction to the Kansai Economy, 2011. Kansai Economic Federation, p 10. Internet: http://www.kankeiren.or.jp/English/economy/pdf/Eibun_Kansai_2010_protect.pdf. Accessed 11 July 2013

Kansai Kokusaika (2011) Joho file. http://www.kansai.meti.go.jp/2kokusai/file2011/New/index2011.htm. Accessed 4 Nov 2011

Kinki En (2014) Boeki gaikyou (general outlook of exports from Kansai Area Japan). Osaka Finance Office

Kobayashi I (2013) Kaigai M & A ni yaku ni tatsu. Guro-baru zenryaku no kandokoro. Usefulness of foreign M & A. Point of global Strategy.Chuokeizai

Olcott G, Oliver N (2014) The impact of foreign ownership on gender and employment relations in large Japanese companies. Work, Employ Soc 28(2)1–19. Published online 11 February 2014, http://wes.sagepub.com/content/early/2014/02/11/0950017013490333.full.pdf+html. Accessed 12 April 2014

Pfoertsch W (2010) Procter & gamble in Japan: from marketing failure to success http://www.pfoertsch.com/wiki/uploads/Main/pgjapancase.pdf. Accessed 11 July 2013

Sekiguchi S (2010) Confucian morals and the making of a 'good wife and wise mother'. Soc Sci Jpn 13(1):95–113

Urata S (2014) Japan's trade policy with Asia. Policy Research Institute, Ministry of Finance, Japan, Public Policy Review, Vol 10(1). March. Internet: https://www.mof.go.jp/english/pri/publication/pp_review/ppr024/ppr024a.pdf. Accessed 12 May 2014

Chapter 4
The Japanese Distribution System

Abstract This chapter focuses on the Japanese distribution system and its recent developments in the retail market. Westerners used to criticize the Japanese distribution system as a closed shop while Japanese in contrast argue that it is of close cooperation, a crucial element for constant harmony which benefits all of society. It will be shown (1) that in recent years the distribution system and the retail market changed remarkably and (2) it will be shown that there are foreign firms enjoying market success in Japan.

4.1 Introduction

For a long time the Japanese distribution system has been criticized by Westerners as being too complex, multilayered and inefficient (Czinkota and Kotabe 2000; Drew et al. 1998; Min 1996; Maquire 2001). While in the late 80s the average retail price in America was 1.7 times the factory invoice price, it was three times the factory price in Japan (Drew et al. 1998). The high prices for consumers—so the Western critics—resulted from a distribution keiretsu where manufacturers controlled wholesalers in their distribution channels through vertical integration, financial linkage and reciprocal dealings (Pirog and Lancioni 1996; Min 1996). Maguire (2001) stated that "…the Japanese market has functioned primarily for the benefit of Japanese producers and not Japanese consumers…." It was reported that the Japanese distribution system was composed of four layers of wholesalers (Min 1996) with around 8000 trading houses, of which the 16 largest were involved in foreign trading (Shao and Herbig 1993; Min 1996) or engaged with non–Japanese firms selling products to Japan (Maguire 2001, p. 247).

In recent years, however, the Japanese distribution system has become more efficient and offers better market access and profits for foreign firms (Schaede 2008). Trading houses like Marubeni (traditionally involved in the grain business) are even more accessible to foreigners as–at least the bigger–Japanese firms which tend to deal their products internationally (Yamaguchi 2009).

This chapter is an updated version of Bebenroth (2011) Ryūtsū kakumei: the Japanese distribution revolution In: Herausforderungen der internationalen marktorientierten Unternehmensführung. Gabler, pp. 525–536

R. Bebenroth, *International Business Mergers and Acquisitions in Japan*,
DOI 10.1007/978-4-431-54989-5_4

This chapter investigates recent changes in the Japanese distribution system and the retail market. Convenience stores supermarkets and department stores will be the center of this investigation, followed by foreign firms in Japan. At the end a conclusion will be drawn.

4.2 Structure of Japanese Retail Market and Regulatory Developments

4.2.1 Overview of the Japanese Retail Market

According to the Japanese census, the Japanese retailing market structure is composed of four big players: First, the stores grouped under the Large-scale Retail Store Law, second department stores, third supermarkets and last but not least fourth convenience stores. In the year 2012 these four groups made up 35.05 % of the total retail trade distribution market (Yearbook Commerce 2013). The mom-and-pop stores accounted for the rest of the Japanese retail market. Stores grouped under the Large-scale Retail Store Law include hypermarkets and other discount stores normally are located outside bigger cities. They had a total market share of 15.6 %. Supermarkets followed with a market share of 9.2 % and department stores, the third biggest player hold a total market share of 6.4 %. Convenience stores had a market share of 5.5 % in the same year of observation.

Looking at the changes in recent years the size of the total retail market almost remained the same. To be specific, from 1998 to 2012 the market size decreased by 0.8 %. However, some groups faced a significant decline in sales volume over the years while others, in contrast, gained sales. Stores grouped according to the Large-scale Retail Store Law faced 15.7 % decline in sales volume in these 14 years. Department stores lost 37.7 % of their turnover in the same period and many of them became a target for takeover (see Fig. 4.1). To retain and attract customers, many department stores lowered prices especially in the apparel sector. In contrast, supermarkets experienced only little change in their turnover (+ 2.9 %) as there were winners as well as losers in that sector. The big winners in gaining sales volume in the last 14 years were the convenience stores, gaining 49.5 % sales volume from 1998 until 2012. From the top of Fig. 4.1, it is clear that convenience stores nowadays play a bigger role in Japan than they did several years ago.

4.2.2 Regulatory Developments: Large-Scale Retail Store Law

The Large-scale Retail Store Law (LSRS) was enacted in 1973 and took effect in March 1974, being introduced for two reasons: First, it "officially" served to protect consumers' interests. Second, it aimed to protect small and independent retailers against new large store openings (Tsuruta and Yahagi 2002). The effect of the law was the restriction of new establishments of large-scale retail stores and it became

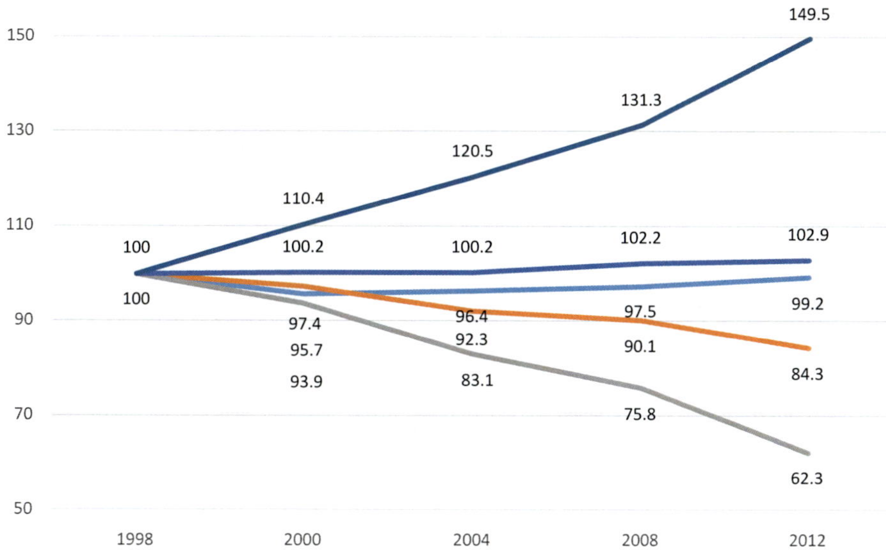

Fig. 4.1 Japanese retail market structure. (Source: Data is taken from several sources (for detailed numbers see Table 4.2))

difficult to open new stores of more than 500 m². In some areas, local prefecture governments had the authority to lower the requirement to 300 and 200m² (Min 1996).

From planning to store opening it took on average about 5–6 years and one way of hampering the establishment of bigger stores was simply to prolong the notification process of formal approval of those planned stores (Tsuruta and Yahagi 2002).

The LSRS law was further strengthened in 1979 by an amendment which led to even more difficulties to open new big stores (Tamura 2000). It is reported that, due to the law, only 11 stores in that category were permitted to open during 1985–1988. Foreign firms who want to invest into the Japanese market need to open bigger stores in order to be profitable. Hence, if foreign retailers come to Japan they hardly can be profitable by opening small or medium sized stores but need to open hyper markets. With the aim to give foreign firms easier access to the Japanese market, the law was replaced in 2000 by the "Large-scale Retail Stores Location Act" and in 2006, a new law, the "City Planning Law", was enacted in order to improve efficiency by decentralizing control with decreased administration.

What were the reasons for this juristically development? First, life should continue in towns and cities. There is clear evidence that developments in other countries (such as the USA etc.) with big shopping centers at the outskirts and very few shops in cities were counter acted. In addition, the ruling party, LDP, has a high voting power at mom-and-pop-store owners.

The amended LSRS led to a liberalization of other retail store categories (department stores, supermarkets and convenience stores). Laws which hindered foreign companies entering Japan have been lowered to some extent in all retailing areas (Meyer-Ohle 2007).

Nonetheless, some foreign companies complain that they are still hindered from doing business in Japan: "Despite a marked expansion of foreign retail activity in the specialty retail channel (albeit with many outlets operated via franchise or under license to Japanese companies), it has proved extremely difficult for foreign retailers to take advantage of global scale logistics when entering the Japanese market" (Buckley 2007).

4.3 Changes at Distribution System

The traditional Japanese distribution system and its retail market has changed in recent years. Some observers call it "ryūtsū kakumei" what can be translated as "Distribution Revolution" (Bebenroth 2011).

One reason why changes took place is the emergence of the internet. Japanese employees with limited time resources, e.g. those who come home late at night and are not able to spare time for shopping, nowadays easily purchase products from their home via the internet. Also newer forms of discount stores have absorbed a big market share. Considering the electronic market, mega-stores like Big Camera, Yodobashi Camera or Yamada Denki emerged (Kano 2010). In the clothing and apparel industry, chain stores, like Fast Retailing with its brand name Uniqlo, have become popular (Daiyamondo 2010; Gekiryu 2010). Their performance is based on nearly 100 % production in China with relatively high quality but competitive low prices. Furthermore, newly developed products like self-heating clothes are successfully introduced into the market against other competitors e.g. Aeon or Seven & I Holdings (Daiyamondo 2009). Besides new competitors, some of the more traditional companies changed their strategy. One of the leading supermarket chains, Ito Yokado which is controlled by Seven & i Holdings for example, increasingly opened convenience stores in the 80s and 90s which turned out as very profitable investments. However, one of their most prestigious department store at Yurakucho in Tokyo was closed at the end of 2009 after 10 years in the red (Suka 2010). In other words, department stores, which were an essential part of Japanese shopping behavior, subsequently run out of business as shopping behaviors of customers changed. Many department stores merged or got overtaken by each other. Isetan department store for example overtook Mitsukoshi in 2009 and started a restructuring program eliminating 1200 employees. Shortly after the deal, the economic situation of both firms weakend and a year after the acquisition there still was no improvement visible (Nikkei Business 2010). However, lately the new firm's performance has improved. The net profit was $ 747.9 million in fiscal year 2012 against merely 30 million in the fiscal year 2011 (Reuters 2013).

4.3.1 Convenience Stores

Convenience store chains are becoming a popular type of retail in Japan. The names associate internationalization. The most popular convenience stores are Lawson, Seven Eleven and Family Mart. However, when looking at the owners of those chains, in all cases they are controlled by traditional firms, like Mitsui, Mitsubishi or Itochu. Thus, traditional firms have used new chains to compete within their own market (Fig. 4.2).

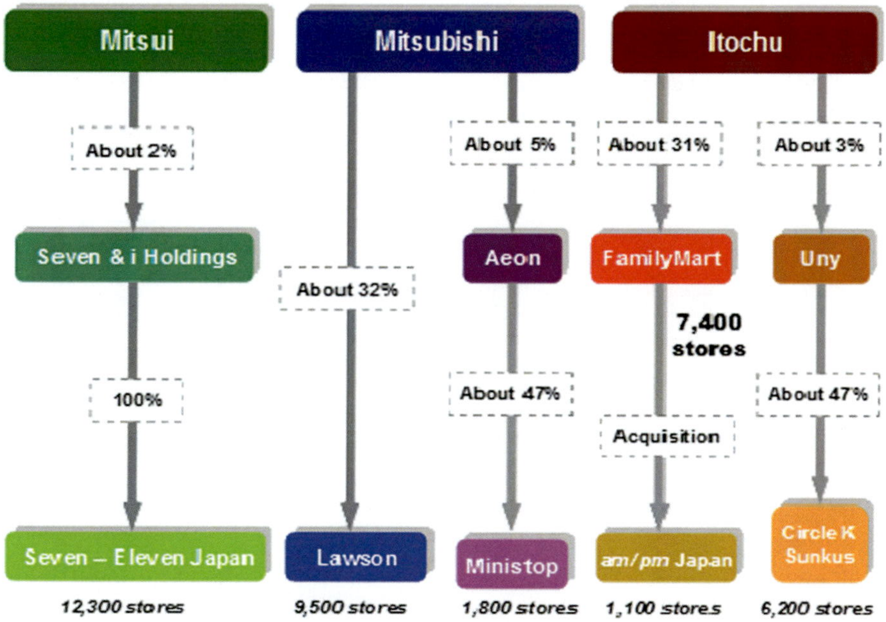

Fig. 4.2 Convenience stores and their traditional parent firms

Japan has about 40,000 convenience store outlets and there are nowadays signs that the market is saturated. Family Mart–which is mostly controlled by Itochu group–overtook AM-PM convenience stores in 2009 for a price of US$ 131.8 million. This transaction happened after Lawson–held by Mitsubishi–withdraw its offer. The strategy of Seven-& i Holdings is to expand by introducing new stores at regions far away from the Kanto or Kansai area, like Fukui, Toyama or Shimane prefectures as well as by focusing on services through an internet portal for convenience stores (Ishibashi 2010).

In contrast to dealing with Japanese traditional department stores, foreign firms report advantages when dealing with Japanese convenience stores. When Nestle Japan for example sells Kitkat, it needs to deal with each department store separately to sell their products. That means, in order to sell Kitkat at department stores, negotiation with about 250 separate store managers, one from each location, was needed. At convenience stores, there is only one person to contact for the whole chain. Price and quality negotiations for a firm like Nestle are therefore easier at the chain-level of convenience stores, which is considered to have a tremendous cost-saving effect (Nestle 2007).

4.3.2 Complexity of the Retail Market

Even if the Japanese market has been becoming more transparent in recent years, it is still a relatively complex network of relationships. To demonstrate the complexity, firm relationships in the food market will be discussed shortly.

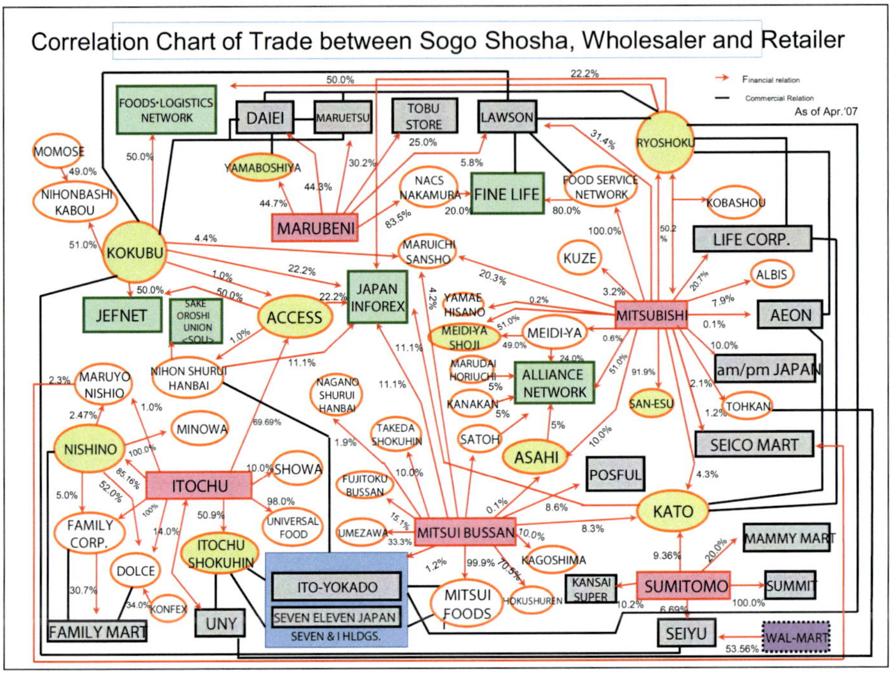

Fig. 4.3 Trade relationships in the food market between wholesaler, retailer and Sogo Shosha. (Source: Data as of April 2007, retrieved from Nestle's Confectionery K.K)

Figure 4.3 shows the web of relationships between different wholesaler, retailer and Sogo Shosha (trading) firms and their interconnectivity vis-à-vis financial and commercial ties for the food market of April 2007. The Sogo Shosha firm Marubeni, for example, enjoys financial connections to department stores and convenience stores like Maruetsu, Tobu or to the Lawson convenience store chain. Ito-Yokado-, another department store chain controlled by Seven and i Holdings–has commercial relations for example with firms like Itochu Shokuhin, Mitsui Foods or Ryoshoku.

4.4 Foreign Market Access to Japan

A recent change in the Japanese retail market is that nowadays more and more foreign firms are selling their products in the Japanese market. Even if there is little satisfaction with some of the laws, foreign access to the Japanese market is clearly increasing.

Some academics keep reminding that there are uncommon structures in Japan and that investors face problems when trying to take advantage of synergy effects. Other researchers are more optimistic and have found successful examples of foreign firms in Japan (Abegglen 2007). All in all, market access to Japan is known to be challenging and there are both successful attempts and failures visible. The largest office equipment seller in the world, the American company Office Depot started its entry into Japan in 1996 as a joint venture together with the Japanese DeoDeo Corporation. As of today, Office Depot has established 16 stores in Japan and without a doubt has a foothold in the market. As another example, the original chocolate and coffee maker Nestle from Switzerland enjoys a profitable stay in Kobe since 1913 until today.

Also Wal-Mart's head of international business, Doug McMillon, is optimistic and has said his company will increase its business in Japan and even consider acquisitions to increase its presence in Japan (Yamaguchi 2012). Even in last years, Wal-Mart hyper-stores reported economic difficulties in connection to the acquisition of Seiyu, the firm is rather optimistic for Japan investment.

In contrast to this, the French company Carrefour hypermarket chain obviously failed to access the Japanese market and sold their eight stores in 2005 after 4 years of their Japan operation to Aeon. A similar pattern was visible for Tesco who also sold their business to Aeon (Yamaguchi 2012).

4.5 Advantages Beyond Foreignness: Market Area Concentration

It is heavily discussed in the literature that foreign firms in Japan enjoy inherent benefits since they stand out against Japanese competitors. As discussed, firms use their brand reputation to sell products in Japan. Beyond that, the Japanese retail market is concentrated in predominantly two regions, namely at Kanto and Kansai area. For foreign retailers this has the advantage of being able to concentrate mainly in the Kanto region (consisting for example of Tokyo, Saitama, Kanagawa, and Yokoyama) as well as in the Kansai region (consisting for example of Osaka and Hyogo prefecture). As Table 4.1 shows, the top six prefectures represent about 64.3 % of the total Japanese retail market. For a foreign firm operating in Japan, this geographic structure is especially advantageous as almost half of the country (except Fukuoka; see Table 4.1) can be covered with two branch offices.

Table 4.1 Retailer sales contribution by prefecture of year 2013

	Area	Total	Percent
1	Tokyo	213671	27.3
2	Osaka	107061	13.7
3	Kanagawa	60030	7.7
4	Aichi	53360	6.8
5	Fukuoka	35948	4.6
6	Hyogo	32579	4.2

2013 Data at: Keizai Sankyo sho: shoukyou hanbai toukei METI (2013):
Report on the current survey of commerce, Table 4 (in Japanese)
http://www.meti.go.jp/statistics/tyo/syoudou/result/pdf/h2sapdfj.pdf

4.6 Conclusion

This report focused on recent changes in the Japanese distribution system and discussed the retail market. It was shown that department stores suffered a reduction in market share while convenience stores gained market share. It can be argued that due to political efforts convenience stores have filled the gap of consumer purchases in the middle of the cities. This development blocked a movement of hyper stores, which would have taken place at the outskirts of cities–and thereby had taken out the "life" and vivid atmosphere of towns and cities. Looking more closely, it was also shown that traditional Japanese firms still control the convenience stores and some critics argue that Japan has actually not changed since the same players still dominate the market.

It was also apparent that foreign hyper markets at retail face serious problems. Other foreign firms enjoy a more open Japanese market access nowadays. Furthermore, foreign firms can make use of a relatively concentrated consumer location to cover almost half of the Japanese market with only having two branch offices, one located in Kanto and the other located in the Kansai region.

Table 4.2 Retail market figures.

	Sales volume (in billion yen)									
	1998		2000		2004		2008		2012	
	Yen	%	Yen	%	Yen	%	Yen	%	Yen	%
Retail trade total	138706	100	132865	95.7	133712	96.4	135257	97.5	137585	99.2
Large-scale retail stores	23248	100	22633	97.4	21467	92.3	20951	90.1	19592	84.3
Department stores	10657	100	10011	93.9	8854	83.1	8078	75.8	6638	62.3
Supermarkets	12591	100	12622	100.2	12614	100.2	12872	102.2	12953	102.9
Convenience stores	6049	100	6680	110.4	7289	120.5	7943	131.3	9044	149.5

Sources:
Yearbook of the Current survey of Commerce (in Japanese):
data for department store and supermarket 1998–2000 figures, p. 3, 8–13.
data for convenience store 1998–2000 figures, p. 204.
Internet:
Department stores and supermarkets 2004–2006 figures:
http://www.meti.go.jp/statistics/tyo/syoudou/result/excel/h2sn101j.xls
http://www.meti.go.jp/statistics/tyo/syoudou/result/excel/h2sn301j.xls
Convenience stores 2004–2006 figures:
http://www.meti.go.jp/statistics/tyo/syoudou/result/excel/h2sn401j.xls
Department stores and supermarkets 2008 figures:
http://www.meti.go.jp/statistics/tyo/syoudou/result/pdf/h2sk002j.pdf
Convenience stores http://www.meti.go.jp/statistics/tyo/syoudou/result/pdf/h2sk003j.pdf
2012 data at: Keizai Sankyo sho: shoukyouhanbai toukei sokuho (2014) METI (2014): Preliminary report on the current survey of commerce, p. 7.
http://www.meti.go.jp/statistics/tyo/syoudou/result/pdf/h2sapdfj.pdf)

Questions

1. Why do Westerners criticized Japan as a "closed shop" while Japanese in contrast to this argued that their own system is of close cooperation to Westerners?
2. Who controls whom at a vertical distribution keiretsu at the retail industry?
3. Has the distribution system and the retail market changed in recent years? How can this development be called?
4. Recall at least two Japanese convenience store chains.
5. Recall an example of a successful firm's market entry into the Japanese market.
6. Which circumstances lead to an increase of convenience stores' sales?
7. Why made the Japanese government it difficult to implement hyperstores?
8. Recall a reason why producers may prefer to deal with convenience stores in contrast to department stores?
9. Why have foreign firms advantages in geographical terms when investing into Japan?
10. Which city has the highest retailer sales volume?

Answers

1. Westerners criticized Japan as a "closed shop" as it was difficult to enter the market. Japanese in contrast to this argued that there are no tariff barriers or any other legal difficulties to enter the market. Non-tariff trade barriers; however, made it difficult to enter the Japanese market.
2. Manufactures control wholesalers in their distribution through a vertical integration.
3. Yes, there is evidence looking at the apparel maker market to see that more and more foreign brands successfully enter the Japanese market and are very profitable. This development can be called ryūtsū kakumei (in Japanese language).
4. Family Mart (by Itochu group); Lawson (by Mitsubishi); Seven Eleven (by Seven&I Holdings from Ito-Yokado, Mitsui).
5. Zara can be seen as one example of a successful firm in the apparel sector to enter successfully the Japanese market.
6. Large-scale Retail Store Law made it difficult for bigger hypermarkets to access Japan. Also mom- and-pop stores shrank. Convenience stores filled the gap and increase their market share.
7. City life should continue to be a vivid one (nigiyaga na seikatsu). Hyperstores at the outskirts take life out of cities and towns. Also, LDP government has traditionally many supporters under mom-and pop-stores.

8. Like a Nestle manager stated, to sell a Kitkat at the whole convenience stores chain it takes only one single negotiation. To sell the same Kitkat at department stores, every single department store needs to be negotiated with.
9. Only two different locations (one at Kanto and the other at Kansai area) are necessary to be present to cover almost 50 % of the Japanese consumer power.
10. Tokyo with 12.2 %.

References

Abegglen J (2007) Seiko suru gaishikei kigyou (Success of Foreign Multinationals in Japan). Kokumin keizai zashi, (J Political Econ Commercial Sci) 196(1):119–133 (Kobe University; original in Japanese)

Bebenroth R (2011) Ryūtsū kakumei: The Japanese distribution revolution. In: Mann A (ed) Herausforderungen der internationalen marktorientierten Unternehmensführung. Gabler Verlag, Wiesbaden, pp 525–536

Buckley DR (2007) Economic integration a new approach to reform: the EBC report on the Japanese business environment. The European Business Council in Japan, Japan, pp 20–21

Czinkota MR, Kotabe M (2000) An overview of Japanese distribution strategy. In: Czinkota MR, Kotabe M (eds) Japanese distribution strategy. Thompson Learning, Belmont, pp 3–5

Daiyamondo (2009) Yunikuro zekkouchou de hi ga tsuita hi–to iryou sensou (Splendid order of heated clothing at Uniqlo [war of heated clothing]). Original in Japanese, Daiyamondo, Tokyo 12(19):14–16

Daiyamondo (2010) Tokucho: yasusa purasu alupha de (Special issue: Inexpensive plus alpha), 2(6):45 (original in Japanese)

Drew M, Howard C, Herbig P (1998) The Japanese distribution system. Eur Bus Rev 2:109–121

Gekiryu (2010) Hankyu no shinso fukei made hokai shita: Shiten rashu—no shozodai (Destroying landscape of Hankyu mental image: Rush of smallness through store closing. 4:68–71 (original in Japanese)

Ishibashi C (2010) Seben netto shoppingu (Seven net shopping). Gekiryu 4:14–17 (original in Japanese)

Kano C (2010) Yamada denki, Yodobashi camera, big camera: okata demise no hitsuzen ga umu shohin to benrisei no sougouka. (Necessity of products from big scale branch stores and adjustments of practical use of general products). Gekiryu 4:46–48 (original in Japanese)

Maguire K (2001) Penetrating the Japanese market: the challenge of non-tariff barriers. Eur Bus Rev 13(4):241–249

Meyer-Ohle H (2007) Veränderungen im japanischen Distributionssystem. In: Andreas M, Anja W (eds) Japans Zukunftindustrien. Springer, Berlin, pp 351–361

Min H (1996) Distribution channels in Japan: challenges and opportunities for the Japanese market entry. Int J Phys Distrib Logist Manage 26(10):22–35

Nestle (2007) Japanese market. Data received from Nestle Confectionery K.K. at Kobe, Japan

Nikkei Business (2010) Mitsukoshi—Isetan no kake: Nebiki ha koukyaku no tame narazu. (The game of Mitsukoshi—Isetan: Discount is not for customer). Nikkei Bus J 2(22):26–38 (original in Japanese)

Pirog III SF, Lancioni R (1996) US-Japan distribution channel cost structures: is there a significant difference? Int J Phys Distrib Logist Manage 27(1):53–66

Reuters (2013) Analyst research report snapshot. https://commerce.us.reuters.com/purchase/showReportDetail.do?docid=53166080. Accessed 24 July 2013

Schaede U (2008) Choose and focus. Cornell University Press, New York

Shao AT, Herbig P (1993) The future of sogo shosha in a global economy. Int Mark Rev 10(5): 37–55

Suka S (2010) Seichi naki tempo heisa de otozuwareru sebun ryu no hyakaten keiei no shinka (Closing of holy dreams of department stores and true management value). Diamondo 17:2–6 (original in Japanese)

Tamura M (2000) Foreword: changing structure and strategy of distribution in Japan. In: Czinkota MR, Kotabe M (eds) Japanese distribution strategy. Thompson Learning, Belmont

Tsuruta T, Yahagi T (2002) The large-scale retail stores act and its "erosion" in the 1970s—1980s. In: Miwa Y, Nishimura KG, Ramseyer JM (eds) Distribution in Japan. Oxford Press, Oxford, pp 114–147

Yamaguchi K (2009) marubeni kokumotsu ngamba uan shosha no yashin hi no maru meja– no genjitsumi. (Ambition of marubeni trading house to become number one in grape business in recent time [round sun major]. Daiyamondo, Tokyo 92–97 (original in Japanese)

Yamaguchi Y (2012) Japan's pain is wal-mart's gain. In: Bloomberg business. Dec. 15th. http://www.businessweek.com/articles/2012-11-15/japans-pain-is-wal-marts-gain. Accessed 17 March 2014

Yearbook Commerce (2013) Yearbook of the current survey of commerce (in Japanese). METI source. http://www.meti.go.jp/statistics/. Accessed October 2014

Chapter 5
Entrance to the Japanese Market

Abstract This chapter examines foreign firms' perceptions of market barriers related to the access, quality of inter-organizational institutions and their market commitment and performance in Japan. Findings suggest that foreign firms that perceive a higher level of macro-level institutional barrier are likely to have an unfavorable assessment of the accessibility of the Japanese distribution system. It was also found that firms with a favorable assessment of the accessibility of the Japanese distribution system are likely to develop better inter-organizational networks. Finally, the findings suggest that firms with a higher level of commitment to and performance in Japan are characterized by a favorable assessment of the accessibility of the Japanese distribution system and having better inter-organizational networks. However, years of experience in Japan or support of Sogo Shosha did not influence firms' perceived institutional barriers.

5.1 Introduction

As stated in Chap. 4, complexities in the Japanese distribution system are well-publicized (Borin et al. 1991; Czinkota and Kotabe 2000; Grewal and Dharwadkar 2002). The country's distribution system is described as 'complex' and 'filled with outmoded business practices' (Japan Economic Studies 2007, p. 23). The system is arguably 'incomprehensible by outsiders' (Aoyama 2007, p. 482) and Japan has long been seen as a problem market for foreign firms to enter and to deal with its distribution system. Its history is replete with cases of both foreign consumer goods companies' and of retailers' painful and frustrating failures. In the mid-1990s, the U.S. government declared the Japanese distribution system as a non-tariff barrier and a structural impediment for U.S.—Japan trade (Aoyama 2007). Many other countries responded in a similar manner. In retailing, the retreat of the French retailer, Carrefour from Japan is a well-known example (Suigai 2009).

Recently, an emerging body of literature has documented changes undergoing the Japanese distribution system (e.g. Meyer-Ohle 2007; Larke and Causton 2005;

This chapter is an updated version of Bebenroth et al. (2014) Foreign firms' access to the Japanese market. European Journal of International Management 8(1): 1–19.

R. Bebenroth, *International Business Mergers and Acquisitions in Japan*,
DOI 10.1007/978-4-431-54989-5_5

Schaefer 2006; Larke and Keri 2007; Haghirian 2007). Practical examples exist of successful foreign companies in Japan, such as Nestle in food industry or P&G (Chap. 4; Tahara 2008). Borin et al. (1991) noted some 20 years ago: '…foreign shampoos are not only receiving comparable level of distribution and in-store merchandising support, but, in many cases receive favorable levels relative to the domestic brands' (pp. 104–106).

Scholars have cited relaxation in the Law for Large-scale Retail Stores in the 1990s as a major trigger for such changes. The deregulation of Japanese laws, especially the Large Retail Store Law undoubtedly eased the opening of new stores. Edelman and Suchman (1997), however, note that 'legal rules 'cause' the organizational practices (or vice versa) is, at best, a gross simplification' (p. 502). In this regard, quality of network relationship with business partners deserves special mention in the Japanese context. Observers have noted that finding prospective agents on the basis of 'cold calls' is a highly ineffective approach in the country. The Japanese often prefer to do business with a party only when the party has been introduced properly and met face-to-face.

However, it would be erroneous to assume that new laws governing the distribution system would automatically make it easier for foreign companies to succeed in Japan. This is because a distribution system involves complex, inter-organizational, and highly- interdependent relationships among various firms. Researchers have called for greater attention to the factors that are likely to drive changes in the Japanese distribution system (Larke and Causton 2005).

From the above observations we can see that analyses of macro-level and intermediate institutions provide necessary and important insights into the Japanese distribution system. Macro-level institutional barriers include regulatory frameworks, roles of government agencies, and culture and social norms. This construct is measured with items like: "Legal regulations were difficult barriers". We refer to this construct as perceived institutional market barriers to enter Japan (abbreviated as PIMB, five items as stated in the appendix).

Our second construct is access to distribution systems (abbreviated as ACCESS, four items as stated in appendix). In this construct, we measure perceptions about access and the complexity of the distribution system. This construct is measured on a mere macro level basis as it includes perceptions of managers considering the Japanese situation in general, not necessarily regarding their own firm. One of the items, for instance, is: "For foreign companies it has become easier to sell products in Japan".

Also trade/professional associations and industry bodies (Morgan 1997) as intermediate institutions are purposeful forms of arrangements created between market and the state by economic actors concerned with the governance of the distribution system (Amin 1999; Mulgan 1994). An appropriate example to investigate the access would be to focus on Japan's multinational trading companies, sōgō shōsha, which were formed to distribute the risks associated with large and complex transactions and to reduce transaction costs through scale economies and efficient use of capital. These intermediate institutions are investigated to what extent they affect foreign firms' access to distribution systems in the Japanese market.

Our third construct concerns the focal firm's quality of inter-organizational institutions with their direct business partners (abbreviated as INTORG, seven items as stated in appendix). We investigate this construct on a micro level asking questions on a firm level basis. This construct measures the extent to which the focal firm is connected within the Japanese distribution network. For instance, one of the items is: "The experiences of our direct business partners in Japan are a valuable support for accomplishing our aims".

Finally, our fourth construct is the focal firm's market commitment and performance (abbreviated as MACP, eight items as stated in appendix). We measure this construct with items like: "Our sales and profit aims have been achieved or will be achieved in the near future". In light of the above observations, this paper empirically examines the following research questions:

Research Question 1 How does a foreign firm's perception of macro-level institutional barriers (PIMB) relates to its access to intermediate institutions (ACCESS), quality of inter organizational institutions (INTORG) and its level of commitment to and performance in the Japanese market (MACP)? (leading to H1–H3)

Research Question 2 How does access to distribution systems (ACCESS) influence the quality of inter organizational institutions (INTORG) and its level of commitment to and performance in the market (MACP)? (leading to H4 and H5)

Research Question 3 How does a foreign firm's quality of inter organizational institutions (INTORG) affect the level of commitment to and performance in the Japanese market (MACP)? (leading to H6)

The paper is structured as follows. We proceed by first providing theoretical background for the above questions leading to the development of some hypotheses. This is followed by the description of the methodology, the analysis and the findings of a preliminary empirical study. We then conduct some additional analyses. The final section discusses implications of the empirical findings for management practices and points out directions for further research.

5.2 Theoretical Background

Market entry and market penetration are among the most researched areas in international management and numerous concepts and theoretical approaches have been applied for explanatory purposes (as e.g. the meta-analysis of Canabal and White III 2008). The major approach used here is institutional theory, which covers de-institutionalization and re-institutionalization of social practices, cultural values and beliefs (North 1990). North (1990) defines institutions as 'macro-level rules of the game' (p. 27). Institutions consist of 'formal constraints (rules, laws, constitutions), informal constraints (norms of behavior, conventions, and self-imposed codes of conduct), and their enforcement characteristics' (North 1996, p. 344). Institutional theory is also described as 'a theory of legitimacy seeking' (Dickson et al. 2004,

p. 81). Legitimacy associated with the above constraints can be mapped with 'legally sanctioned behavior', 'morally governed behavior' and 'recognizable, taken-for-granted behavior' (Scott et al. 2000, p. 238) respectively.

It is important to note that inter-organizational networks (e.g., business networks) and competition are also driving forces behind an organization's input, output, as well as beliefs, norms and traditions (Dickson et al. 2004; Kimberly 1981). Organizations are embedded within larger inter-organizational networks, which generate formal and informal pressures (Pfeffer 1981). For instance, companies often imitate host country firms' or other established competitors' behavior to legitimize their activities thus acting in a polycentric way (Wind et al. 1973). Likewise, Abrahamson and Fombrun (1994) argue that the structure of inter-organizational value-added networks 'both induces and reflects the existence and persistence of more homogeneous macro-cultural beliefs about boundaries, reputations, and strategic issues' (p. 730), which may have important consequences for 'inter-organizational inertia and change, innovation, diffusion, and strategic similarity' (p. 749).

In this paper, we argue in favor of institutional inertia and state that changes in institutions occur very slowly (Clark and Soulsby 1999; Ibrahim and Galt 2002; Zweynert and Goldschmidt 2006). North (1990, p. 6) further noted that 'although formal rules may change overnight as the result of political and judicial decisions, informal constraints embodied in customs, traditions, and codes of conduct are much more impervious to deliberate policies'. As to foreign market accessibility to the distribution system, the real issue thus concerns overcoming institutional inertia related to informal institutions.

That is not to say, however, that institutions do not change at all (Parto 2005). As we have seen, laws concerning the Japanese distribution system were amended and there are visible efforts by the Japanese government to open up the distribution system to foreign firms. Opening the distribution system to foreign firms would lead to positive competitive effects such as more choices and better product offerings. A fiercer competition would not only positively influence prices for Japanese consumers, but could also encourage Japanese firms to become lean and stronger (Tahara and Inoue 2009).

Network, process and learning approaches are some of the other concepts that are applicable to the quality of business network relationships. The network approach explains foreign market entry and penetration through the establishment of 'docking nodes' in existing and sometimes overlapping network relationships in particular markets (Johanson and Mattsson 1989). Cooperation with all market players including distributors becomes crucial with external influences playing an important role in a firm's internationalization process (Welch et al. 1998; Hadley and Wilson 2003). In this regard, compared to the West, the distinguishing mark of Japanese distribution system is that foreign firms are less likely to be included in the networks.

There may be a real and/or perceived difficulty to enter rather closed networks with different rules and values such as the Japanese distribution system. Process considerations, as earlier discussed by Johanson and Vahlne (1977), are loosely connected with network approaches. The international development of companies in several stages from export to overseas production represents a gradual internationalization process and it can become more elaborated if the network aspect is integrated (Jansson and Sandberg 2008). This becomes more relevant with higher perceived psychic distance of the foreign market (Prime et al. 2009). For Western companies, the Japanese distribution system is likely to be characterized by a higher psychic distance and hence would require deeper knowledge.

5.3 Hypotheses

In this section, we propose several hypotheses that might explain relationships among our various constructs: perceived institutional market barriers (PIMB) at a macro level of institutions to enter the Japanese market, access to distribution systems (ACCESS), quality of inter organizational institutions (INTORG) and finally the level of market commitment and performance (MACP). The empirical analysis focuses first on direct interrelationships of perceived institutional market barriers (PIMB) to market commitment and performance (MACP). Also the effects of access to distribution systems (ACCESS) and quality of inter organizational institutions (INTORG) on perceived institutional market barriers (PIMB) and market commitment and performance (MACP) are analyzed. Furthermore, we investigate if access to distribution systems (ACCESS) affects the quality of inter organizational institutions (INTORG).

5.3.1 Effect of Perceived Institutional Market Barriers

The network theory states that international expansion becomes crucial with external influences. This argument is based on macro level observations. Internationalization often starts with low-risk, indirect exporting to 'psychically close' or similar markets (Johanson and Vahlne 1977). Over time and through experience, firms increase their foreign market presence. They acquire general and market specific knowledge about language, culture, laws, and information sources, which would increase their commitment to 'psychically distant' markets (Johanson and Vahlne 1990). Even if psychic distance is considered to be the distance between the home market and a foreign market (Evans et al. 2000), a paradox arises from the fact that operating in a psychically close country does not necessarily lead to a superior performance of a given firm (O'Grady 1996). To put things in context, we would argue that a market with a high perceived institutional entry barrier is likely to be regarded as a high risk market. Put differently, if past experiences associated with entering the Japanese market are judged negatively, businesses are likely to be reluctant to engage in efforts to expand their operations and penetrate the local market.

Firms entering into an international market vary widely in terms of resource stock such as the level of knowledge in the sense of preparedness (Delios and

Makino 2003). Recent research shows that flagship stores of luxury brand retailer reinforce and enhance relationships with distribution partners (Moore et al. 2010).

Inter-firm differences in perceived institutional entry barrier may well be related to their initial stock of resources which may subsequently lead to variations in the evaluations of investment uncertainties and perceptions of the need to acquire new capabilities as well as augment and improve existing capabilities (Delios and Makino 2003). As noted earlier, formal constraints as perceived institutional entry barrier should lead to a lower market commitment and performance. As we mentioned earlier, institutional market barriers will also negatively affect access to distribution systems as well as the quality of the network relationship. Based on above discussion, the following three hypotheses are presented:

H1 A foreign firm's perceived degree of institutional barrier at a macro level to enter the Japanese market is negatively related to the access to distribution systems.

H2 A foreign firm's perceived degree of institutional barrier to enter the Japanese market is negatively related to the quality of inter organizational institutions with business partners.

H3 A foreign firm's perceived degree of institutional barrier at a macro level to enter the Japanese market is negatively related to its country market commitment and performance.

5.3.2 Effects of Access to Distribution Systems

Scott (1995, p. 40) observes the existence of external and internal dimensions in institutions by stating that values and norms "…are both internalized and imposed by others". Inter-firm differences in behavior can be explained in terms of an "institutional filter", which determines the extent to which specific environmental demands affect an organization's system of norms and values and therefore are adopted (Bresser and Millonig 2003). Macro-level heterogeneity can thus arguably be attributed to "homophilic microlevel rules" (Macy and Wilier 2002, p. 13). Dienhart (2000, p. xvi) illustrates how macro- and micro-level institutions are related:

[M]arkets.are embedded in social institutions that guide behavior, involve organizations, that have internal structures (institutions) that guide behavior, and involve individuals making decisions in the context of market and organizational institutions and relationships.

Moving to our specific context of the Japanese distribution system, it is worth noting that relationships and the network approach are of special interest in the Asian context. This is also reflected to a certain extent in some of the well-known dimensions of Hofstede (2001), which placed Japan third behind China and Hong Kong in long term commitment. Business networks provide firms operating in Asia with various competitive advantages in the form of social capital (Pil and Leana 2009). It is thus argued in the Asian context that having good and longstanding relationships is of high value (Sano 1995).

We would argue that managers who place a high level of importance to the access to distribution systems at the macro level (ACCESS) are likely to have a better quality inter organizational institutions with direct business partners on a micro level (INTORG). In a similar manner, a high level of market accessibility (ACCESS) would most likely lead to a better commitment and performance (MACP). These considerations lead to the following two hypotheses:

H4 A foreign firm's perceived access to distribution systems is positively related to the quality of inter organizational institutions.

H5 A foreign firm's perceived access to distribution systems is positively related to its commitment to and performance in the Japanese market.

5.3.3 Effects of Inter Organizational Institutions

Viewed from the lens of the network approach, firms operate through various types of business relationships with suppliers, competitors and other organizations. Cunningham and Calligan (1991) argue that networking combines two abilities to be a source of competitive advantage. First, it creates a net of relationship with the potential for all parties involved to benefit complementarily. Second, it harnesses the synergistic potential of the net in pursuit of the common goal (O'Farell et al. 1998). As entering and working in networks depend on resources, it can be argued that businesses that have well-developed relationships and networks tend to place a higher level of importance on the Japanese market to enter and are likely to spearhead more efforts to market commitment and performance (Johanson and Vahlne 1992). We therefore formulate the following hypothesis from the standpoint of foreign firms operating in Japan:

H6 A foreign firm's quality of inter organizational institutions with direct business partners in Japan are positively related to the commitment to and performance in the Japanese market.

As a visual aid, Fig. 5.1 schematically represents the above hypothesized relationships in the following model:

5.4 Methodology: Questionnaire Development and Administration

A cross-sectional survey was conducted in July 2008 among German firms with various levels of presence to the Japanese market. A questionnaire was developed based on exploratory research conducted by the authors in Tokyo and in Kobe through a range of interviews in December 2007 and finally sent out with an accompanying letter to 2095 German firms, which could be classified as consumer goods companies. These firms were taken from Hoppenstedt database, in which all relevant

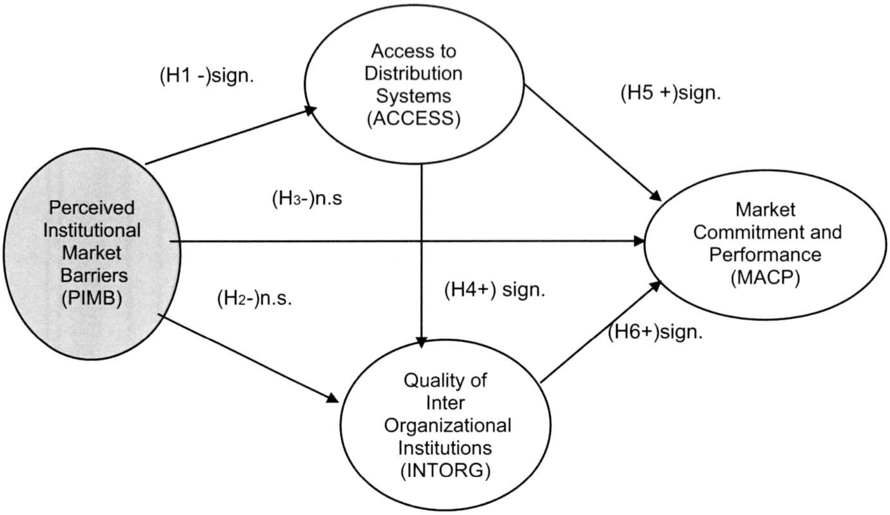

Fig. 5.1 Model for commitment to and performance in Japan. (sign. = significant, n.s. = not significant)

industries were segmented. The back translated and pre-tested questionnaire was sent out in three languages, German, English and Japanese, to give the firms possibility to let also non-German and Japanese managers respond to the questionnaire.

We received 173 questionnaires (8.26 %) of which 160 turned out to be usable. However, because of missing values, we only had 24 to 45 observations in our regression analyses. For our statistical analyses, we applied factor analyses and OLS regressions to this sample of firms. Profiles of respondent firms regarding their entry into the Japanese market, commitment to this market, size, etc. are presented in Table 5.1.

5.5 Analyses

Multiple items were used to measure German firms' perceptions of various attributes related to the Japanese market commitment and performance. Thus we employed an exploratory factor analysis (EFA) of the items used to measure perceived institutional market barrier, access to distribution systems, quality of inter organizational institutions and their market commitment and performance. Since the study deals with a new dataset, an EFA helped us to provide a factor structure and to detect "misfit" variables.

A method of iteration suggested by Rai et al. (1996) was employed to derive a stable factor structure (Table 5.2). Items with factor loadings less than 0.5 (Churchill 1979); or those with cross-loadings on two or more factors greater than 0.35 (Kim

Table 5.1 Profile of respondent firms

		No. of firms
First exports to Japan (Year)	1900–1969	8
	1970–1979	15
	1980–1989	19
	1990–1999	21
	2000-	19
Number of brands/products exported to Japan	1–2	51
	3–6	17
	8–20	7
Original entry into the Japanese market (Year)	1900–1969	7
	1970–1979	14
	1980–1989	18
	1990–1999	21
	2000-	21
Number of countries in which the company is doing business.	1–10	40
	11–20	30
	21–30	18
	31–40	14
	41–50	13
	Over 50	28
Total number of employees	1–20	10
	21–50	19
	51–100	11
	101–500	68
	501–2000	30
	over 2000	9
Proportion of business in Japan related to the whole business (%)	<1	13
	<5	26
	5–10	21
	>10	6

and Mueller 1978) were eliminated. Scales and items retained after factor analysis are presented in the Appendix.

We employed metric measures to assess German firms' perceptions of various aspects of the Japanese distribution system. Seven-point Likert scales (strongly agree = 1, strongly disagree = 7) were used in measuring each construct. All results are expressed in terms of the original scores rather than z-transformed scores. Perceived barriers of market entry were originally measured with eight items. The analysis of items resulted in a five item solution, with a reliability estimate of 0.816. This factor was termed 'perceived institutional market barriers (PIMB)'. Difficulties when doing business in Japan were measured with 12 items. However, the factor

Table 5.2 Result of factor analysis

	No. of items used in the survey	No. of items after the final iteration	Cronbach's Alpha
Perceived institutional market barriers (PIMB)	8	5	0.816
Difficulties when doing business in Japan	12	1	NA
Access to distribution system (ACCESS)	8	7	0.844[a]
Quality of inter organizational institutions (INTORG)	13	7	0.852
Market commitment and performance (MACP)	11	8	0.870

[a] For this factor, we further deleted three factors due to a low response rate and finally came up with a 4-item solution. This value corresponds to the four retained items

analysis failed to converge on a solution with a stable factor structure. Therefore, we did not apply this factor to our analysis.

Firms' access to the Japanese distribution system was measured with eight items. It yielded a solution of seven factors with a reliability coefficient of 0.844 (Cronbach's Alpha). Because of a low response of the firms, however, we deleted three factors. The other factors were not answered to a satisfied extent and did not permit an unequivocal interpretation; its meaningfulness on conceptual and psychometric grounds was questionable. As such, these measures were deleted from all subsequent analyses (see Zeithaml et al. 1996 for a similar approach). Therefore, we came up with a 4-item solution for an intermediate institutional level, referred as "access to distribution systems" of the Japanese market (ACCESS).

The quality of inter organizational institutions in Japan was measured with 13 items. The results from a factor analysis indicated a one factor solution of seven items (Cronbach's Alpha = 0.852). This factor was labeled as 'quality of inter organizational institutions' (INTORG).

Details of the commitment to and performance of a company's business in Japan were measured with 11 items. A factor analysis yielded an eight—item, single factor scale with a reliability coefficient of 0.875. This factor was labeled as 'market commitment and performance" to the Japanese market (MACP)'. Overall, the scales have excellent internal consistency, which is evidenced by alphas ranging from 0.816 to 0.875. These clearly exceed the threshold of 0.7 that Nunnally (1978)

Table 5.3 Mean, standard deviation, and correlation matrix

	1. PIMB	2. ACCESS	3. INTORG	4. MACP
1. PIMB	–	–	–	–
2. ACCESS	−0.617[c]			
3. INTORG	−0.069	0.341		
4. MACP	−0.058	0.209	0.661[a]	
Mean	4.43	4.53	3.15	3.33
SD	1.51	1.19	1.13	1.26

suggested. In the following, we present our descriptive statistics, correlation matrix and then OLS regression results.

5.6 Findings

5.6.1 General Tests

Descriptive statistics and correlation matrix of the variables used in the analyses are presented in Table 5.3. The key dependent variable of our regressions includes commitment to and performance in the Japanese market (MACP). The two variables explaining the market commitment and performance are access to distribution systems (ACCESS) and quality of inter organizational institutions (INTORG). Our independent variable consists of perceived institutional market entry barriers (PIMB).

Our descriptive results show that foreign firms have on average positive perceptions about institutional market barriers. For instance, legal regulations are not anymore considered as tough barriers to enter the Japanese market (Mean=4.43, S.D.=. 1.51). Furthermore, foreign firms are positive about the quality of their direct business partners (Mean=3.15, S.D.=1.13). However, foreign firms have negative perceptions of the access of the Japanese distribution system (Mean=4.53, S.D.=1.19). Firm's market commitment and performance is below the neutral point of 4.0 and hence is perceived as positive (Mean=3.33, S.D.=1.26).

As presented in Table 5.3, perceived institutional market barriers has a significant negative correlation with the access of foreign firms (−0.617, $p<0.01$). Likewise, the variable related to inter organizational institutions positively correlated to commitment and performance of foreign firms in Japan (0.661, $p<0.01$). In table 5.4, we first consider the OLS regression results with access to distribution systems (ACCESS) as the dependent variable and perceived institutional entry barriers (PIMB) as the independent variable (Model I). There is a significant and negative relationship as predicted in our hypothesis 1. We thus found support for our hypothesis that lower perceived entry barriers are likely to lead to higher access to distribution systems.

Our second variable as quality of inter organizational institutions (INTORG) is not statistically significant to perceived institutional market barriers (PIMB) as

Table 5.4 Determinants of market commitment and performance, perceived accessibility and quality of inter-organizational institutions

IV	Model I DV: ACCESS	Model I DV: INTORG	Model III DV: MACP	Model IV: DV: ACCESS	Model V: DV: MACP	Model VI: DV: MACP
Intercept	*23.454* *(9.239)*[a]	*2.954* *(2.748)*[a]	*3.775* *(5.726)*[a]	*12.483* *(5.382)*[a]	*2.525* *(3.710)*[a]	*0.995* *(2.748)*[a]
PIMB	−1.729[b] (2.858)	−0.040 (0.712)	−0.055 (0.7)			
ACCESS					*0.081* *(2.203)*[b]	
INTORG				*1.551* *(2.320)*[b]		*0.882* *(8.212)*[a]
N	24	31	36	38	45	51
R^2	0.271	0.005	0.004	0.130	0.101	0.579
Adj-R^2	0.238	−0.030	−0.025	0.106	0.081	0.571
F	*8.165*[a]	0.139	0.151	*5.384*[b]	*4.854*[b]	*67.444*[a]
Hypothesis tested	$H_{1:}$ supported	$H_{2:}$ not supported.	$H_{3:}$ not supported.	$H_{4:}$ supported	$H_{5:}$ supported	$H_{6:}$ supported

[a] significant at 1 % level
[b] significant at 5 % level
[c] significant at 10 % level

suggested in our hypotheses 2; that is, we failed to reach a level of significance above chance (Model II). Heavy institutional barriers (PIMB) do not show a significant negative effect to quality of inter organizational institutions (INTORG).

Next, we discuss our OLS regression results for our dependent market commitment and performance (MACP) in table 5.4 (Model III). The direction of the effects of market entry barriers is negative as predicted by hypothesis 3 but not significant. That means, our data failed to provide evidence that higher market barriers lead to a lower commitment to and performance in the Japanese market for foreign firms. We then tested the effect of the variable access to distribution systems (ACCESS) on the quality of inter organizational institutions (INTORG) and found support for hypothesis 4. This means that firms with a favorable perception of the access to distribution systems tend to have a better quality of inter organizational institutions (Model IV).

Now, we take access to distribution systems (ACCESS) and quality of inter organizational institutions (INTORG) as independent variables and test the effect on market commitment and performance (MACP). The findings in table 5.4 (Model V) also support our hypothesis that the perceived access to distribution systems has a statistically significant positive effect on market commitment and performance (MACP). Likewise, the result in table 5.4 (Model VI) is supportive of our hypothesis regarding the effect of the quality of inter organizational institutions (INTORG) on market commitment and performance (MACP) (Tables 5.3, 5.4).

Table 5.5 Comparison of INTROG and ACCESS for firms distributing products in Japan via and without Sogo Shosha

	N	Mean (INTROG)	*N*	Mean (ACCESS)
Without Sogo Shosha	32	2.9241	11	4.0758
Via Sogo Shosha	14	3.3878	9	4.5741
t-test	($t=-1.18$, $p=0.255$)			

Table 5.6 Comparison of PIMB for firms entered into the Japanese market before and after 2000

Company's original entry into the Japanese market	*N*	Perceived institutional barriers (PIMB)
Before the year 2000	30	4.36
Year 2000 or after	8	4.68
t-test	$t=0.518$ (df=36)	

5.7 Additional Tests

Two additional tests were performed (Table 5.5) to investigate if Sogo Shosha (Japanese trading firms) positively influence foreign firms to perceive a better "quality of inter organizational institutions" (INTROG) or to perceive a better "access to distribution systems" (ACCESS). To put different, do companies distributing products via or without Sogo Shosha receive a more positive quality of relationships and a better distribution accessibility in Japan?

Table 5.5 indicates that companies distributing products to Japan do not significantly differ in terms of the ACCESS and INTROG scores when employing a Sogo Shosha. For ACCESS, the difference of -0.498 failed to reach significance ($t=-1.18$, $p=0.255$)[1] meaning there is no improvement when Sogo Shosha are included in the distribution system.

Another area of interest was to compare firms' changes in regard to their perceived barriers to market entry in recent years. As the Large-Scale Retail Store Location Act was enacted in 2000, our independent samples t-test was performed to determine whether foreign firms entering the Japanese market before/after 2000 differed in terms of the perceived market entry barriers. As Table 5.6 indicates there is no significant difference in terms of the perceived barriers of market entry for firms before and after 2000.

5.8 Discussion

A review of the distribution literature as well as anecdotal evidence indicates changes in conditions related to foreign companies' market access in Japan. For this, we test the direct relationship between German firms' perceived institutional market

[1] Equal variances were assumed.

barriers and their market commitment and performance. We refer this first construct as formal institutions. Our tests also involve two variables related to informal institutions: German firms' perceived access to distribution systems and the quality of inter organizational institutions. We refer these as formal institutions. Our tests also involve two variables related to informal institutions: German firms' perceived access to distribution systems and the quality of inter organizational institutions.

Applying considerations mainly from institutional theory and the network approach, some new light is shed on recent developments. Despite governmental supports to attract foreign firm investments to Japan, foreign firms still consider the Japanese market as far from accessible. Our direct test concerning the effect of German firms' perception of institutional market barriers on their market commitment to and performance (MACP) in Japan did not show statistically significant results.

The findings of this research thus support the view that legal changes alone do not automatically lead to a better market commitment and performance. We then tested the effects of the two informal constructs, access to distribution systems (ACCESS) and quality of inter organizational institutions (INTORG) on MACP. We can see that there are significant positive effects of both of these variables on MACP. Thus, our findings indicate that firms with a better access to distribution systems and a better quality of inter organizational institutions are likely to show a higher market commitment to and performance in Japan.

One way to encourage foreign firms' investments in Japan would be to help them deal with the informal institutions, for instance, by offering smoother ways for them to improve their relationships with Japanese firms and to support access to the market. In light of the stereotypically expectations that surround the Japanese distribution system, it is worth noting that firms have good relationships with their Japanese business partners and report positively about their cooperation partners. In this sense it is no surprise to us that a higher level of access to distribution systems and a high quality of inter organizational institutions leads to a stronger market commitment and performance. Also, access to distribution systems seems to positively influence the quality of inter organizational institutions.

Our findings have important implications for public policy. The above analysis indicates the importance of informal rather than formal institutions for increasing commitment and performance of foreign firms operating in Japan. In this regard, a December 2004 survey conducted among Japanese citizens by Nomura Research Institute deserves mention. Over 30% of respondents said that foreign companies' image had improved compared to a decade before whereas less than 9% thought that it had worsened (Suginohara 2008). To encourage further foreign investments in Japan, the Japanese government may need to go beyond changing just legal regulations. As macro-level political issues do not seem to influence German firms' market commitment and performance, measures need to be taken to help them have an improved access to the distribution system or deal with Japanese firms in order to facilitate their operations in the country. There is also evidence in our sample that the quality of network of foreign firms in Japan influences market commitment and performance. It thus seems that firms having a solid network are likely to have a higher level of market commitment to and performance in Japan.

5.9 Limitations and Future Research

A first limitation of our research concerns the limited geographical basis of respondent firms as this study relates only to German firms operating in Japan. Also, due to unit non-response and item non- response, we were left with a small sample size and, thus, limited statistical power to compare firms' perception of the Japanese distribution system and the effects of various explanatory variables. A third limitation concerns the fact that only cross sectional data were collected. For investigating changes of perceptions over time longitudinal data would be more appropriate. A fourth limitation of the paper is that our findings are based on the accounts of events as perceived by a single organizational member, which has a potential to lead to a single-source bias. Finally, the gap between perception and reality may be due to various reasons such as lack of interest and information, strong prejudice and country image, non-representative opinions of people and media, and selective information processing. Besides cultural distance was sorted out as we just investigated German firms, psychic distance of managers can be defined in broader terms. This is an individual-level phenomenon and attitudes towards a given market may thus differ from person to person (Sousa and Bradley 2006). As we lacked necessary data, we were not able to emphasize the issue of psychic distance.

The perspective developed here suggests many exciting directions for future research. Specifically, this study gives some insights into changes of a country's distribution system. The focus of this paper was on the consumer goods industry and Japan-based German firms. The distribution problems facing foreign firms in the B2B sector is likely to be different from those in the B2C sector.

Future research based on this paper's framework can be extended to firms from other geographic areas (e.g. North America, Asia, etc.) operating in Japan. Firms from other geographic regions may have different expectations as to the Japanese distribution system and hence may assess the recent changes differently. Another interesting avenue for future research is to examine how national regulatory framework related to distribution systems triggers changes in informal institutions related to such systems. One such example concerns the changes in the Chinese distribution system following China's entry into the World Trade Organization (WTO).

Finally, future researchers could study how interrelationships among the above constructs vary across industries and business sectors in Japan. Analysts, for instance, have noted that deregulation in Japan have taken place more rapidly in areas such as consumer goods compared to industrial goods leading to more explosive growth of the former compared to the later. A comparison of foreign firms in consumer goods and industrial goods sectors in terms of perceived institutional entry barriers, level of market commitment and performance, access to distribution systems and quality of inter organizational institutions with business partners thus might be worthwhile target of study.

5.10 Conclusion

This paper examined interrelationships among foreign firms' perceptions of market barriers in Japan. Questions were related to the access, quality of inter-organizational institutions and on foreign firms' market commitment and performance in Japan. There is evidence that foreign firms that perceive a higher level of macro-level institutional barrier are likely to have an unfavourable assessment of the accessibility of the Japanese distribution system.

Also, firms with a favourable assessment of the accessibility of the Japanese distribution system are likely to develop better inter-organizational networks with other firms in Japan. Furthermore, the findings suggest that firms with a higher level of commitment to and performance in Japan are characterized by a favourable assessment of the accessibility of the Japanese distribution system and to have better inter-organizational networks. Years of experience in Japan or support of Sogo Shosha; however, did not matter for foreign firms to have lower perceived institutional barriers.

Questions

1. How do you explain problems of foreign consumer goods companies' and of retailers' to enter the Japanese market?
2. Has foreign firms' perceived accessibility to the Japanese distribution system changed in a favorable direction in recent years?
3. What factors seem to cause problems for foreign firms to successfully enter the Japanese market?
4. Are Japanese Sogo Shosha (Japanese trading houses) helpful for foreign firms to successfully enter the Japanese market?
5. Have market barriers reduced for foreign firms in recent years?

Answers

1. Japanese domestic competitors are not interested in having foreign competition. Failures are visible in the retreat of the French Carrefour supermarkets from Japan.
2. Foreign firms still perceive the Japanese market as difficult to enter.
3. Relationships with Japanese firms seem to determine whether or not a foreign firm has success in Japan. The better the relationship with Japanese firms, the more positive are foreign firms about the Japanese market.
4. Evidence suggests that Sogo Shosha are not helpful for foreign firms to enter the Japanese market. There is a little better relationship with business partners visible and a better access to the market. However, this is not statistically significant.
5. No, to split firms in two groups before and after the year 2000, there is no evidence that a lowering of market barriers has happened.

Appendix

Scales and Items Retained After Factor Analysis

Perceived Institutional Market Barriers to Enter Japan (PIMB) (cronbach's Alpha = 0.816)

The following statements apply to our company′s original entry into the Japanese market ___ (year):

- Legal regulations were difficult barriers.
- Taxes were too high.
- The assistance of governmental institutions was unsatisfactory/bureaucratic barriers were high.
- The Japanese distribution system was extremely complex (intransparent/too many levels/too costly etc.).
- Language and cultural differences caused problems.

Access to Distribution Systems in the Japanese Market (ACCESS) (cronbach's Alpha = 0.844)

In our opinion the following statements apply as follows:

- The distribution system in Japan is becoming less complex.
- For foreign companies it has become easier to sell products in Japan.
- The dealing with Japanese trading companies has become more convenient.
- It is more convenient getting access to the Japanese distribution system.

Quality of Inter Organizational Institutions with Direct Business Partners in Japan (INTORG) (cronbach's Alpha = 0.852)

In our opinion the following statements apply:

- All of our direct Japanese business partners actively promote our products.
- Some of our direct Japanese business partners have made special expenses for our business.
- Our direct Japanese business partners are satisfied with the economic results of our cooperation.
- The business views of our direct business partners correspond to our strategic plans.
- The experiences of our direct business partners in Japan are a valuable support for accomplishing our aims.

- Our products are essential for the market success of our direct business partners.
- We are satisfied with our business results due to the cooperation of most of our Japanese business partners.

Market Commitment and Performance in Japan (MACP) (cronbach's Alpha = 0.870)

The following statements apply to our company:

- The business we are doing in Japan is of outstanding importance within our international business activities.
- Generally, our Japanese retail partners engage themselves in selling of our products.
- Japanese retail partners understand our corporate and sales philosophy.
- The Japanese consumer is very different from the European consumer
- Our sales and profit aims have been achieved or will be achieved in the near future
- It was a good decision doing business in Japan.
- Long-term relationships can be built easily with our direct and indirect customers.
- Our products in Japan are of high brand equity.

References

Abrahamson E, Fombrun CJ (1994) Macrocultures: determinants and consequences. Acad Manage Rev 19(4):728–755

Amin A (1999) An institutionalist perspective on regional economic development. Int J Urban Reg Res 23:365–378

Aoyama Y (2007) Oligopoly and the structural paradox of retail TNCs: an assessment of Carrefour and Wal-Mart in Japan. J Econ Geogr 7(4):471–490

Bebenroth R, Kshetri N, Huenerberg R (2014) Foreign firms' access to the Japanese market. Eur J Int Manage 8(1):1–19

Borin N, Vranken CV, Farris PW (1991) A Pilot test of discrimination in the japanese distribution. J Retail 67(1):93–106

Bresser RKF, Millonig K (2003) Institutional capital: competitive advantage in light of the new institutionalism in organization theory. Schmalenbach Bus Rev 55(3):220–241

Canabal A, White GO III (2008) Entry mode research: past and future. Int Bus Rev 17:267–284

Churchill AG (1979) A paradigm for developing better measures of marketing constructs. J Mark Res 16(1):64–73

Clark E, Soulsby A (1999) Organisational change in post-communist Europe. Routledge, London

Cunningham MT, Calligan K (1991) Competitiveness through networks of relationships in information technology product markets. In: Paliwoda SJ (ed) New perspectives on international marketing. Routledge, London, pp 509–524

Czinkota MR, Kotabe M (2000) Entering the Japanese market. Ind Mark Manage 29:483–491

Delios A, Makino S (2003) Timing of entry and the foreign subsidiary performance of Japanese firms. J Int Mark 11(3):83–105

Dickson MW, BeShears RS, Gupta V (2004) The impact of societal culture and industry on organizational culture: Theoretical explanations. In: House RJ, Hanges PJ, Javidan M, Dorfman PW, Gupta V (eds) Culture, leadership, and organizations : the GLOBE study of 62 societies. Sage, California, pp 74–90
Dienhart JW (2000) Business institutions, and ethics. Oxford University Press, New York
Edelman LB, Suchman MC (1997) The legal environments of organizations. Annu Rev Sociol 23:479–515
Evans J, Treadgold A, Mavondo F (2000) Psychic distance and the performance of international retailers: a suggested theoretical framework. Int Mark Rev 17(4/5):373–391
Grewal R, Dharwadkar R (2002) The role of the institutional environment in marketing channels. J Mark 66(3):82–97
Hadley RD, Wilson HIM (2003) The network model of internationalization and experiential knowledge. Int Bus Rev 12:697–717
Haghirian P (2007) Markteintritt in Japan. Orac-Wirtschaftspraxis, Vienna
Hofstede G (2001) Culture's consequences: comparing values, behaviors, institutions and organizations across nations. Sage, Thousand Oaks
Ibrahim G, Galt V (2002) Bye-bye central planning, hello market hiccups: institutional transition in Romania. Cambridge J Econ 26(1):105–118
Jansson H, Sandberg S (2008) Internationalization of small and medium sized enterprises in the Baltic Sea Region. J Int Manage 14:65–77
Johanson J, Mattsson LG (1989) Internationalisation in industrial systems—a network approach. In: Hood N, Vahlne J-E (eds) Strategies in global competition. Routledge, London. pp 287–314
Johanson J, Vahlne JE (1977) The internationalization process of a firm- a model of knowledge development and increasing foreign market commitments. J Int Bus Stud 8:23–32
Johanson J, Vahlne JE (1990) The mechanism of internationalization. Int Mark Rev 7(4):11–24
Johanson J, Vahlne JE (1992) Management of foreign market entry. Scand Int Bus Rev 1(3):9–27
Kim JO, Mueller CW (1978) Factor analysis: statistical methods and practical issues. Sage, Beverly Hills
Kimberly JR (1981) Managerial innovation. In: Nystrom PC, Starbuck WH (eds) Handbook of organizational design. Oxford University, New York, pp 84–104
Larke R, Causton M (2005) Japan—a modern retail superpower. Palgrave Macmillan, Basingstoke
Larke R, Keri D (2007) Recent changes in the Japanese wholesale system and the importance of the Sogo Shosha. Int Rev Retail Distrib Consum Res 17(4):377–390
Macy MW, Willer R (2002) From factors to actors: computational sociology and agent-based modeling. Annu Rev Sociol 28:143–166
Meyer-Ohle H (2007) Veränderungen im japanischen Distributionssystem. In: Moerke A, Walke A (eds) Japans Zukunftindustrien. Springer, Heidelberg, pp 351–361
Moore CM, Doherty AM, Doyle SA (2010) Flagship stores as a market entry method: the perspective of luxury fashion retailing. Eur J Mark 44(1/2):139–161
Morgan K (1997) The learning region: institutions, innovation and regional renewal. Reg Stud 31(5):491–503
Mulgan G (1994) Democratic dismissal, competition, and contestability among the quangos. Oxford Rev Econ Policy 10(3):51–60
North DC (1990) Institutions, institutional change and economic performance. Harvard University, Cambridge
North DC (1996) Epilogue: economic performance through time. In: Alston LJ, Eggertsson T, North DC (eds) Empirical studies in institutional change. Cambridge University Press, Cambridge, pp 342–355
Nunnally JC (1978) Psychometric theory (2nd Ed). McGraw-Hill, New York.
O'Farell PN, Wood PA, Zheng J (1998) Regional influences on foreign market development by business service companies: elements of strategic context explanation. Reg Stud 32(1):31–48
O'Grady, Shawna L, Henry (1996) The psychic distance paradox. J Int Bus Stud 27(2):309–333
Parto S (2005) Economic Activity and Institutions: Taking Stock. J Econ Issues 39(1):21–52
Pfeffer J (1981) Management as symbolic action. Res Organ Behav 3:1–52

Pil F, Leana C (2009) Applying organizational research to public school reform: the effects of teacher human and social capital on student performance. Acad Manage J 2009:1101–1124
Prime N, Obadia C, Vida I (2009) Psychic distance in exporter-importer relationships: a grounded theory approach. Int Bus Rev 18:184–198
Rai A, Borah S, Ramaprasad A (1996) Critical success factors for strategic alliances in the information technology industry: an empirical study. Decis Sci 27(1):141–155
Sano Y (1995) Human resource management in Japan. Keio University, Tokyo
Schaefer P (2006) Handel in Japan—Strukturen und Entwicklungstendenzen. In: Zentes J (eds) Handbuch handel. Gabler, Wiesbaden, pp 209–231
Scott WR (1995) Institutions and organizations. Sage, California
Scott RW, Ruef M, Mendel PJ, Caronna CA (2000) Institutional change and healthcare organizations: from professional dominance to managed care. University of Chicago, Chicago
Sousa CMP, Bradley F (2006) Cultural distance and psychic distance: two peas in a Pod? J Int Mark 14(1):49–70
Suginohara M (2008) The politics of economic nationalism in japan: backlash against inward foreign direct investment? Asian Surv 48(5):839–859
Suigai S (2009) Kokusai kigyo karefu-ru ni hiru honkokku no kishingo [Yellow light on the country for an international company like Carrefour]. Gekiryu 7:136–140
Tahara K (2008) Eraberareruten no himitsu [The secret of a choosen shop]. Daiamondo 10(18):30–38
Tahara K, Inoue K (2009) Yotsu mega hyakaten no senryaku to nandai [Strategy and problems of four mega department stores]. Daiamondo 10(18):36–38
Welch DE, Welch LS, Young LC, Wilkinson IS (1998) The importance of networks in export promotion: policy issues. J Int Mark 6(4):66–82
Wind Y, Douglas SP, Perlmutter HV (1973) Guidelines for developing international marketing strategies. J Mark 37:14–23
Zeithaml VA, Berry LL, Parasuraman A (1996) The behavioral consequences of service quality. J Mark 60(2):31–46
Zweynert J, Goldschmidt N (2006) The two transitions in central and eastern europe as processes of institutional transplantation. J Econ Issues 40(4):895–918

Part II
Mergers and Acquisitions

Chapter 6
Setting the Stage for Mergers and Acquisitions

Abstract This chapter deals about "setting the stage for Mergers and Acquisitions. It will be discussed that the shareholder structure has changed in Japan. Regional and City banks decreased their share ownership, while foreign investors increased it to almost 30 %. Also, several legal changes were implemented into the M&A relevant laws to foster an increased M&A. There are many reasons for undertaking an M&A, some are globally identical, for example, to create synergies or to save costs. However, there are also some Japan specific reasons to mention. One of them is that a (Japanese) firm needs to divest because it is too conglomerated. That would give also foreign firms a chance to easily access the (Japanese) market.

6.1 Introduction

There is a long-standing argument that Japan is difficult for foreign firms to enter. There is also some evidence, that the current situation is more relaxed and that restrictions have been lowered for firms to enter Japan. In this, the development of the shareholder structure in the last years is discussed. Also, legal changes in Japan concerning Mergers and Acquisitions (M&A) are introduced. Then the focus will be on M&A, after a definition, theories for them are discussed. Also, bidder motivations are highlighted and it is to ask to what extent M&A actually create value.

6.2 Shareholder Structure

In a wave of increased liberalization of the Japanese economy back in the 80s and 90s, the shareholder structure of Japanese listed firms changed drastically. In the 80s, individual shareholders decreased their holdings in Japanese firms. In contrast, during the mid-80s, financial institutions rapidly increased their holdings. From the early 90s, the role of foreign shareholders became more dominant in the Japanese market. For example, in the early 1990s, foreign investors held merely 4 % of shares

R. Bebenroth, *International Business Mergers and Acquisitions in Japan*,
DOI 10.1007/978-4-431-54989-5_6

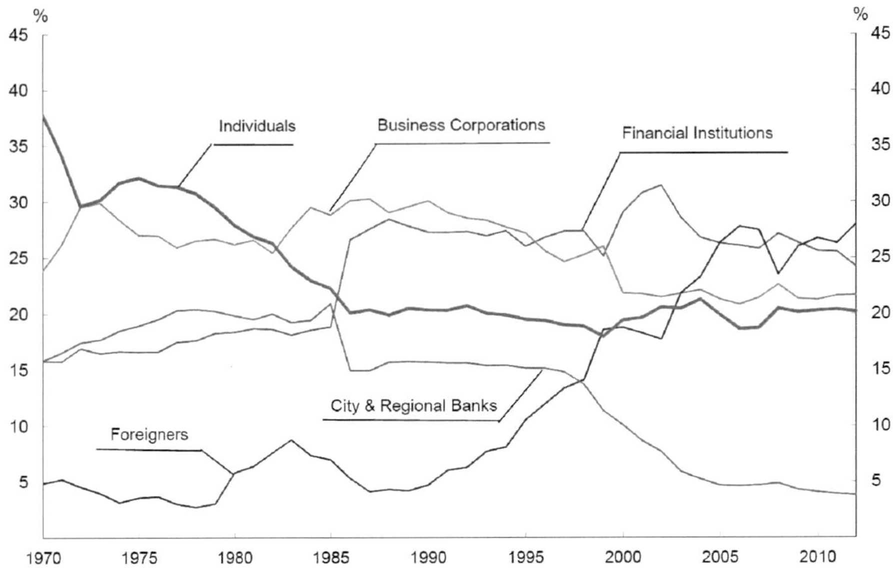

Fig. 6.1 Changes of market value by shareholder types

at Japanese firms. In 2012, foreign investors held 28 % of the shares at Japanese firms (Fig. 6.1). In the past few decades, the cross shareholding system has been dismantled resulting in a decreased amount of shareholding by business corporations. For example, from the late 1980s, business corporations held about 30 % of the shares; however, by 2012, that percent decreased to about 21 %. Japanese financial institutions had a peak in early 2000 but have since weakened to less than 25 % in the year 2012.

The group which had the highest decrease in holdings of Japanese firms were regional banks and city banks. They reduced their share portfolio drastically in the last years. For example, until the Plaza Agreement in 1985, City banks and Regional banks held about 20 % of all shares of listed Japanese firms. In the late 1980s, regional banks and city banks still held about 15 % of the shares. However, this number decreased to 3.8 % in the year 2012.

The changes in the structure of the shareholdings may have been a result of the behavior of firms to conduct M&A more frequently. It can be hypothesized that these changes in the ownership of Japanese firms led to more pressure for firms to increase profits. Previously, Regional banks and City banks aimed to create long-term relationships with the management of the firms rather than pressure these firms to increase profits. Foreign investors were especially outspoken and more forceful in urging the firms' management to continually strive for gains in profit.

6.3 Legal Changes

6.3.1 *Examples of Legal Changes*

In Japan, M&A's are regulated by the Ministry of Economy, Trade, and Industry, the Ministry of Justice, and the Financial Services Agency. The fact that there were so many different regulatory bodies may have caused the Japanese takeover market to be ridden with many complicated regulations. There were many efforts by the government to harmonize regulations as well as to regulate counter measures against acquisitions and the protection of minority shareholders (Igaki and Yamaguchi 2011).

Previously, firms dealing in large M&A transactions had to undertake a pre and a post notification process. Prior notification was required for the largest and more important deals. For example, if a takeover occurred in one of the more sensitive industries, like the energy industry, firms had to submit a pre-notification. If a firm acquired more than 5 % of outstanding shares of a firm, only a post notification had to be submitted. Additionally, most inbound direct investments required post-notification if the investor was a national of any country other than Japan (Igaki and Yamaguchi 2011)[1]. This has changed in recent years. Nowadays, there are normally only post-notifications required, which are easier for firms to handle because the deal itself is normally not affected. Post-notifications have to be submitted, within 15 days from the day the transaction closed, through the Bank of Japan to the Ministry of Finance and, depending on the industry, through other organizations as well (Igaki and Yamaguchi 2011).

6.3.2 *Overhaul of Commercial Code*

In the year 1997, the ban on holding companies by the Anti-Monopoly law was lifted. This ban was implemented by the US after WW2 to prevent a reemerging strong Japanese war industry (Chap. 2). As a result, the Japanese M&A market grew especially because spin-offs and transfers of businesses which did not relate to the firms' core businesses (Aoki 2000; Milhaupt 2006). Also, lawmakers began in 1998 to introduce annual revisions to several different laws concerning M&A, which resulted in a new Corporation Law in 2006. Under this law, whole industries became severely deregulated. For example, in 1977 under the previous Prime Minister Hashimoto, the financial industry was deregulated to make financial institutions more efficient. This deregulation was dubbed the "Big-Bang". Due to the "Japanese Big-Bang" in the financial industry, many other industries were also affected. Deregulations followed in the healthcare and oil industries. Also, industries with a high overseas competition, like pharmaceuticals, were deregulated.

[1] This notification regime was the result of the amendment of the Foreign Exchange Law in Jan. 1992.

In October 1999 the Commercial Code was amended to allow payments to be made solely with stocks. This is also called equity swap, when firms pay for a takeover with their own shares instead of using money. Until 2000, most Japanese firms practiced unconsolidated accounting, which meant that affiliated firms, like subsidiaries, were not included in the balance sheets. This made it easy for firms to hide inefficient subsidiaries, which were not visible to the outside. Announced in 1998 and effective from 2000 obligatory consolidated accounting was introduced. There is evidence by Onji et al. (2012) that before these amendments were created, subsidiaries were often motivated by the need of the management to shift access personnel to other firms. These accounting amendments also led to an increased takeover market.

The previous, time-consuming merger process was also simplified in April 2001 (Kunimaru 2010, p. 35). In May 2007, triangle mergers were introduced (Ishikawa 2013). In this scenario, for example, a Japan based German subsidiary could acquirer a Japanese firm and have the German head-quarter pay or exchange their shares. As a result, the M&A market has grown rapidly in the last years (Chap. 6).

In Dec. 2008, amendments to Financial Instruments and Exchange Law came into effect and introduced changes to the takeover bid rules and procedures for "combined transactions" (Igaki and Yamaguchi 2011). In 2010, modifications on tax regime were introduced to streamline in-group transactions of firms. That meant, the tax preference given to in-group capital transactions was dropped.

6.4 M&A and Other Types of Market Entry

6.4.1 Definitions of M&A

The typology of M&A can be split in two separate units, in Mergers (*Gappei*) and in Acquisitions (*Baishu*)[2]. Acquisitions refer to a takeover where one firm, the bidder acquires (at least parts of) another firm, the target (Oesterle 2012, p. 4). In this vein, normally (but not always) the stronger firm acquires the weaker one. An acquisition can also be described as an absorption or a buyout. Examples of acquisitions would be Takeda Pharmaceuticals buying Nycomed from Switzerland or Daikin buying Goodman from the US.

In contrast to acquisitions, mergers happen when two firms merge together to form a new one. In this scenario, theoretically both firms would be of equal size and equal power at the beginning and after the deal[3]. That means, after the deal, both firms would continue to share equal power. This is a highly theoretical construct and an example would be the previous unsuccessful attempt of merging the German

[2] Definitions however vary according to the authors. Aurora et al. (2011), for example, defines "mergers" as "mergers through consolidation" and "acquisitions" as "mergers through absorption", pp. 81–82).

[3] Oesterle (2012, p. 3) defines mergers as follows: "In a merger, the owners of separate firms of not too dissimilar sizes pool their interests in a singly firm".

car maker Daimler Benz together to the US American car maker Chrysler. That deal having a volume of US$ 36 billion was called a "Merger of Equals" to signal that both parties shared the same power. It ended up in failure and Chrysler was sold for US$ 7.4 billion at the end to Cerberus Capital Management (80.1 %), an institutional investment fund (Mateja 2007).

At a majority acquisition the bidder firm obtains the majority of shares that means more than 50 %. However, in some cases, only a 30 % share would be enough to have a majority acquisition. At some larger firms, a shareholding of 30 % signals de facto the power over the firm. In this scenario, the bidder sizes voting power at the target to control it or to integrate it into their own business. Some deals are acquisitions but could also be interpreted as capital participations; especially in the case of bigger transactions, where the amount of outstanding shares is too high (and too costly) for a bidder firm to conduct a majority acquisition. In the car market, for example, when Nissan was taken over by Renault or Mitsubishi Motors was taken over by previously Daimler Chrysler in early 2000, the amount of shares taken over was about 20–30 %. It was higher than 5 % but did not a reach majority of 50 %. However, both firms were able to substantially influence their Japanese partners' business. In the case of Nissan, it led to a great success, but for the case of Mitsubishi to an economic failure (Yoshida and Bebenroth 2006). Besides majority acquisitions, there are other possible types of acquisitions. These other types are integrated into Japanese M&A statistics (e.g. Recof M&A Database and can be divided into a capital participation, a capital increase, and in a business transfer.

The capital participation occurs when a bidder firm participates at a target, but with only a small amount of shares. The amount is normally under 5 % of all outstanding shares. This is the cut off line because in many countries, as well as in Japan, if an investor purchased more they would have to go public (Igaki and Yamaguchi 2011). Capital participations occur when bidders either do not want to or may not be able to take full control of the target. For example, some firms test their engagement at a given target first with a small amount of shares. Additionally, they have only a relatively small amount of money at stake. With a capital participation, a firm may wait to see, whether the investment should be increased.

A capital participation may also be grounded in governmental regulations and laws. In some industries, a government may not allow bidders to overtake more than a certain amount of shares at a given target. This is especially relevant for cross border deals. A Japanese example of that would be when Delta Airlines acquired a small amount of shares form one of the two largest Japanese airline carriers, Japan Airlines (JAL) in 2009. The reason for only having a capital participation was that the Civil Aeronautics Law prevents cross border acquisitions giving foreign firms full control over one of the two existing airline carriers. In other words, the reason that laws do not allow majority acquisitions is that of economic dependency on foreign countries. Foreign persons, or corporations cannot register ownership of any aircraft in Japan having more than one-third of the voting rights (Igaki and Yamaguchi 2011). This is put in place because bringing Japanese and foreigners in and out of the country is of a high strategic importance. If an airline carrier went bankrupt just because a foreign investor withdrew their money there would be a tremendous negative effect on the whole country's economy—not just on the airline industry.

Another type of acquisition is capital increase. If a bidder already participates in the target, with a small amount of shares and the bidder is satisfied they would simply increase their investment, which is called a capital increase. Depending on the case, some bidders, but not all, want to take full control over their target in the second or even third step of their investment. An example where this form of capital increase took place in Japan is when the French yoghurt maker Danone increased their capital participation at Japanese yoghurt maker Yakult from 5 to 19 % (Business Journal 2012).

Finally, the third type besides a majority acquisition is the business transfer. It occurs when merely a part of a business is sold to another firm (Nonaka 2013, p. 28). This form happens frequently in Japan at traditional, older, and larger Japanese firms as these firms want to (or need to) focus on their core business (in Japanese: Sentaku to Shuchu; choose and concentrate) and; therefore, separate some of their units which do not anymore belong to their main field of business. These transactions are not full firm takeovers, rather a part of the firm is transferred to the bidder firm. There is recent evidence for the US that—in contrast to complete firm takeovers, shareholders of the bidder firms obtain positive and significant wealth gains of about 2–3 % when conducting a business transfer (Eckbo and Thorburn 2008). Ushijima and Schaede (2014) find for Japanese business transfers, that most of their sellers were larger, more diversified and less profitable than their buyers. Also, buyers received positive abnormal returns after the deal. Put differently, after absorbing business transfers, bidder firms gain. Furthermore, only 20 % of their sellers were in financial distress, concluding that business transfers in Japan are not having the focus on bailing out financially distressed firms.

Mergers and acquisitions can be divided into three types: vertical, horizontal and diagonal. Horizontal acquisitions happen in the same line of business. For example, M&A in the Japanese banking industry happen normally horizontally. In this, one bank merged or overtook another bank in the same line of business. In vertical acquisitions, a bidder would either overtake their supplier, for example, to ensure access to raw materials. That would be called an upstream or vertical acquisition. There is also a downstream vertical acquisition. If a car manufacturer, for example, overtakes a car dealer to generate direct profits from selling cars. That would be an example for a downstream vertical acquisition[4]. In diagonal acquisitions, the business of the bidder is not connected to the business of the target. In the late 1980s, at the time of the Japanese bubble economy, many diagonal acquisitions were seen (for example when Sony overtook Columbia Pictures Entertainment in 1989). More recently, Japanese firms conduct M&A in the same industry. Kang et al. (2000) shows that 80 % of their acquisitions occurred in the same 2-digit industry.

[4] Monden (2010, p. 69) argues instead of undertaking an acquisition as a single firm to better construct some vertical inter-firm network with suppliers and customers.

6.4.2 Other Types of Market Entry: Joint Ventures

Besides M&A there are other ways that companies can allocate resources. A firm could divest, for example, to sell unprofitable entities or it could join into Strategic Alliances (Aurora et al. 2011, pp. 296–337). To transfer knowledge to other parts (Minbaeva et al. 2014), for example to have a business in other countries, another way would be to establish a joint venture, which is used widely, especially as a means to enter foreign markets. Joint ventures are a popular method to enter the Japan market, as well as for Japanese firms to invest abroad. Often, Joint ventures are established between two different country's headquarters. One firm has a technical advantage (and puts their knowledge into the venture) and the other one offers their sales force for providing market entrance into the country. A Joint venture is when two firms join forces to set up an entity, which is independent but at the same time economically reliant on its mother firms. One firm usually has a technical advantage (and puts their knowledge into the venture) while the other one offers their customer base to provide entry into a country's market. Some employees from each of the mother firms would join forces to become one unit. For example, Bosch has several joint ventures in Japan with different Japanese firms to sell their technology to the Japanese. An example of a Japanese firm abroad would be Toyota who formed a joint venture with Renault in The Check Republic to jointly sell their cars. This means that even if Toyota and Renault are fierce competitors in the rest of the world, in that particular case, they joined forces to save costs and to outperform other competitors.

Firms conducting Joint ventures enjoy several advantages. Firms can share the risks and the associated costs of entering into a new market. In the Toyota-Renault case, the Joint venture saves cost for selling cars in The Czech Republic. Besides cost advantages in the distribution, joint repair stations save additional costs and provide better service to customers in that country.

Nowadays, many Japanese firms conduct Joint ventures with Chinese firms to successfully enter the Chinese market. Toshiba for example formed a Joint venture with the Chinese firm Greentech, for producing and selling their LED light (light-emitting diode) technology in the Chinese market.

It should be mentioned; however, that there are also some disadvantages associated with Joint ventures. One of the biggest hurdles is that one of the partner firms often becomes redundant after a while. In most cases the partner offering technical knowledge becomes redundant when the other partner in the target country is able to produce the same, or even better, products. Why, then should the Joint venture partner in the target country not take all the profit of the business for themselves? It is also possible that one of the mother firms changes their strategy. If a headquarters, for example, decides to exit a geographical area, the Joint venture may not be necessary anymore. Also, Joint ventures could result in bringing the mother firms' business in competition to their own products.

Previously, M&A to Japan were often legally restricted. Even if transactions were legally not prohibited or hindered, for foreign firms it was difficult to overtake a

Japanese firm because Japanese firms were not interested in being taken over. Many firms went into so-called cross shareholdings. In a cross shareholding situation, several firms would hold each other's shares and would not give them out to any other investor (Chap. 2). This means that foreign firms could not overtake Japanese firms even when legally allowed. Previously, there was no other choice than to accept a Joint venture for foreign firms to enter, for example, the Japanese market. Nowadays, the M&A market opened up for firms to come to Japan and to overtake Japanese firms, than solely to get in the market by support of local firms. In this, acquisitions of foreign firms to enter the Japanese market are nowadays quite common.

6.5 Hubris, Selection and Market Changing Theory

The hubris theory states, that managers are overconfident in themselves and in their actions in regard to transactions (Yamamoto 2010, pp. 94–95). Roll (1986) explains this theory in the case of a tender offer bid. For example, managers from the bidding firm, would offer a price higher than what the market values the company due to their overconfidence in their own ability to manage the target firm more effectively than the old managers. This is based on their past experiences. In other words, managers from the bidding firm would undertake deals even if there is evidence that the majority of the deals end in failure, or do not fulfill their strategic goals (Knilans 2009). Sirower (1997) found that only 33 % of the deals added value for the acquired shareholders. Seldon and Colvin (2003) state that 70–80 % of all acquisitions fail. Kimata states that there is 50–70 % failure rate for firms entering the Japanese market (Kimata 2010, p. 331).

The "selection theory" can also be applied when investigating cross border M&A. Which firm would a foreign investor overtake compared to a local bidder, a better or a worse one? The selection theory states that foreign bidders will overtake better performing targets. In this case, a foreign bidder has more at stake and higher costs than a comparable presumptive domestic bidding firm. On the same line of argument, transactions by foreign firms will only be undertaken in cases where a target is especially lucrative and would be a good fit for the business of the bidder firm (Paprzycki and Fukao 2008, p. 7). Bebenroth (2009), on the other hand comes to the opposite conclusion. Foreign bidders seemed to get served at a later stage. Put differently, domestic firms select their targets before any foreign bidder knows about it. If no firm is interested in the target; however, the sphere may be widened to the foreign bidders' audience (Bebenroth 2009).

Finally, the market changing theory addresses the question, why do acquisitions occur. This is based on the theory of the firm by Ronald Coase (1937) and refers to industry changes because of technological factors such as new communications technology or changes in transportation technology. Also Jensen (1983) elaborates on political, economic, and technological changes that are responsible for mergers and even for merger waves. That there are merger waves is not a new phenomenon. The first merger wave in the US occurred already after the Great Depression of 1883. The wave peaked at firms in mining industries from 1898 to 1902 (Aurora et al. 2011).

For example, during the oil shock in the 70s, technical improvements and deregulations in some industries led to waves of M&A. In other words, as soon as markets and industries change, firms need to adapt to the new environment. This leads to merger waves. Some firms become bidders, these are the winners, become stronger and may use new opportunities. Other firms may lose clients and market share until they are finally taken over. There is scientific evidence by Mitchel and Mulherin (1996) for example, that mergers in the merger wave of the 80s were industry specific and happened especially in deregulated industries. This means that in the frame of the market changing theory, often competitors in the same industry overtake each other, what happened e.g. to Sanyo Denki when they got taken over by Panasonic in the electronics industry.

6.6 Bidder Motivations

What motivates a bidder firm to overtake a target? Globalization is one phenomena that encourages firms to expand their business rapidly into another country's market. In the globalized world of today, there are many advantages to international diversification. Firms can all of a sudden access new markets without time consuming internal growth, for example, the workforce of the overtaken firm can immediately sell the bidding firms' products. Undertaking an acquisition can also lead to a more diversified product range which might make firms less dependent on products but even more independent in their home markets. Market expansion is a driving force for external growth. A German solar energy firm (SMA) at Kassel, for example, knows that without governmental subsidy, a prosperous future would be difficult or even impossible. This means that before the German government downsizes the subsidies, the firm will aim to have a stronger presence in other parts of the world. The same logic can be applied to Japanese firms such as Toshiba or Panasonic with their reliance on governmental subsidies for their solar energy units. Therefore, firms are eager to become global players with their leading technology to balance out domestic challenges because of a fear that changes may occur, like future subsidy decreases. Another reason for globalization is tax avoidance and to reduce manufacturing costs (Ota 2013). Japanese car manufacturers, for example, try to circumvent import taxes for their cars sold in Europe. Toyota, is said to have built, mainly for this reason, a car manufacturing plant in Poland. Another advantage for Toyota (having a factory in Poland) is that the cost for manufacturing and the labor is much lower in Poland than in Japan. In this vein, car manufacturers preferably want to produce their cars in that country or at least in that region where they intend to sell their units (see also Table 3.1 in Chap. 3). Exports from Japan to Eastern Europe are very costly and can be avoided by producing cars in Eastern Europe directly.

Another advantage of an acquisition is called "economies of scale and scope". A firm that increases their production volume has lower costs per unit produced. The reason is that the fix costs hardly increase at all. Only the variable costs (per unit) have to be accounted for. If firms' amalgamate, their combined R&D costs decrease and cuts in overhead costs are possible. This phenomena is called "economies of scope." An example of this can be seen in the recent department store acquisition by Isetan of Mitsukoshi. Isetan saves money because both firms buy their products jointly together. Boots, for example, will not be bought separately anymore but together as one order. After the acquisition; therefore, the power of the new firm increased against its suppliers. A higher power in negotiation means a better (lower) price for products. The same principle could be seen in car manufacturers. After Renault acquired Nissan Motors, for example, the costs for buying the parts from both of their suppliers decreased by about 30 % because they could order them together (Tochi 2014).

Advantages of size are some of the main reasons for an acquisition. The bigger a firm becomes, the lower their costs. These phenomena can be described in the pharmaceutical market. The R&D costs of pharmaceuticals make up about 20 % of the turnover price. It is suggested that one of Takeda's incentives, for example, to overtake Nycomed from Switzerland was to realize synergies in combining research activities to save costs. Also, an expansion of the business into other areas could raise synergies. Nonaka (2013, pp. 20–22) explains this using the case of an Udon (noodle) store, which overtakes a Pasta store in Chiba prefecture, to realizing synergy effects.

Acquisitions can also change firms' strategies. For example, before the previously second biggest German mobile phone maker Mannesmann was taken over by British Vodafone, it was a travel agency and before that it operated as a steel pipe maker. This firm is an example of how acquisitions and external growth led to a strategic transformation of the core business into totally different areas of business (Mannesmann 2014).

Finally, some acquisitions occur to exploit technological capabilities of the targets. That means, by acquisitions new sources of knowledge can be created (Greenberg and Guinan 2004; Ranft and Lord 2002; Empson 2007). It is said that when Panasonic overtook Sanyo Denki, one of the major driving factors was that Panasonic could acquire Sanyo Denki's lithium-ion battery technology. It is important to mention that Sanyo Denki was the world's market leader in that technology. The fact that firms are cash rich could also be a driving factor to carry out acquisitions. This means that the target firm has a large amount of savings, a presumptive bidder firm would own it after the deal (Hasegawa 2007)

6.7 Value Creation Through M&A

One of the fundamental questions in M&A research is whether or not M&A creates value (Devos et al. 2009). Early research on this question by Jensen and Ruback concludes that the source of gains in M&A are "elusive" (1983, p. 47). Following research concludes that on average, M&A creates value for the combining firms (Mulherin and Boone 2000; Andrade et al. 2001). In that, target shareholders receive profits from transactions. However, bidder shareholders end up with higher costs than with a profit. This is supported by King et al. (2004) who points out a negative impact on the acquirer's financial performance. Whittington and Bates (2007) state: "The finance perspective has identified an elephant in the M&A domain" (p. 28) and ask, despite the negative results do M&A continue? Smith (2007) also concludes in his article "M&A as illusion" that most acquisitions destroy value for shareholders of the acquiring firm (p. 63).

Another stakeholder group are the banks, which have equity and debt interests in the deal. Having technical expertise, they evaluate the target firm which means that banks also often set the prices for the deal, the value to be paid for a target. Banks also act as a go-between to complete the deal (Sheard 2002). Banks; however create value mainly for themselves in the consulting business. This function is also in Japan often undertaken by financial advisors, which might be coming from banks, investment houses, or M&A consulting firms (Kimata 2010, pp. 45–58).

M&A are more than just financial transactions. M&A are rather long term processes which significantly affect not only the people in the firms but the managers and all employees at both firms, the target but also (often times) bidder firms themselves. It is well documented in the literature that M&A often lead to a downsizing, which leaves employees of target firms in stress, fear, and anxiety (McBain 1999). This means, often (but not always) the M&A process has a negative effect, especially on the target employees. This was also described as "merger syndrome". In this sense, a systematic effort has to be made to create an internal climate of fairness between the target employees and the bidder firm (Fairfield 1992).

Whether or not an M&A is successful will be seen years after the deal in the integration period. There is scientific evidence, that the communication of the bidder management to all employees is an important factor for the success of the M&A (Bryson 2003). Especially the human side has to be treated with respect. As Aurora et al. pointed it out: "For the merged entities to work together harmoniously, it is important that the corporate culture of both companies go hand in hand" (p. 279). Firms doing cross-border acquisitions face even more problems than firms undertaking domestic deals (Very et al. 1996).

Despite economies of scale and other benefits associated with acquisitions; however, Kobayashi (2013) points out that in cross border acquisitions, costs often increase to more than expected. Also compared to cross border acquisitions of Western firms (from the US or from Europe), when Japanese firms acquire foreign firms they normally have a comparatively low profitability (pp. 1–2). There is evidence that executives of acquired cross-border firms are more likely to quit their jobs than executives of acquired domestic firms (Krug and Hegarty 2001). In this sense, cross-border targets are more challenging to handle than domestic ones.

6.8 Conclusion

This chapter focused on an introductory topic to "set the stage for M&A". It could be seen that the shareholder structure in Japan changed to a more international one. Recently, foreign investors in Japan held almost 30% of the shares. This is said to be one of the changes responsible to have Japanese firms become more profit oriented. That means, previous concerns about turnover and number of employees got transformed to a rather profit orientation.

Also, recent legal amendments facilitate conducting deals. Besides some theories discussed for reasons why a firm might be motivated to overtake another firm, this chapter also shed some light on the topic of value creation that means whether or not M&A actually create value. There is some evidence that the shareholders of bidder firms end up rather paying for the acquisition. In contrast, the shareholder of the targets take out a profit—and at the end most of the deals end in failure.

Questions

1. How changed the shareholder structure at Japanese firms in the last years?
2. Recall a legal change what may have increased the M&A market.
3. Give a definition for a merger, an acquisition, a capital participation, a capital increase and a business transfer
4. Give reasons why an investor should conduct a capital participation?
5. Why was a joint venture previously attractive for foreign firms to enter the Japanese market?
6. What does the Hubris theory stands for in M&A discussion?
7. What are reasons that American Delta Airlines only did a capital participation at JAL but not a majority acquisition?
8. Recall bidder motives for conducting an acquisition?
9. Recall the winner at M&A
10. Recall the loser at M&A

Answers

1. There are changes in the shareholder structure of Japanese firms, that City banks and Regional banks sell their shares and foreign investors increase their shares, recently almost up to 30 %.
2. Harmonization of different regulatory bodies may have led to a simpler process. Especially foreign firms appreciate an easier application process.
3. A merger is when both firms melt together having equal size and equal power. In reality, this is very uncommon. An acquisition is when the bidder firms acquires a target. At majority acquisitions, the bidder obtains the majority voting power over the target. A capital participation is when an investor only obtains a minority shareholding, often under 5 %. A capital increase is when an investor acquires shares after an initial capital participation. Reason for this might be that the investor is satisfied with its initial investment and wants to take more stake at the firm. A business transfer is when a firm sells parts of it. This preferably happens when a firm wants to streamline their business activities and to focus on their

strategic field of business. Also, business transfers may happen if firms face financial difficulties and need to sells parts of it to raise money.

4. A reason to conduct a capital participation might be to lower the risk of failure, to slowly get acquainted with a target, or because laws do not allow a majority acquisition.
5. Joint Ventures were previously attractive for foreign firms to enter Japan because high financial risks could be lowered. Also, there was often hardly any other way to enter the Japanese market. Acquisitions were often not allowed or difficult to conduct because Japanese firms went into cross shareholdings, so that foreign bidders could not acquire shares.
6. Hubris theory argues that managers are overoptimistic in regard to their acquisition performance. Researchers state that 70 to 90 % of all deals end in failure, however, managers do not listen to these advices because of their over optimism and further conduct acquisitions.
7. The Japanese government did not allow Delta Airlines as foreign investor to hold more shares. The danger is that a bankruptcy of an airline would hurt the whole Japanese economy as people can not anymore brought back and forth to Japan.
8. Some of the bidder motives for conducting acquisitions are: economies of scale and scope, e.g. to get bigger in size or to increase power. To use synergies, e.g. to have the previous sales force to sell complementary products of the firm. To use globalization advantages, e.g. that products are build and sold at the country of origin. To expand the market, e.g. products can be sold at other countries after the acquisition of a firm in that given country. Also an increase in the variety of products and a technology transfer can be considered as a motive for an acquisition.
9. Winner at M&A are the shareholders of the target firm. In case of unfriendly takeovers the premium is highest.
10. Loser at M&A are normally bidder shareholder and the people involved at the target firm. Not only managers at the target but also regular employees are exposed to changes.

References

Andrade GM, Mitchel M, Stafford E (2001) New evidence and perspectives on mergers. J Econ Perspect 15:103–120

Aoki M (2000) Information, corporate governance, and institutional diversity: competitiveness in Japan, the USA, and the transnational economies. Oxford University Press, Oxford

Aurora RS, Shetty K, Kale SR (2011) Mergers and acquisitions. Oxford University Press, India

Bebenroth R (2009) Foreign M&A in Japan: do foreign firms cherry pick Japanese targets? Kobe Econ Bus Rev 54:1–16

Bryson J (2003) Managing HRM risk in a merger. Empl Relat 31:347–53

Business Journal (2012) Yakulto Baishu de okaka soudou! Hanbai Gaisha ga Furansu Danone to kumu (Yakult house disturbance because of a takeover! Bidder firm is French Danone at Internet: http://biz-journal.jp/2012/11/post_1027.html. Accessed 25 April 2014

Coase R (1937) The nature of the firm. Economica 4:386–405
Devos E, Kadapakkam PR, Krishnamurthy S (2009) How do mergers create value? A comparison of taxes, market power, and efficiency improvements as explanations for synergies. Rev Financial Stud 22:3. (In: Mulherin JH (ed) Mergers and acquisitions. The International library of critical writings in economics 270. Edward Elgar Publishing, 2012, pp 3–35)
Eckbo EB, Thorburn KS (2008) Corporate restructuring. Break ups and LBOs. In: Eckbo EB (ed) Handbook of empirical corporate finance, vol 2. Amsterdam
Empson L (2007) M&A as knowledge. In: Angwin D (ed) Mergers and acquisitions. Blackwell Publishing, Malden, pp 229–255
Fairfield K (1992) 10 myths of managing a merger. Across the Board 13–15
Greenberg D, Guinan PJ (2004) Mergers and acquisitions in technology-intensive industries: the emergent process of knowledge transfer. In: Pablo AL, Javidan M (eds) Mergers and acquisitions: creating integrative knowledge. Blackwell Publishing, Oxford
Hasegawa T (2007) Baishu Boei to M&A hanrei shuu. Casebook on M&A and defense of corporation. LexisNexis Japan
Igaki T, Yamaguchi Y (2011) Japan. In: Campbell D (ed) Mergers and acquisitions in North America, Latin America, Asia and the Pacific: Selected issues and jurisdictions. Center for International Legal Studies. Wolter Kluwer, pp 359–393
Ishikawa N (2013) Sankaku gappei nado no kaikin to sankaku gappei nado taiou zeisei no gaiyou. (Lifted ban on triangle mergers and tax summary) 257–267. Ota Y (ed) M&A kigyou soshiki saihen no suki-mu to zeimu (Organizational reorganization at M&A and Tax. 2nd edn. Okura Zaimu Kyoukai
Jensen MC (1983) The modern industrial revolution, exit, and the failure of internal control systems. J Financ 11:5–50
Jensen MC, Ruback RS (1983) The market for corporate control: the scientific evidence. J Financ 11:5–50
Kang JK, Shivdasani A, Yamada T (2000) The effect of bank relations on investment decisions: an investigation of Japanese takeover bids. J Financ 55:2197–2218
Kimata T (2010) kigyou baishuu no jitsumu purosesu. Process of acquisition business. Chuo Keizai
King DR, Dalton DR, Daily CM, Covin JG (2004) Meta-analyses of post-acquisition performance: indicators of unidentified moderators. Strat Manage J 25:187–200
Knilans G (2009) Mergers and acquisitions: best practices for successful integration, Employment Relations Today. The Global Consulting Partnership
Kobayashi I (2013) Kaigai M&A ni yaku datsu. Guro-baru senryaku no kandokoro. Usefulness of foreign M&A. Point of global Strategy. Chuo keizai sha
Krug JA, Hegarty WH (2001) Research notes and commentaries: predicting who stays and leaves after an acquisition: a study of top managers in multinational firms. Strateg Manage J 22:185–196
Kunimaru T (2010) The method of payment in takeovers and earnings management. In: Y Kurokawa (ed) M&A for value creation in Japan. Monden Institute of Management. Japanese Management and International Studies, vol. 6. World Scientific Publishing Co. Pte. Ltd, Singapore, pp 35–52
Mannesmann (2014) Mannesmann AG. Homepage. http://www.fundinguniverse.com/company-histories/mannesmann-ag-history/. Accessed 16 April 2014
Mateja J (2007) How Chrysler marriage failed. Chicago Tribune, May 15th 2007. http://articles.chicagotribune.com/2007-05-15/news/0705141000_1_daimler-benz-cerberus-capital-management-carmakers. Accessed 19 March 2014
McBain R (1999) Human resource management. Manage Updat 11(1):22–30
Milhaupt CT (2006) A lost decade for Japanese corporate governance reform? What has changed, what hasn't, and why. In: Blomstroem M, La Croix S (eds) Institutional change in Japan. Routledge, Abingdon, pp 97–119
Minbaeva D, Pedersen T, Bjoerkman I, Fey CF, Park HJ (2014) MNC knowledge transfer, subsidiary absorptive capacity and HRM. J Int Bus Stud 45:38–51

Mitchel Ml, Mulherin HJ (1996) The impact of industry shocks on takeover and restructuring activity. J Financ Econ 41:193–229
Monden Y (2010) M&A and its incentive system for the inter-firm organization. In: Kurukawa Y (ed) M&A for value creation in Japan. World Scientific Publishing Co. Pte. Ltd, Singapore, pp 67–89
Mulherin JH, Boone AL (2000) Comparing acquisitions. J Corp Financ 6:117–139
Nonaka K (2013) M&A no jimu roudou kanri (Personnel management of M&A). Chuo Keizai
Oesterle DA (2012) The law of mergers and acquisitions (American casebook series), 4th edn. West, Westminster
Onji K, Vera D, Corbett J (2012) Capital infection, restructuring targets and personnel management: the case of Japanese regional banks. J Jpn Soc Int Econ 26 495–517
Ota Y (2013) M&A kigyou soshiki saihen no suki-mu to zeimu (Organizational reorganization at M&A and Tax, 2nd edn. Omura Zaimu Kyoukai)
Paprzycki R, Fukao K (2008) Foreign direct investment in Japan. Cambridge University Press, New York
Ranft AL, Lord MD (2002) Acquiring new technologies and capabilities: a grounded model of acquisitions implementation. Organ Sci 13(4):420–442
Roll R (1986) The hubris of corporate takeovers. J Bus 59(2):197–216
Seldon C, Colvin G (2003) M&A needn't be a loser's game. Harvard Bus Rev 81(6):70–79
Sheard P (2002) Main banks and the governance of financial distress. In: Aoki M, Patrick H (eds) The Japanese main bank system—its relevance for developing and transforming. Oxford University Press, New York
Sirower MC (1997) The synergy trap: how companies lose the acquisition game. Free Press, New York
Smith C (2007) M&A as illusion. In: Angwin D (ed) Mergers and acquisitions. Blackwell Publishing, Malden, pp 63–86
Tochi S (2014) Gon shi machi no tougou. Gon waiting for Integration. Asahi Shinbun April 16th, p 6
Ushijima T, Schaede U (2014) The market for corporate subsidiaries in Japan: an empirical study of trades among listed firms. J Jpn Int Econ 31(3):36–52
Very P, Lubatkin M, Calori R (1996) A cross-national assessment of acculturative stress in recent European mergers. Int Stud Manage Organ 26:59–88
Whittington M, Bates K (2007) M&A as success. In: Angwin D (ed) Mergers and acquisitions. Blackwell Publishing, Malden, pp 27–62
Yamamoto T (2010) The impact of market inefficiency on TOB in Japan. In Y Kurokawa (ed) M&A for value creation in Japan. Monden Institute of Management. Japanese Management and International Studies, vol. 6. World Scientific Publishing Co. Pte. Ltd, Singapore, pp 91–102
Yoshida H, Bebenroth R (2006) Nissan jidosha to Mitsubishi jidousha no keiei zaiken ni okeru koudou bunseki- koporetogabanansu no shiten kara (analysis of restructuring—Nissan motors versus Mitsubishi motors). Kokumin Keizai Zashi 194(3)(in Japanese language):75–87

Chapter 7
Mergers and Acquisitions in Japan

Abstract This chapter focuses on Mergers and Acquisitions (M&A) in Japan. The development of the Japanese M&A market will be shown and two examples are discussed. The first example discussed is the acquisition of Nycomed by the Japanese pharmaceutical maker Takeda. The second example discussed is the acquisition of US firm, Goodman, by Daikin in the air conditioner maker field.

7.1 Introduction

As previous chapters discussed (especially Chap. 6: setting the stage) Mergers and Acquisitions (M&A) has a long history and it is very common in the West. This chapter deals with M&A concerning the Japanese market. It will shed light on the developments of Japanese M&A from around 1986 to the present day. It will show that M&A were previously uncommon in Japan with the exception of the Japanese bubble economy of the late 1980s. It will also show the Japanese M&A market has increased in its popularity since the late 1990s until now. Furthermore, strategic investors will be separately discussed from solely institutional investors. Then, the development of institutional investments coming into Japan will be discussed. In this chapter, cross border acquisitions will be highlighted. Finally, two examples of Japanese acquisitions will be discussed, Takeda and also Daikin which both invested an enormous amount of money to takeover foreign firms.

7.2 Development of Japanese M&A Market

The development of the Japanese M&A market is discussed starting from the year 1986 (Fig. 7.1) and divided into three types of acquisitions. In this terminology, first, in-in type refers to domestic transactions, where Japanese firms took over other Japanese firms. Second, in-out acquisition type refers to Japanese firms which went abroad to take over foreign firms. Third, out-in type transactions are opposite to in-out and refer to foreign firms coming to Japan and taking over a Japanese firm. In the year 1986 there were a mere 400 acquisitions (Fig. 7.1). This number

R. Bebenroth, *International Business Mergers and Acquisitions in Japan*,
DOI 10.1007/978-4-431-54989-5_7

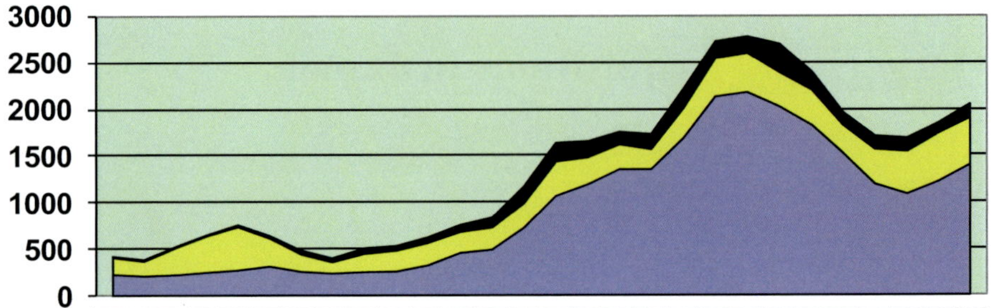

	1986	1987	1988	1989	1990	1991	1992	1993	1994	1995	1996	1997	1998	1999
■ OUT-IN	14	18	14	12	23	28	44	43	60	54	62	76	110	182
□ IN-OUT	181	158	291	388	463	301	186	120	196	222	239	224	236	266
■ IN-IN	223	206	218	245	268	309	253	234	249	255	320	453	488	721

	2000	2001	2002	2003	2004	2005	2006	2007	2008	2009	2010	2011	2012	2013
■ OUT-IN	201	174	136	163	210	185	179	308	198	138	145	143	112	149
□ IN-OUT	368	289	264	213	320	411	421	366	377	299	371	455	515	499
■ IN-IN	106	119	135	135	168	212	217	202	182	152	119	108	122	140

Fig. 7.1 Development of Japanese M&A. (Source: Recof M&A Database, several Issues 1986–2014)

increased in the late 1980s to more than 750 deals where the bubble period of the Japanese economy pushed more Japanese firms to invest abroad rather than in the home market (Chap. 2). There was a trend at the end of the bubble economy for Japanese firms to seek takeovers of foreign firms as opposed to domestic (other Japanese) targets. In technical terms, in-out acquisitions scored higher than in-in acquisitions. It is prudent to mention that transactions normally take a long time from the start of negotiations to get signed and realized. The first peak of all types of M&A was seen in the year 1990 with over 750 transactions. As the bubble burst in 1989, the peak of Japanese takeovers of firms from other countries was in fact delayed by 1 year. In the following years after the bubble burst, the Japanese M&A market slowed down in the number of deals and reached its lowest level in 1993 with under 400 transactions. From 1998 there is an increase visible to a peak in 2006 with 2775 transactions. In the following year, still around 2700 M&As were undertaken, of which 308 were foreign investors, meaning non-Japanese bidders taking over Japanese target firms (Recof M&A Database, Print Issues 1985–2014). Through the financial crises and the Lehman shock in 2008, the market decreased again to around 2400 M&A with 198 by foreign bidders taking over Japanese firms (Recof M&A Database, Print Issues 1985–2014). For the year 2009, still around 2000 acquisitions were made with 138 out-in transactions. In 2010, the whole acquisition market decreased to a level of around 1700 transactions, with 143 out-in transactions. In 2011, the total number of acquisitions was almost unchanged; however, a decrease of in-in deals was compensated for by an increase of in-out deals, leading to 455 in-out deals. In 2012 the market recovered in terms of the overall numbers and a record high of in-out acquisitions was visible, which counted 515 deals. Therefore, on 515 occasions a Japanese firm went abroad to take over a non-Japanese firm. Never in Japanese M&A history have Japanese firms taken over more foreign firms than in 2012. The year 2013 showed a recovery in terms of the total number of acquisitions to a level again of over 2000 cases (exactly 2048) with still many in-out acquisitions, exactly 499 cases.

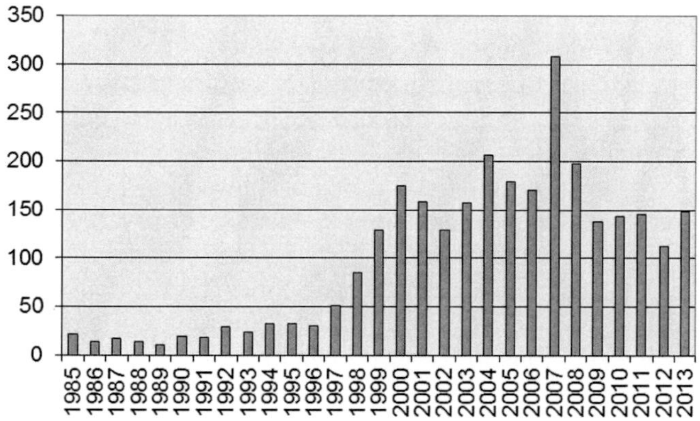

Fig. 7.2 Development of out-in acquisitions. (Source: Recof M&A Database, Print Issues 1985–2014 (in numbers of deals))

Figure 7.2 presents out-in acquisitions separately to more easily demonstrate their development.[1] From the time period of 1985 to 1996 there was never a year when more than 40 out-in transactions were undertaken. In 1997, for the first time ever, out-in acquisitions counted for more than 50 transactions per year. Put differently, before 1997 Japan never experienced more than 50 acquisitions by foreign firms. It can be said, that it was uncommon for Japanese firms to get taken over by foreign firms. The increase in 2007 is clearly visible, showing many institutional investors (which are mainly financially oriented, mainly from Great Britain) included in the data. For the time afterwards, in the years of 2009 to 2012, there is some stability at about 1400 transactions per year. The number reduces in the 2012 observation to 112 transactions but recovers again to 149 transactions in the year 2013.

7.3 Strategic Versus Institutional Investors

There are differences between strategically driven and financially driven M&A. A bidder firm is referred to as strategically driven when the firm has knowledge of the target firms' operative business. In strategically driven acquisitions, there is a tendency to combine weaker with stronger firms to realize synergies and to have a more prosperous firm at the end (Chap. 6). With strategic acquisitions, firms often belong to the same industry groups, having relationships before the deal. Most acquisitions in Japan are motivated by strategic considerations (Kester 1991; Higgins 2013). As a point in case, when Renault took over Nissan Motors they could help the Japanese firm in strategic ways because the bidder firm (in this case Renault) knew how to produce and sell cars more efficiently and could obviously help Nissan Motors to get a turnaround (Yoshida and Bebenroth 2006). As was the case with Nissan Motors and Renault, it is commonly assumed that Japanese M&A occur at firms

[1] This would be the black ink line from Fig. 6.1

in trouble (Fukao and Amano 2004; Fukao et al. 2005). In other words, targets get taken over to improve their unsatisfactory performance. In this sense, acquisitions are a way, for example, of rescuing a firm (Horiuchi and Okazaki 1994). Other newer research states that acquisitions also occur because targets want to refocus and restructure their business (Schaede 2008; Ushijima and Schaede 2014).

In contrast to strategic acquisitions, institutional investors have no strategic but a merely financial interest in the target firm (Shleifer and Vishny 2003). There exist a wide variety of institutional investors. In this vein, institutional investors are always financially driven but can be placed in a range between friendly and unfriendly ones. Prior research suggests that friendly institutional investors can be divided into so-called "dedicated" and "transient" ones (Porter 1992). Dedicated investors are seen as rather long-term-oriented investors consisting of pension funds (e.g. Californian Pension Fund, CalPers). In contrast, transient investors are seen as rather short-term-oriented, having merely tactical interest in the target firm. However, both investors are friendly in their attempt to take over a target firm. Meaning the target management is in favor of the deal and value can be created in different ways (Uotila et al. 2009).

In contrast to both of these friendly types of institutional investors, they may also purchase equity stakes in targets as part of hostile attempts. For the US, there is some evidence that activist hedge funds lead to a stronger managerial discipline. One of the reasons for an increased performance is that hedge funds lobby for change at the firms they invest in, for example, because they promised their investors an increase in their capital. Recent US research shows that there is improved shareholder wealth when hedge funds stock equity is invested in firms (Klein and Zur 2009; Becht et al. 2009; Helwege et al. 2012). Also for Japan, there is some evidence by Inoue and Kato (2007) that hedge funds targeted inefficiently managed and undervalued Japanese firms (Bebenroth 2009). In the long run, the discipline that foreign funds bring, improves the function of the Japanese firms' management (Inoue 2010, p. 130; Arai 2008).

However, results are mixed and other researchers did not find clear empirical evidence, that unfriendly takeovers by investment funds increase the value of target firms (Feito-Ruiz and Menéndez-Requejo 2011). At the end of the chapter, a case discussed will be Steel Partners, a so-called vulture fund, as an example of this kind of firm acting in Japan.

7.3.1 Strategic Versus Institutional Inbound M&A to Japan

Research on M&A and Japan has predominantly relied on case studies (e.g. CalPERS by Jacoby 2007) or on Japanese investments abroad (e.g. in Europe by Yeh 2011). Prior research revealed that institutional investors' characteristics differ according to their country of origin (Bae et al. 2006). At a higher level of analysis, structures, responsibilities and functioning of corporate boards differ widely across firms according to their country of origin (e.g., Charkham 1994; Shleifer and Vishny 1997). Such characteristics can translate into differences in institutional investors' behavior.

Figure 7.3 provides an overview of the timely development of out-in acquisitions in Japan, contrasting strategically and institutionally driven M&A. It is clearly

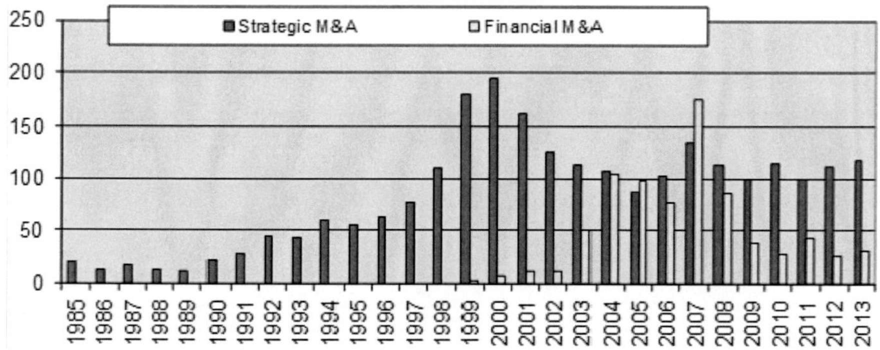

Fig. 7.3 Development of strategic vs. institutional M&A to Japan. (Source: Recof M&A Database, several issues, latest on Febr. 2014, p. 30 (in number of deals))

visible that institutional acquisitions did not exist before 1999. Therefore, strategic acquisitions occurred in Japan earlier than equity share purchases by institutional investors. From the year 2003, financially driven investments by institutional funds reached 50 cases for the first time. In the year 2007, financially driven acquisitions by non-Japanese funds outperformed in numbers even strategically driven acquisitions. Within this, an additional 174 stock equity purchased investments by institutional investors led to the highest ever out-in market (in 2007). It is also visible that stock equity purchases by institutional investors declined in the year of the Lehman shock. From the year 2008, strategic acquisitions dominate again in their volume against the financially driven M&A by institutional investors. This trend also remained in the following year. In the year 2013, there were only 32 financially driven acquisitions conducted by institutional investors against 117 strategically driven transactions.

7.3.2 In-Out Acquisitions

We now investigate the opposite direction, namely in-out acquisitions. We also analyze it separately to easily see their timely development.[2] There is a first peak in the year 1990 with 463 acquisitions. That means with a short time delay after the economic bubble period, many Japanese firms went abroad to take over foreign firms.

It is clear that the M&A market slowed down during the so called "lost decade" and bottomed out in 1993. After that, Japanese firms again became more active in taking over cross border targets. It is also remarkable, that there was only a small decrease of in-out acquisitions at the time of the Lehman Shock. In 2012, there was a record on cross border acquisitions, where Japanese firms acted as bidders. Still in 2013, there are 499 deals of this type (Fig. 7.4).

[2] This would be the yellow ink line in Fig. 7.1

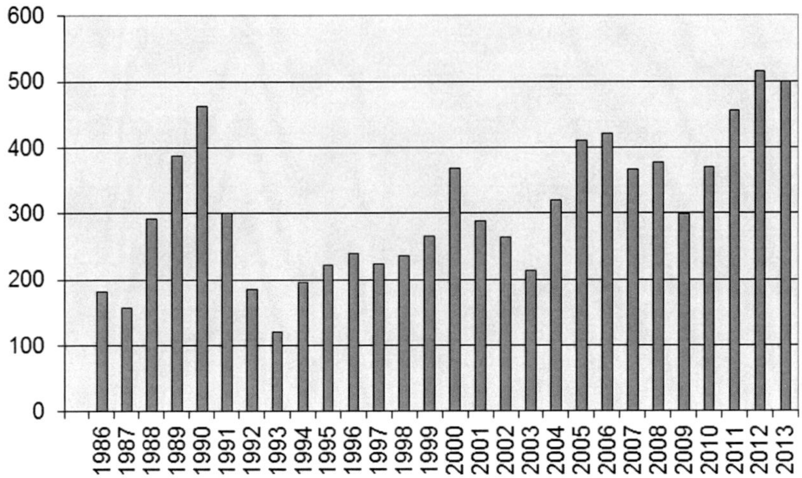

Fig. 7.4 Development of in-out acquisitions. (Source: Recof M&A Database 1987–2014 (in numbers of deals))

7.3.3 Cross Border M&A

Next, cross border investments (covering in-out deals as well as out-in deals) are split into three geographic regions, USA, Europe and the rest into "others", mainly coming from Asia. It becomes evident that recently not the USA or Europe but firms from "other" countries, mainly from Asia, dominate the Japanese cross border M&A market (Fig. 7.5).

US cross border investments with Japan increased from the year 2002 until the Lehman Shock in 2008. Therefore, the highest number of deals between the USA was in the year 2007. In 2013, for the US, 172 transactions were counted. European investments were on a lower but stable level over these years with a volume of 70 to 160 deals that were cross border investments. In 2013, European firms had 137 cross border transactions with Japan. The third geographic group called "others" is mainly composed of Asian firms. It is clearly visible that this group has recently become the dominating cross border acquisition partner of Japanese firms. These firms called "others" accounted for 326 deals in 2013, of which 74 transactions were undertaken by firms from China and from Hong Kong. That means, even though Japanese media reports frequently to focus on US or European firms cross border acquisitions, the market has in fact changed to an increase in cross border acquisitions with firms from "other" countries, mainly with those from Asia.

Looking at the Japanese cross border M&A market in regard to firms solely from European countries (Fig. 7.6), it is visible that until the year 2012, only three European countries were dominating the market. Such as Great Britain, France and Germany. Great Britain has the highest number of cross border acquisitions with Japan. The second biggest cross border partner is Germany with more than

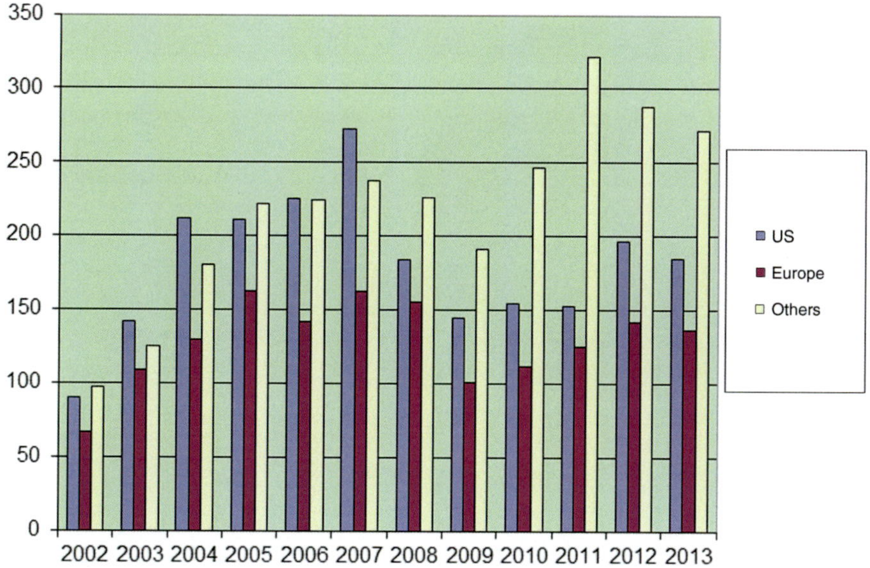

Fig. 7.5 Development of cross border M&A to USA, Europe and to others. (Source: Recof M&A Database, years 2003–2014, various issues)

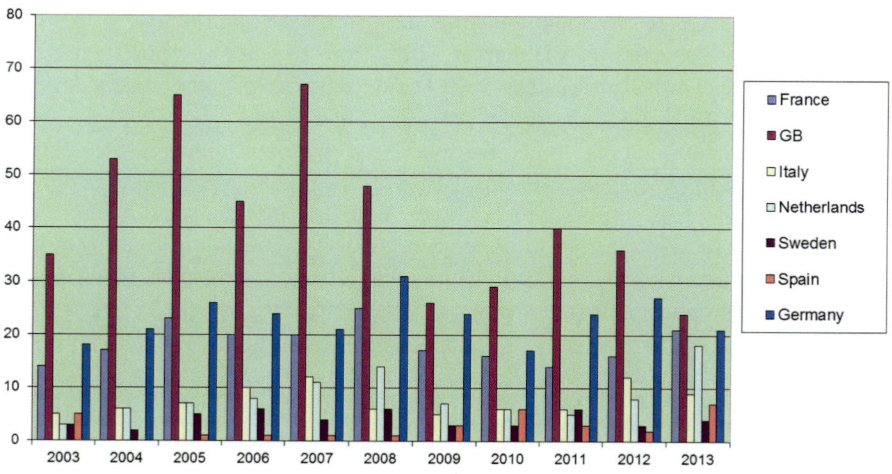

Fig. 7.6 Country specific Japan M&A from European countries (*in-out and out-in together*). (Source: Recof M&A database 2004–2014, various issues)

20 deals yearly. France ranks as the third largest investor nation with about 10–20 cross border acquisitions. All other European countries are represented with very low numbers of cross border acquisitions with Japan. That means, neither Japanese firms went to these countries to take over firms, nor did firms from these countries come to Japan to take over Japanese firms.

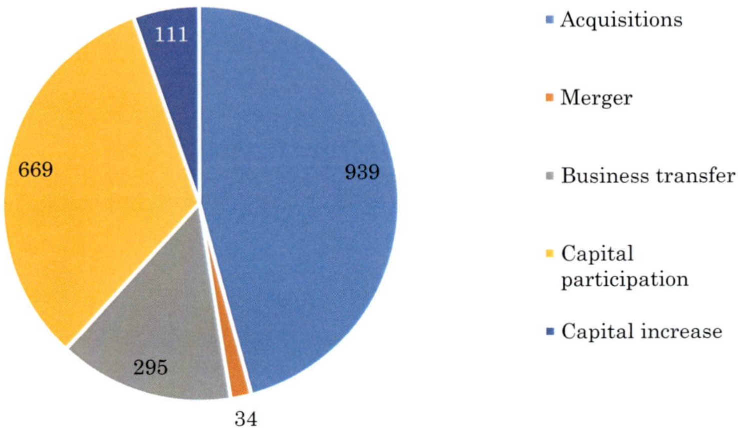

Fig. 7.7 Types of M&A. (Source: Recof M&A database, Febr. 2014, p. 21 (data for the year 2013))

The Netherlands, for example, came only recently to a higher cross border M&A activity with Japan. In the year 2013, there were 18 cases registered but except in the years of 2007 and 2008 no more than 10 cross border cases with Japanese firms were counted. Looking in more detail into deals with the Netherlands, however, almost all deals were led by Japanese firms. It seems that the primary aim for the Japanese firms was to enter the EU market. Firms from all other European countries are quite inactive in cross border deals with Japanese firms. Italy only reached more than 10 cross border acquisitions in the years 2007 and 2012.

It should be mentioned that the British system of retirement funds is different to the continental European system. In this, British firms put their employees' savings into the funds of private firms which invest them into markets worldwide. This leads British financial investors to conduct preferably financially driven acquisitions. That is an approach in contrast to continental European firms, which normally acquire firms with a strategic intent (more at Chap. 11).

7.4 Different Types of M&A

Next, the numbers and the percentages of different types of M&A transactions in Japan are presented. This will only cover the year of 2013 (Fig. 7.7). It is visible that so called "majority acquisitions" make up about half of the cases of the 2048 completed deals in the year of 2013. This means, in total, 939 acquisitions were majority acquisitions with a share participation of more than 50 %. Put differently, around 45.8 % of all M&A were conducted in order to gain control over a target firm. Another big part of M&A consists of capital participations. With capital participations investors only participate with a minority of shares. In other words, even if firms get acquired, according to the statistics, the bidder does not receive full control over the target. These types of transactions occurred in 2013 exactly 669 times (32.7 %). This is also a common way, especially for foreign firms, to enter the Japanese market. If strategically conservative in its intent, the high risk of a failure can be lowered and an early retreat is still possible. Capital participations are also common for institutional investors such as hedge funds or pension funds as they intend to purchase equity stock rather than to take over the whole target firm to strategically control it. Institutional investors have an interest in participation in case the shares are at a low price (see Chap. 11). Transactions of business transfers happened in 2013 exactly 295 times (14.4 %) and (in the same year observation) there were 111 transactions typed as capital increases (5.4 %). Interestingly, mergers occurred only 34 times (1.7 %). It should be noted, that these 34 transactions at least "sell" their transaction as a merger. It is not certain; however, that these deals were indeed mergers, where both parties in practical terms share the same power. It could be assumed, that some of the so called mergers were in reality acquisitions. It should be clear from the number of transactions that even if the name M&A always appears as one single phrase, mergers are relatively untypical phenomena.

7.5 Examples of Recent In-Out Acquisitions

In the following, two examples of in-out acquisitions are discussed. The first example consists of Nycomed being taken over by Takeda in the pharmaceutical sector. The second example is Daikin, which took over Goodman in the air conditioning industry. As described earlier, the Japanese M&A market is mainly driven by in-in acquisitions that means Japanese acquire other Japanese firms without any involvement of foreign firms (Muramatsu 2007). However, in-out acquisitions—that Japanese firms go abroad to take over other non-Japanese firms—received a record number of 515 cases in 2012 (Recof M&A Database, Print Issues 1985–2014) and still scores high with 499 cases in 2013 (Recof M&A Database, Print Issues 1985–2014). The Takeda—Nycomed deal is one of the deals which should be; therefore, discussed in more detail below.

7.5.1 Example 1: Nycomed Takeover by Takeda

7.5.1.1 Introduction

As a short case study, this will shed light on the acquisition of Nycomed (a pharmaceutical firm from Switzerland) by Takeda Pharmaceutical (a Japanese pharmaceutical maker). In this case study, challenges and what the future might bring for Takeda, having undertaken this acquisition, will be discussed.

7.5.1.2 Takeda and Nycomed

At first, a brief introduction of the firms will be provided with some background information. The bidder, Takeda, is the largest pharmaceutical firm in Japan as well as throughout Asia (Takeda Homepage 2014a; Inagaki and Simmes 2011). Takeda was founded in 1781 at a very early time when the country was still closed to Western influences (see Chap. 2). Similar to other pharmaceutical firms, Takeda has a long history. Takeda's research and production facilities are established all over the world, even if Japan remains the most important market for the firm. Already in1914, Takeda established a center for conducting up-to-date research. Takeda became incorporated in 1925 and was listed at the Tokyo and Osaka stock exchanges in 1949. The corporation's first overseas operations started in the early 1960s. Today, Takeda operates in 70 countries around the world.

According to some experts in the pharmaceutical industry, before Takeda acquired Nycomed the Japanese firm was under represented in Europe. Establishments defined as research, development, and/or manufacturing sites were only found in Ireland, the UK, and in Italy. To all other European countries Takeda mainly exported goods.

The target, Nycomed was a private pharmaceutical firm based in Zurich, Switzerland with a strong presence in Europe and in emerging markets (Takeda Homepage 2014a). Nycomed was established in 1874 conducting many takeovers in its recent history until 2007. Before Nycomed was acquired itself, it was actively taking over other firms. In 2007 e.g. two pharmaceutical firms were acquired by Nycomed; the German Altana Pharmaceutical and Bradley Pharmaceuticals, a US based firm. In 2011, Nycomed itself became a target of the largest Japanese pharmaceutical maker, Takeda.

In contrast to the poor Takeda presence in Europe, Nycomed, based in Switzerland, had a presence also in Belgium, Austria, Germany, Denmark, Norway, Poland, Estonia, and in Russia. The increased presence in the European market is estimated to have doubled Takeda's sales in Europe. Nycomed was; furthermore, not only present in Europe but was also aggressively growing in emerging markets (Takeda Homepage 2014a). Since Takeda already had a foothold in China, the Nycomed deal gave the firm a strategic market entrance to other emerging markets where Nycomed (but not Takeda) had previously established business relationships from joint ventures with local offices and even to subsidiaries. These countries are for example Brazil, India and Russia. Acquiring Nycomed could be considered, therefore, as a good strategy to target BRIC countries. Also sales in China are expected to increase through the Nycomed acquisition. The overall aim is to have a long term strategy of 25 % of the employees based in Japan, 25 % in America, 25 % in Europe, and 25 % in emerging markets. In other words, Takeda's long-term goal is to grow globally. In May 2013, Takeda officially released its Vision 2020, which is aligned under the key theme of "Better Health, Brighter Future". This vision consists of the following three elements: "Business: Committed to Improving Health", "Organization: Strength from Diversity," and "People: Powered by Passion" (Takeda News 2013b).

The Osaka based firm was led until recently by CEO Yasuchika Hasegawa and is now led by the newly introduced Christopher Weber, a 47 year old Frenchman, headhunted from GlaxoSmithKline. Weber is approved by the Takeda board of directors to take the role of COO (chief of operations) starting from April 2014 (Sasaki 2014). He is nominated to become the next CEO to lead this firm to become a global player. Hasegawa will change to become the chairman (Takeda News 2013a; Sasaki 2014).

7.5.1.3 Challenges

There is evidence that the acquisition of Nycomed also has its challenges. On Sept. 30th 2011, Takeda announced officially that the acquisition of Nycomed was performed on the same day, with a price of 9.8 billion € (Takeda Homepage 2014b). Takeda might have overpaid for the target in financial terms for Nycomed, knowing that the turnover of that firm was a mere 3.2 billion €. Besides, the target was owned by a group of four big institutional investors that might have led to a rather weak Nycomed management. When an institutional investor controls a firm, the management is under pressure to bring positive results every quarter. In other words, the Nycomed management could not plan for a longer time span and; therefore, was in rather a weak position to implement strategic changes which were favorable to the long term future of the firm (Juve 2011).

What may have been other reasons for this takeover? Japanese firms are often stated to care more about having a high turnover and a higher number of customers than having a high profit. That might be one of the reasons for Takeda to acquire Nycomed. Through the acquisition of Nycomed, Takeda had a foothold in both Europe and in emerging markets.

It should also be mentioned that before the Nycomed acquisition took place, Takeda held reserves of $ 10.6 billion against merely $ 200 million in debt (Lachapelle and Gammeltoft 2011). These figures outperformed all other major pharmaceutical companies which normally have more debt than reserves. It could be argued that Takeda might have looked for an opportunity to spend their cash for investment. That means the main motive of this acquisition was probably to spend money rather than because Nycomed was an attractive target firm. As Takeda accumulated such an enormous amount of cash, the deal of acquiring Nycomed could be financed almost entirely in form of cash reserves.

Prior to taking over Nycomed, Takeda had already experienced problems with another major acquisition in 2008 when Takeda took over Millenium Pharmaceuticals, an American biotech firm. This firm had promising cancer research based in Cambridge, Massachusetts. The acquisition cost Takeda $ 8.9 billion dollars. It was the most expensive pharmaceutical deal by a Japanese firm of its time (Feuerstein 2008). That deal was heavily criticized as a mistake for Takeda because it resulted in a 27 % loss of Takedas' share value (Lachapelle and Gammeltoft 2011). With this history in mind, there is anxiety that the Nycomed acquisition could become a failure too.

Like all stock listed firms, Takeda has to obtain a credit rating. A credit rating has to be obtained to see to what extent a firm is able to fulfill its financial obligations, especially the certainty of the fulfillment of paying back outstanding loans. A downgrade causes a higher interest rate when taking on new loans and leads to the fact that a firm, like Takeda after the Nycomed deal, may be considered to be a riskier company. Of the three agencies on the market, S&P, Fitch, and Moody's, two of them, namely S&P and Moody's gave a credit rating to Takeda. S&P has given Takeda an AA rating for many years, which is one note under the highest scores available, the triple A. At the acquisition process of Nycomed, S&P's credit rating watch and Moody's too announced consideration of a multi-notch downgrade for Takeda (Inagaki 2011). However, on July 10th, 2013, Moody's released its rating for Takeda giving it an AA3, which is not any worse than before the deal was signed in 2011 (Moody's 2013).

To fulfill financial obligations, besides rather short term share price changes or credit ratings, long term effects have to be taken in account. Some of the unseen problems that Takeda might face with such an acquisition are cultural misunderstandings between managers of both firms. A mismanagement in terms of a different style of decision making or challenges in turning decisions into action could be responsible for future problems. Takeda's management style may differ significantly from Nycomed's. This issue will probably remain, even when having Mr. Weber now at the top of the firm. The marketing strategies of Takeda managers may not work the way Japanese managers want them to and employees in Europe or in emerging markets may not follow the orders given by the Japanese headquarters. Loyal customers and a strong brand are important aspects of a successful firm. However, local firms in emerging markets might be closer to their customers and better understand their specific needs. They might be faster in establishing their own brand and specific products to their clients. It is questionable whether Takeda can compete with local firms even with the support of Nycomed to have an early entrance into these markets.

There are also positive effects to register. Both firms, Takeda and Nycomed unanimously made the decision in favor of the acquisition and shared a feeling it was a fair deal. Even with the relatively high price paid by Takeda, both parties feel the deal was worth the action. Yasuchika Hasegawa, previous CEO at Takeda promised at that time to control cultural problems and to focus on more internationalization in the near future. With the headhunted Christopher Weber to lead this rather traditional firm, he did much more for a globalized Takeda than anyone ever assumed. Again, projections are no guarantees and anything is possible in the global pharmaceutical market. There is hope that Takeda succeeds in its integration challenges with Nycomed and that this acquisition ends successfully in growth but even more in profits.

7.5.2 Example 2: Daikin Takeover of US Goodman

7.5.2.1 Introduction

Another acquisition from the in-out type is seen in the air conditioning business when Daikin took over one of the largest US American air conditioning firms, Goodman. This is in line with the general phenomenon for mergers and acquisitions in

Japan, that Japanese firms take over (non-Japanese) target firms. There has been a continuous increase of cross border M&A deals involving Japanese firms. The Daikin & Goodman case is one of the representative in-out acquisitions, where the Japanese firm takes the lead. The deal was signed in 2012 and shows Daikin's efforts to enter the North American market in the air conditioning business.

7.5.2.2 Daikin and Goodman

Daikin Industries (Daikin) was founded in 1924 in Osaka. The firm is headquartered at Osaka and its current CEO is Noriyuki Inoue. Overseas offices are located in New York, Duesseldorf, Beijing, Shanghai, and Guangzhou. Daikin owns four major plants in Japan and provides services for air conditioning and refrigerators. Other parts of Daikin's business deals with oil hydraulics, defense systems, chemicals, and new operations. However, Daikin's revenues from April of 2012 to March of 2013 show that 87% stems from the air conditioning business. Only 10% of the business is in Chemicals and the remaining 3 to 4% is stated as other fields of business (Daikin Homepage 2014). In other words, the business of Daikin mainly consists of air conditioning.

In the process of Daikin's globalization efforts starting in the year 2006, Daikin purchased OYL Industries, a Malaysia based firm headquartered at Kuala Lumpur (Daikin News 2006) to become the largest air conditioning manufacturer in Asia. Daikin are known for their innovations in the air conditioning market. In technical terms, the market can be split into air conditioners for firms and bigger buildings and into those implemented in private homes. In Japanese homes, for example, the so called "split system of air conditioning" can be found everywhere. In this, individual air conditioning devices dominate in private housing due to the lack of a central cooling or heating system in Japan. One of the examples would be the rectangle-shaped air conditioners usually installed on the walls of private houses. Besides individual units, bigger offices and department stores etc. rely on the so called "variable refrigerant flow" which is a technology that allows one outdoor condensing unit to be connected to multiple indoor devices. These variable refrigerant flow units work only at the needed rate, meaning only if the temperature for example goes higher than 25 degrees, will they go into operation. That as well as other technical implementations allow a substantial energy saving of up to 55% over comparable unitary equipment units. These and other technological advantages are Daikin's strengths which makes them the worldwide leader in the air conditioning business. There is reason to believe, that Daikin's technological advantages greatly influenced their acquisition process behavior.

The target firm, Goodman Global Inc. was founded in 1975 in San Antonio, California, USA by Harold V. Goodman. The firm is headquartered in Houston, Texas and possessed five major domestic plants and factories. The CEO at the time of the acquisition was David Swift, running the firm since 2008. Goodman Global Incorporations business covers, besides air conditioning, heat pumps, gas furnaces, packaged units, controls & thermostats, air handlers & coils, and so called mini-split systems. To summarize, Goodman consists of four divisions, "Goodman air conditioning & heating, Amana heating & air conditioning, Quietflex, and Amana PTAC". Goodman air conditioning & heating is the kernel of the original firm. All other divisions can be considered as additions to the main strategic field of business, as they were added to the corporation through acquisitions at a later stage. Although the parent company is Goodman Global Inc., all three divisions had their own brand strategies and names. The firm was known to have a strong distribution network, low cost product knowhow, and lean management expertise in the North American market. Both firms' divisions of air conditioning provide a solid basis to join forces.

There were several steps necessary until the acquisition of Goodman by Daikin was accomplished in August 2012. Already in 1997 Goodman acquired Raytheon Appliances (which was a predecessor of Amana Corporation). In 2001 Goodman separated its appliances business from its air conditioner business to sell their appliances business to Maytag Corporation. In the year 2004, Goodman was acquired by a finance fund, called Apollo Management, which undertook 2 years later (in 2006) an initial public offer to bring Goodman into a listing on the New York Stock Exchange. In 2007, Goodman management agreed to be acquired by an institutional investor named Hellman & Friedman. This is a hedge fund and primarily interested in short term profits (Chap. 11). In 2012, Daikin Industries took over the Goodman shares mainly from this institutional investor, Hellman & Friedman. Therefore, it is noteworthy that Daikin took over shares from an institutional investor, instead of stable shareholders of the acquired firm (here Goodman).

7.5.2.3 Challenges

The objectives and benefits from the deal can be summarized as follows: First of all, Daikin Industries intended to enter the North American air conditioning market focused on globalization efforts. Without acquiring Goodman, it would be hardly manageable for Daikin to internally establish a distribution network in the US. Second, Daikin has, due to a larger profile in the world market, advantages to save costs and may be able to use economies of scales. The market for air conditioning can now be served from within the US. Put differently, Daikin does not need to export their products anymore, eliminating the need to pay taxes, and has lower transportation fees (inclusive of the cost for insurances). The acquisition could also benefit the new firm strategically and in terms of general efficiency in dealing with clients. The acquisition also helps to grow the business by introducing Daikin's new technological advantages like energy saving power management technologies. Daikin might take advantage by learning how to run a business more efficiently in the US, especially with previous Goodman clients.

However, some challenges should be mentioned. The acquisition of Goodman cost Daikin 3.7 billion US$. This is until now by far the most expensive deal Daikin has ever undertaken. Further questions arise. Why should Daikin, even with a world leading technology in the field of air conditioners, be successful in the US market when Goodman was obviously not? It could be argued that for Japanese firms the US market is rather difficult and challenging due to cultural differences. Also, Japanese managers at the headquarters in Osaka are costly to send over to the US. If they are sent over, they may cause more friction with the US managers rather than bringing benefits. This would be of special importance if Japanese managers speak little English or if they do not want to speak it. US managers at the subsidiaries may feel that they do not have enough authority in their decision making. Finally, technological advantages can be imitated by other firms relatively easily. There is the challenge that not only technological advantages fade away but also that previous Goodman managers will leave the firm—possibly going to the competitors.

Furthermore, unique characteristics that distinguish Japanese businesses from global businesses have both benefited and harmed Japanese firms over the years. The most notable traits of Japanese firms mostly come from how businessmen think of the firm they belong to. There is a saying about Japanese businessmen at Daikin that these employees are extremely traditional in their belief systems. This can harm the procedures and outcomes in mergers and acquisitions between Japanese and foreign firms, especially if the cultures of both firms differ too much.

7.6 Conclusion

This chapter discussed Japanese M&A. It was shown that there has recently been a high level of activity in the M&A market. Also, most of the deals are rather domestic ones. This is against the belief system of many Japanese who assume M&A to be connected to foreign firms. When compared with domestic deals, there are recently many more Japanese firms investing abroad to take over foreign firms (with a peak of 515 deals in 2012). Conversely, foreign investors coming to Japan to take over a Japanese firm is rather rare, especially compared to domestic deals.

Two small case studies shed light on Japanese firms which took over a foreign one and discussed some of their challenges. Also, it became evident, that even though M&A normally appear at one phrase, mergers almost never happen. For the year 2013, only 34 mergers were reported and even with these deals it can be assumed that some firms called the deal a merger so as not to lose face when they were indeed a target.

Questions

1. From 2048 M&A in the year 2013, how many of them (approximately) were majority acquisitions?
2. How many mergers occurred in the year 2013?
3. Describe the Japanese M&A market from 1986 until now, what is striking?
4. How would you describe the out-in situation with acquisitions nowadays, foreign companies acquiring Japanese entities?

5. Which European countries' firms are active in the Japanese M&A market? Recall at least three of them.
6. What is a characteristic of British takeovers against Continental European ones?
7. What is the difference between "transient" and "dedicated" institutional investors?
8. How would you describe the development of foreign institutional investors coming to Japan, from 1999 until today?
9. Give reasons why Takeda overtook Nycomed from Switzerland?
10. Why did the air conditioner firm Daikin take over the US American firm Goodman?

Answers

1. In 2013, there were 939 majority acquisitions undertaken, which counted for about 46 % of all M&A
2. In 2013, there were merely 34 mergers, 2 % of all M&A deals.
3. What is striking is that there was a low M&A market in 1986 with around 400 deals. At the end of the 1980s', there was an increase in the number of deals, especially the in-out deals increased to a peak. Many Japanese firms went at that time out of Japan to take over non-Japanese firms. Some of the deals especially in the USA became famous examples of failures, for example when Mitsubishi took over Rockefeller Center in down town New York. In 2006, there was a peak with more than 2600 deals. After the Lehman Shock in 2008, there was a decrease in the number of deals to around 1800 deals a year. Also, in the last 20 years, most of the acquisitions are in-in deals. That means, M&A in Japan is rather a domestic issue. Recently, there is an increase visible of in-out deals (Japanese firms taking over foreign ones). In the year 2012, there was a record of 515 cases reported and even in 2013 there were still 499 Japanese firms which took over foreign firms.
4. On average, there are more than 100 out-in acquisitions in the last few years, fewer than in-out but higher than at the 1980s and 1990s. In the year 2013, there were 149 deals reported.
5. In the last decade, Japanese cross border M&As occur mainly with firms from only three European countries. On the top, Great Britain with the highest number of transactions (in the year of 2013 with 24 deals). The second most important country is Germany and France comes third. Finally, acquisitions with firms from the Netherlands have only increased in 2013 to a substantial amount of deals. All other European countries have very few cross border M&As with Japanese firms.
6. The British retirement system is a fund based system. It provides funds to participate at target firms worldwide. Continental European acquisitions are rather strategically oriented.

7. "Transient" institutional investors on the one hand are short term oriented investors. When share prices increase, a transient investor would sell them. "Dedicated" investors, on the other hand, would still hold the shares. Dedicated investors are often composed of pension funds with an intended long term relationship to take a stable profit out of the target firm.
8. Previously, foreign institutional investors were almost unknown in Japan. Since 1999, the first few stock equity participations were recorded by foreign institutional investors to Japan. Only in the year 2007, did inbound investments of institutional investors happen more often than investments by strategic investors. Recently, stock participations by institutional investors decreased again to lower levels.
9. One reason for Takeda to take over Nycomed was to access the European market in order to sell their products through Nycomed, but also to produce in Europe. This saves transportation costs and avoids taxes (for exporting to the EU). Another important reason was to use Nycomed's systematic build-up of network subsidiaries in emerging markets, especially in the BRIC countries to save time and effort to get into these markets.
10. Daikin aims to sell its world leading technology with air conditioners globally but also in the US market. Also, a strong yen made it difficult for Daikin to export their products to other countries. In return, it became financially attractive to take over a foreign firm, like Goodman. Finally, as Goodman was controlled by a short term oriented institutional investor, managers were obviously happy to have a stable strategic investor again.

References

Arai T (2008) M & A to shihon shijou—kouritsuteki de kouhei na shihon shijou wo motomete (M & A and financial markets—request for efficient and equal financial markets: 1–18. In: Shadan houjin M (ed) A jidai no fando to kabunushi rieki. Juridicial person: M & A fund period and shareholders' profits. March, Tokyo

Bae, K-H, Yamada T, Ito K (2006) How do Individual, Institutional, and Foreign Investors Win and Lose in Equity Trades? Evidence from Japan. How do Individual, Institutional, and Foreign Investors Win and Lose in Equity Trades? Evidence from Japan. *International Review of Finance*, Vol. 6 (3/4):129–155

Bebenroth R (2006) In the Wave of M&A: Europe and Japan. Iudicium, Munich

Bebenroth R (2009) Foreign M&A in Japan: do foreign firms cherry pick Japanese targets? Kobe Economic & Business Review, 54th Annual Vol 1, 1–16

Becht M, Franks J, Mayer C, Rossi S (2009) Returns to shareholder activism: evidence from a clinical study of hermes UK focus fund. Rev Financ Stud 22:3093–3129

Charkham J (1994) Keeping good company: a study of corporate governance in five countries. Clarendon Press, Oxford

Daikin Homepage (2014) Corporate profile. http://www.daikin.com/company/gaiyou.html?ID=daikin_jpn. Accessed 19 Mar 2014

Daikin News (2006) Corporate news. http://www.daikin.com/press/2006/060518_2/. Accessed 19 March 2014
Feito-Ruiz I, Menéndez-Requejo S (2011) Cross-border mergers and acquisitions in different legal environments. Int Rev Law Econ 31(3):169–187
Feuerstein A (2008) Japan' Taka Will Pay $9B for Millennium. The Street. Oct. 4th 2008. http://www.thestreet.com/story/10411425/1/japans-takeda-will-pay-9b-for-millennium.html. Accessed 16 April 2013
Fukao K, Amano T (2004) Tainichi chokusetsu toshi to nippon keizai [Direct investment in Japan and the Japanese economy]. Nihon Keizai Shinbunsha
Fukao, K, Ito K, Kwon HU (2005) Do out-in M&As bring higher TFP to Japan? An empirical analysis based on micro-data on Japanese manufacturing firms. J Jpn International Econ 19:272–301.
Helwege J, Intintoli VJ, Zhang A (2012). Voting with their Feet or Activism? Institutional Investors' Impact on CEO Turnover, *Journal of Corporate Finance*, 18, (1):22–37
Higgins NH (2013) Do stock-for-stock merger acquirers manage earnings? Evidence from Japan. J Acc Public Policy 32:44–70
Horiuchi A, Okazaki R (1994) Capital markets and the banking sector: efficiency of Japanese banks in reducing agency costs. In: Sato R, Levich RM, Ramachandran RV (eds) Japan, Europe, and International Financial Markets. Cambridge University Press, Cambridge
Inagaki K (2011) Takeda buys Nycomed for $ 14 Billion. The Wall Street Journal. May, 20th 2011. http://online.wsj.com/article/SB10001424052748704904604576332561259734564.html#. Accessed 16 April 2013
Inoue K (2010) Do M & A in Japan increase shareholder value. In: Y Kurokawa (ed) M & A for value creation in Japan, Monden Institute of Management. Japanese Management and International Studies, vol 6. pp 117–132
Inagaki K, Simmes J (2011) Takeda Pauses in M&A. The Wall Street Journal Online. Oct. 17th 2011. http://online.wsj.com/article/SB100014240529702040023045766310020224387 60.html. Accessed 16 April 2013
Juve (2011) Zehn-Milliarden-Deal: Takeda baut bei Nycomed-Übernahme auf CMS-Verbund. May 20th 2011. http://www.juve.de/nachrichten/deals/2011/05/zehn-milliarden-deal-takeda-baut-bei-nycomed-ubernahme-auf-cms-verbund. Accessed 16 April 2013
Kester WC (1991) Japanese takeovers: the global contest for corporate control. Harvard Business School Press, Boston
Klein A, Zur E (2009) Entrepreneur shareholder activism: hedge funds and other private investors. J Financ 64:187–229
Lachapelle T, Gammeltoft N (2011) Takeda-nycomed roiling investment suffering 40 % loss: Real M&A, Bloomberg, May 20th 2011. http://www.bloomberg.com/apps/news?pid=2065100sid=abab8JpV2a_c. Accessed 16 April 2013
Moody's (2013) Homepage, internet https://www.moodys.com/research/Moodys-assigns-Aa3-rating-to-Takedas-Japan-bonds–PR_276225. Accessed 19 March 2014
Muramatsu S (2007) M & A in Japan—Past and present. In: Bebenroth R (ed) In the wave of M&A: Europe and Japan. Iudicium, Munich, pp 70–93, (p 93, Fig. 4)
Porter ME (1992) Capital choices: changing the way America invests in industry. Harvard Business School, Boston
Sasaki G (2014) Global Takeda dohanba—jiko kaikaku itasu kankyu wo tsukuru. Sachiraito [Takeda half way to Globalization. Environment of self-reform]. Searchlight. Nikkei Sangyo Shinbun, March 30th: 14
Schaede U (2008) Choose and focus: Japanese business strategies for the 21st century. Cornell University Press, New York
Shleifer A, Vishny RW (1997) A survey of corporate governance. J Financ 52(2):737–783
Takeda News (2013a) Takeda appoints Chief Operating Officer, Nov. 30th 2013. http://www.takeda.com/news/files/20131130_en.pdf. Accessed 19 March 2014

Takeda News (2013b) Takeda pharmaceutical company limited announces mid-range growth strategy starting from the fiscal year 2013 (Ending March 31, 2014) Growth strategy as a new Takeda. http://www.takeda.com/news/2013/20130509_5767.html. Accessed 19 March 2014
Takeda Homepage (2014a) Building a global pharmaceutical company http://www.takeda.co.uk/uk/about-takeda/nycomed-acquisition/. Accessed 19 March 2014
Takeda Homepage (2014b) Takeda completes acquisition and names new CEO of Nycomed. http://www.tpi.takeda.com/media/news-releases/2011/takeda-completes-acquisition-and-names-new-ceo-of-nycomed/. Accessed 19 March 2014
Uotila J, Maula M, Keil T, Zahra SA (2009) Exploration, exploitation, and firm performance: analysis of S&P 500 corporations. Strateg Manage J 30:221–231
Ushijima T, Schaede U (2014) The market for corporate subsidiaries in Japan: an empirical study of trades among listed firms. J Jpn Int Econ 31(3):36–52

Chapter 8
Cross Border Bidders Versus Domestic Ones

Abstract This chapter investigates differences in targets overtaken by cross-border bidders versus domestic ones. The literature from the selection theory argues that there is "cherry picking." That means, cross-border bidders overtake the comparably better performing targets in contrast to domestic bidders, which acquire weaker targets in a sort of "rescue mission." Targets in the study were investigated to see if this statement holds true.

The results show that cross-border targets did not perform better but performed worse than domestic ones. According to my sample, I have to conclude that there is no "cherry picking" of Japanese firms at cross-border acquisitions. This lends support to the idea that foreign bidders probably come to the acquisition target at a later stage. To put it differently, Japanese firms get overtaken by foreign bidders in case where no domestic firm is interested in overtaking the target. Reasons are discussed.

8.1 Introduction

Cross border M&A has been historically seen as a means for firms from developed countries to enter less developed ones (Wilson 1980). Nowadays, this has changed, as cross-border M&A also appear to target companies in developed countries (Shimizu et al. 2004). In contrast to domestic acquisitions, cross-border acquisitions face additional challenges of evaluating, negotiating and integrating targets (Shimizu et al. 2004). Uncertainty and information asymmetry in foreign markets lead firms to difficulties in adjusting and learning both the local market and the target firm (Kogut and Singh 1988; Zaheer 1995).

There has been much research done in the international field (Goehlich 2009), especially to investigate post-acquisition performance with positive short term results for acquirers (Barnes 1984; Gregory 1997, Meshi and Metais 2006). In the long run, however, acquirers are predicted to have negative financial performance and there are mixed results for acquired target firms (King et al. 2004). These results

This chapter is an updated version of Bebenroth (2010) Inbound M&A to Japan: cherry picking versus rescue mission? Kobe Economic & Business Review 54: 1–16

R. Bebenroth, *International Business Mergers and Acquisitions in Japan*,
DOI 10.1007/978-4-431-54989-5_8

are supported by recent studies,where acquisitions were researched in a longitudinal study framework (Barkema and Shijven 2008). Also when investigated in life cycles of M&A booms, with early mover advantages for acquisitions at the beginning of a boom, the performance of the bidder companies in the long run was generally negative (McNamara et al. 2008).

The M&A area is well researched. Using patent data on pharmaceutical M&A, Ornaghi finds that mergers are more likely to be signed between firms with relatively similar technologies and drug portfolios and that performance implications depend on the similarity of bidder and target (Ornaghi 2009). Rhodes-Kropf and Robinson (2008) show that financial indices of bidders and targets are quite similar. Bidders with a high market-to-book-ratio acquire targets with a similar pattern. There is also research available about the post-merger effects of target enterprises (Olatunji and Uwuigbe 2009). The predominant target-oriented M&A research starts 1 year before the acquisitions occur (Eero and Boeckerman 2008; Munoz-Bullon 2008). An understudied topic, however, is target performance and employment effects the years before the acquisitions take place.

This research aims to shed light on the pre-acquisition period of targets by comparing two groups of Japanese target firms taken over either by a foreign (non-Japanese) bidder or by a domestic one. This is of importance, as employee downsizing activities, as well as the M&A market in general, are recently more active in countries like Japan (Lee 1997; Fukao and Murakami 2005). The wave of M&A nowadays clearly includes Japan and not only Japanese investments abroad—which were previously described as undertaking investments predominantly through Greenfield ventures but only to a lesser extent through M&A (Bebenroth 2007; Hebert et al. 2005). This relatively unknown phenomenon to Japan, therefore, served as the bases for this investigation.

It is stated in the literature that cross-border bidders "cherry pick" targets, choosing comparably better performing targets against domestic acquisitions (Bandick and Karpaty 2007). In the case of Japan, Paprzyki and Fukao (2008) state: "…on a closer inspection, it turns out that foreign firm's superior performance partly owes to the fact that they acquire Japanese firms that already perform better than the average local firms." (p. 7.) This "cherry picking" argument can also be found at Fukao et al. 2005 stating: "…we found that foreign firms acquire Japanese firms with higher TFP levels and higher profit rates. In contrast, in-in M&As ('domestic') [remark by the author] seem to have the characteristics of rescue missions. Small firms with a higher total liability/total asset ratio tend to be chosen as targets of in-in M&As" (p. 298).

I challenge this view by asking two questions: (1) Do foreign bidders "cherry pick" in the sense that they choose financially better performing targets compared to domestic bidders? (2) Does the downsizing pattern of targets differ between foreign and domestic acquisitions? For this, I looked into the target companies on a yearly basis, starting 7 years before the acquisitions took place and ending with the target's last financial statement before the acquisition event.

In the next two chapters theoretical arguments for cross-border acquisitions and downsizing effects in the Japanese M&A context are described. Chapter 5 presents hypotheses. Then data and results are empirically examined and presented. Chapter 8 ends with a discussion and conclusion of the results.

8.2 Theoretical Arguments for Cross Border Acquisitions

The theoretical framework of this study is based on the theory of multinational firms. This research is separated from the "inefficient management hypothesis" that states that targets were poorly managed and got replaced by bidder firms (Mandelker 1974).

According to this basic understanding, M&A might enhance creating value if companies put their expertise and know-how into an acquired firm (Buckley and Casson 1976; Rugman 1981). Departing from this inefficient management hypothesis, a theoretical construct can be provided, describing why headquarters undertake acquisitions. The "learning theory" states that a target will benefit from a bidder through financial help and advances in technology. Therefore, through expertise from the foreign headquarters in financial, technical or other areas, a target will benefit from being acquired.

Beyond domestic transactions and cross-border transactions, there is a "selection theory" which states that a foreign bidder will overtake a better performing target. The reasoning behind this is that a cross-border bidder has more at stake and higher costs than a comparable domestic one. Therefore, transactions will only be undertaken in cases where a target is especially lucrative.

Cross-border acquisitions may face even more severe problems than domestic ones (Very et al. 1996). Executives of acquired cross-border firms are more likely to quit their jobs than executives of acquired domestic firms (Krug and Hegarty 2001). In this sense, cross-border targets, so the theory, are more challenging to handle than domestic targets. Light will be shed on the differences of both kinds of transactions for investigating the targets' performance and to look into the downsizing behavior of the targets to see whether foreign bidders "cherry picking" their targets (Bandick and Karpaty 2007) can be proved or disproved.

8.3 Japanese Inbound M&A

Potential economic benefits of inward foreign direct investments (inward FDI) are highly appreciated by all countries' governments. A reason for this is that, through inward FDI, competition between local companies' increases, leading to lower prices for consumers and job-creation in the local economy (Fleming and Johnson 2008). Also, Japanese officials highly appreciate foreign direct investment to Japan. The Japanese government has launched a number of political measures to promote inward FDI. Former Prime Minister Junichiro Koizumi promised several years ago in his general policy speech to the Diet in 2003 to double the cumulative amount of inward FDI until 2008 (Fukao et al. 2005). The largest part of this inward FDI has been realized through M&As (Schaede 2008, p. 117). However, the inward FDI to Japan is not yet seen as high enough. Japan had only 5% inward FDI stock compared to the USA in 2012 (chapter 2) and, therefore, the lowest inward FDI ratio of the world's leading economies.

The Ministry of Economy, Trade and Industry (METI) proposed amendments in 2007. Several changes were implemented, e.g. harmonizing Japanese regulations to other leading countries' for improved inward FDI to Japan. Some of the amendments are fostering inward FDI, while others seem to be counterproductive. One example is regulatory changes. Before the amendments, companies were regulated according to industries and after, according to products. Some companies then became more severely regulated after the amendments in cases where they produced goods sold to defense forces (Nagashima et al. 2008).

On May 20th 2008, the Expert Committee on FDI Promotion, an advisory group to the Minister of State on Economic and Fiscal Policy, presented five recommendations to the Council on Economic and Fiscal Policy to increase foreign inward FDI to Japan. This has been maintained for the last years with the Invest Japan Office (WIP Japan 2014). In spite of relatively small Japanese inward FDI, the number of transactions in the Japanese M&A market has recently been increasing. This trend is visible since 2000 (see the Fig. 1). In this terminology, in-in refers to domestic transactions, in-out to acquisitions of Japanese firms abroad and out-in transactions to foreign firms overtaking Japanese firms. In 2007 there occurred over 2700 M&As, out of which 308 were foreign (non-Japanese; out-in) bidders overtaking Japanese target companies (Recof M&A Database et al. 2008). This was the highest number of Japanese inbound M&A reported ever. In 2008, there were still 2400 M&A undertaken with 198 by foreign bidders (Recof M&A Database et al. 2009). In 2013, there were still 2048 deals undertaken, having 149 of them performed by foreign firms.

8.4 Foreign Bidders to Japan

Foreign bidders overtaking Japanese companies are quite a new phenomenon and it has not yet been researched to a satisfying extent. Until now, Japanese research mainly covered domestic transactions, where a decline in productivity, ROE and ROA was found in the acquirer (Yeh and Hoshino 2001). Also, some long term studies of domestic acquisitions are available where employment was positively related to post-merger performance (Kruse et al. 2007).

Available in Japanese, there is research on M&A and foreign direct investments to Japan (e.g. Fukao and Amano 2004). The English literature, however, provides only few investigations in this area, e.g. Paprzycki and Fukao (2008) and Fukao et al. (2005). In their valuable contribution, they show evidence that cross-border acquisitions with a Japanese target differ from domestic ones.

In the case of Japan, there is some evidence suggesting "cherry picking" of cross-border target firms (Fukao et al. 2005). Fukao and Murakami find that cross-border target companies show a 10 % higher TFP as well as higher earnings and a higher return on capital compared to domestically-acquired targets (2005). The profit/sales ratio is 1.5 % higher at foreign companies compared to local companies. They also find significantly higher capital/labor ratio which leads to a higher labor productivity at foreign-owned firms. Finally, Return on Capital and the annual wages of employees were comparably higher at foreign firms.

8.5 Hypotheses

The structure of the targets for the financial performances and for downsizing was investigated. In each area I came up with one hypothesis comparing target enterprises of cross-border acquisitions to domestic ones.

In general, sources of the financial performance of targets, as well as arguments for downsizing, are similar. Foreign investors face challenges, such as "liability of foreignness" (Zaheer 1995) and a so called "double-layered acculturation" (Barkema et al. 1996). In this case, that would suggest that cross-border bidders pay a higher price for their targets and have cultural disadvantages versus domestic bidders. This is supported by Lin et al., who find evidence in the banking sector that shows that bank acquisitions in the same state in the US have a higher performance than out–of–state acquisitions (2006).

Foreign bidders have comparably higher costs. This starts with receiving information about the target. At the negotiation stage, costs for traveling to the target, translation services and costs for consulting expertise will be much higher than for a domestic acquirer. Also, the target's management should have a better negotiating position at foreign bids as foreign bidders are not as familiar with the Japanese market as domestic competitors are. All these facts lead to higher costs for cross-border bidders. Foreign buyers pay higher premiums in acquiring targets than domestic ones (Shimizu et al. 2004). Interestingly, Dewenter (1995) found some evidence that the level of premiums paid between foreign and domestic bidders differ according to whether the acquisition is hostile or not. However, only in cases of hostile takeovers, will foreign bidders pay a higher premium than rival bidders. Otherwise their premium would be even lower. The arguments lead to the conclusion that foreign bidders should be compensated with financially more attractive Japanese targets.

In my understanding of an acquisition, however, a potential Japanese target company suffered economically for some time before it was finally taken over by a domestic company. Apart from cost factors, it is to suggest that, in regards to information exchange, Japanese companies are closer to each other than foreign companies are to Japanese ones. In case of financial difficulties, therefore, potential domestic bidders should realize the chance of making an acquisition earlier than foreign bidders. Therefore, it is to state the following: Only in cases when no domestic company is interested in acquiring a suffering company whatsoever will foreign bidders have a chance of being able to make a bid on a Japanese target company.

Therefore, I assumed that the performance of the cross-border targets in this study is not better compared to domestic ones. That is to say, targets of cross-border acquisitions might outperform domestic acquisitions in the time after the acquisition has taken place. However, the reason is not that they are the potentially better companies, but that they start from a lower base. To put it different, targets overtaken by foreign firms suffer for a longer time. As foreign bidders come to the target relatively late in the process, target performance is already very weak and surviving becomes more and more questionable. After an acquisition is accomplished, a turnaround would offer more chances for recovery compared to domestic acquisitions. Therefore, in contrast to existing research results in this field, I did not assume that there is "cherry picking" in the case of Japan, but a question of the critical stage where the target company went in before being acquired. The hypothesis is stated as:

H.1. Foreign bidders come to the target in a later stage. Therefore, the financial performance of the target in the time period before the acquisition will be lower compared to targets at domestic acquisitions.

The second area of interest consists of target downsizing before the acquisition. Management literature deals with downsizing since the 1980s, where organizations use it as a tool to cut costs or to improve profitability and productivity (Iverson and Pullman 2003). There is clear evidence that target companies in M&A reduce the number of employees after the acquisition event (McGuckin and Nguyen 2001; Lichtenberg and Spiegel 1990). In Europe, unions are relatively strongly organized and powerful in protecting their employees against the management. M&A could be seen as a way for some firms to "legally" downsize their workforce. It was less surprising that Gugler and Yurtoglu found European companies downsizing by 10 % when involved at M&A (2004).

For the post-acquisition period, some scientific evidence reports that target-downsizing will be more severe in cross-border acquisitions than in domestic ones (Krug and Hegarty 2001). A reason for this could be that cross-border acquisitions are more costly. Therefore, to balance out these high costs and to make a success out of the target acquisition, a foreign bidder would need a stronger focus on the core business that results in higher synergy effects. One obvious way to receive this synergy effect would be possible through heavier downsizing of the target. Another explanation for higher downsizing of cross-border targets would be that foreign acquirers are less committed to countries like Japan so that acquisitions could lead to comparably more job losses in the acquired firms than in domestically acquired ones.

Post-acquisition downsizing could also be seen from a different perspective however. A domestic bidder is already supposed to be present in the market (at least in cases of horizontal M&As) and does not only provide production facilities but also services and distribution. This could result in even higher synergy effects through employee downsizing. Also Fukao and Murakami did not find evidence in Japan for foreign investors reducing employment significantly more than domestic bidders (2005). In summation, a domestic bidder may be even more likely to consolidate target activity and downsize employees.

In contrast to conventional research, in this research downsizing activities of the targets is investigated in the time before the acquisition takes place. Assuming that the foreign bidder company comes to the target in a later stage, target employees should have been downsized to a greater extent before the acquisition compared to targets of domestic acquisitions. The hypothesis is:

H.2 Foreign bidders come to a target in a later stage. Therefore, the downsizing of the target's employees in the time period before the acquisition will be higher in cross-border acquisitions compared to targets in domestic acquisitions.

8.6 Data and Method

The year of 2007, provided 308 inbound M&A, the highest number ever. The author could collect the data from the monthly printed issues of Japanese Merger Acquisition Research Report used by (Recof M&A Database 2008 issue).

In the next step, all stock-listed target firms were collected from the sampling as non-listed firms data could not be retrieved. Also all cases of business transfers got eliminated because in that particular case, a target firm separates only an entity to an acquirer. After these two processes were done, 241 stock-listed firms were left which underwent acquisitions, capital participations as well as capital increases. Then data for these firms were retrieved from the electronic database of NEEDS financial request. All of these forms count as M&A according to Recof and were collectively used in this research as M&A targets. Finally five holding companies, five regional banks, three city banks and two security targets were dropped from the sample, as their financial accounting is different from the sample. In the end, I was left with 226 target firms. Split into two groups, there were 158 domestic targets and 68 cross-border targets.

The companies were investigated starting from the year 2001 to the last annual financial statements in 2007. Most of the companies have their annual financial statements report at the end of March with an acquisition thereafter. However, in two minor cases, exceptions needed to be made. Some companies had their annual financial statements reporting after March, e.g. in September.

As variables for financial performance, revenue, operating profit, profit per share and ROE as well as ROA was used (Yeh and Hoshino 2001). To investigate other variables, like downsizing developments, the number of employees, labor productivity, director salary and bonuses and the labor equipment ratio was investigated. Also the foreigner share ratio of the targets was investigated.

For the method, a descriptive approach of investigation was used and data for all companies each year collected by dividing them into domestic and cross-border acquisitions. Data for financial performances and downsizing developments was retrieved. As a second step, three logistic regression analyses with dependent variables in the range of domestic to cross-border acquisition were employed. These models relate to the probability of having a foreign investor overtaking a Japanese firm to performance and with downsizing variables X. The regression analyses include return on assets (ROA), labor productivity (LP) and return on equity (ROE). Industry segmentation serves as control variable.

$$\text{prob}(\text{cross border ac} = 1) = \text{Exp}(\alpha + \beta \text{Xi}) / (1 + \exp(\alpha + \beta \text{iXi}))$$

8.7 Results

The aim of this research was to shed light on whether cross-border and domestic bidders differ in picking their target. I explicitly wanted to investigate if cross-border bidders really “cherry pick” Japanese targets.

Table 8.1 Japanese In-in-acquisitions: average of financial performances

Year	Revenue	Operating profit	Profit per share	ROE	ROA
2001	215907.8	8112.1	193.7	−0.9	4.7
2002	199691.5	5274.6	1787.5	−9.5	3.7
2003	201072.1	7508.4	1865.5	−0.5	4.4
2004	196573.9	8652.3	1741.8	3.4	5.0
2005	204598.0	11023.2	1981.8	−6.4	5.3
2006	218286.5	12912.1	698.3	−0.3	5.4
2007	225274.1	12358.2	743.3	4.6[a]	4.9[a]
Obs.	*154–158*	*154–158*	*149–156*	*149*	*152–158*

Source: Recof M & A Database, Print Issue, MARR, several issues, latest 2008

Table 8.2 Japanese out-in-acquisitions: average of financial performances

Year	Revenue	Operating profit	Profit per share	ROE	ROA
2001	88685.9	5401.1	23514.5	2.5	5.2
2002	83426.9	3412.3	13308.2	0.6	4.4
2003	80555.8	3512.2	8381.7	1.8	6.1
2004	77020.8	4376.9	3404.5	5.3	6.0
2005	78902.6	6188.9	1824.4	−6.0	6.9
2006	81576.8	6191.1	1218.4	−0.2	5.3
2007	82529.5	4387.9	719.3	−19.9[a]	3.3[a]
Obs.	*62*	*66–68*	*64–67*	*64*	*64–67*

Source: Recof M & A Database, Print Issue, MARR, several issues, latest 2008

The two samples differ tremendously in their company sizes, in revenue and in number of employees. The domestic sample of target firms in this research was about double in size compared to cross-border acquisition targets. This is clearly different when compared to the results of Fukao et al. (2005). The operating profit was therefore understandably also higher at the domestic acquisition targets (Tables 8.1 and 8.2). However, while the operating profit for the cross-border targets decreased, at least in the last annual financial statement before the acquisition, the domestic targets showed an increase of operating profit for the last 3 years.

Both samples had a positive ROA for cross-border targets all 7 years before the acquisition, ranging from 6.9 % in the year 2005 to only 3.3 % in 2007. Looking at ROE data, there were negative values for domestic targets with only 2 positive years in 2004 and 2007, the last year before the acquisition occurred. Cross-border acquisitions, on the other hand, had a more positive development at the beginning of the observations, starting in the first years from 2001 until 2004 with positive values and then turning into negative values the last 3 years, with even a negative of 19.9 % in 2007. These descriptive results for ROE clearly showed that the cross-border targets took a turn for the worse the last 3 years before the acquisitions occurred.

The ROE as well as ROA data in this research showed significantly lower values for cross-border targets in the year 2007. That is statistically significant (Tables 8.5 and 8.6). Looking at the number of employees, there is evidence that both groups

Table 8.3 Japanese in-in-acquisitions: downsizing developments

Year	No. of employees	Lab. productivity	Director sal. and bonuses	Labor equipment ratio	Foreigners shares ratio
2001	2203.8	1874.3	197.7	3442.2	0.0014
2002	2129.9	1859.2	193.9	3708.8	0.0017
2003	2077.7	1920.4	183.8	4061.1	0.0025
2004	2014.2	2113.7	178.1	4336.4	0.0037
2005	1948.8	2366.8	210.5	4563.7	0.0036
2006	1898.6	2567.2	202.3	4833.4	0.0033
2007	1907.5	2657.8[a]	209.6	4686.0	0.0040
Obs.	*154–158*	*152–158*	*142–146*	*152–158*	*2–20*

Source: Recof M & A Database, Print Issue, MARR, several issues, latest 2008

Table 8.4 Cross border (out-in) acquisitions: downsizing developments

Year	No. of employees	Lab. productivity	Director sal and bonuses	Labor equipment ratio	Foreigners shares ratio
2001	1435.5	1977.9	178.2	4276.1	0.0037
2002	1341.5	2099.4	164.5	4437.9	0.0096
2003	1225.3	2223.1	166.7	5012.1	0.0105
2004	1192.5	2313	167.2	5127.3	0.0101
2005	1171.3	2482.6	170.5	5054.4	0.0094
2006	1163.1	2797.9	177.7	5178.9	0.0174
2007	1171.7	2108.9[a]	209.6	5327.4	0.0243
Obs.	*65*	*65–68*	*59–63*	*64–66*	*3–6*

Source: Recof M & A Database, Print Issue, MARR, several issues, latest 2008

downsized their workforce (Tables 8.3 and 8.4). Domestic targets downsized from 2203 employees in 2001 to 1907 in 2007. Cross-border targets downsized from 1435 employees in 2001 to 1171 in 2007. Labor productivity increased in both groups with statistically significant lower results for cross-border targets in the year 2007. Director and salary bonuses as well as the labor equipment ratio did not show any differences between groups (not stated in table). Looking at the ratio of shares held by foreigners, one sees that the level in both groups was very low. What is surprising here is that until the year 2001, only three cross-border targets were foreign-owned and that increased to only six targets by 2007.

The hypothesis about financial performance received preliminary support for the last year of the observation in 2007. The ROA (Table 8.5) as well as the ROE have a negative sign and are statistically significant to 1 %. Also the hypothesis about downsizing at least in the area for labor productivity (Table 8.6) is statistically significant to 1 %. Other downsizing variables, e.g. no. of employees did not receive any significant result (not reported at the tables). However, I also did not find evidence for stronger downsizing at cross-border firms, as is stated in the literature.

Table 8.5 ROA logistic regression

Out-In	Coef.	Std. error	z	$P>\|z\|$	95 % conf. interval	
ROA2001	0.01	0.20	0.64	0.52	−0.21	0.04
ROA2002	−0.05	0.03	−1.62	0.11	−0.13	0.01
ROA2003	0.06	0.05	1.33	0.18	−0.30	0.16
ROA2004	0.03	0.06	0.64	0.53	−0.78	0.15
ROA2005	−0.05	0.05	−0.98	0.33	−0.16	0.05
ROA2006	0.12	0.06	1.88	0.06	−0.01	0.24
ROA2007	−0.14	0.05	−2.95	0.00	−0.24	−0.05
Industry1	0.16	0.65	0.25	0.81	−1.12	1.45
Industry2	0.80	0.55	1.46	0.15	−0.28	1.88
Industry3	0.44	0.65	0.68	0.50	−0.83	1.71
Industry4	−0.20	0.57	−0.35	0.73	−1.32	0.92
Industry5	0.68	0.75	0.91	0.36	−0.78	2.14
Industry6	1.52	0.74	2.06	0.04	0.08	2.97
Industry7	0.28	0.63	0.45	0.66	−0.96	1.51
Cons	−1.30	0.43	−3.03	0.00	−2.15	−0.46

Dependant variable, out-in; independent variable, return on assets (ROA) on a yearly basis; control variable, industry

Logistic regression: Number of Observations=216, LR Chi2 (14)=22.41, Prob>Chi2=0.0706, Pseudo R2=0.0854

Log likelihood=−120.05633

Cross-border targets find themselves in weaker shape compared to domestic targets. This leads to the idea that the cross-border bidders come to the target at a later stage.

The industry classification shows that only in the service industry (no. 6 in the industry classification at the Tables 8.5, 8.6 and 8.7) has significant impact for takeovers. However, all other industries do not significantly impact the results in this study.

8.8 Discussion

I would not call the acquisitions by foreign bidders "cherry picking" and find evidence from my data that both groups varied in size considerably, with the smaller firms being the cross-border targets.

According to the data used in this study, cross-border targets were not the better performing firms in the years before the acquisition event but generally weaker than domestic targets. That means cross-border acquisitions in Japan do not occur because the foreign bidder merely invests its money for a lucrative investment. My understanding is that potential Japanese targets were left over, not getting taken over by any domestic firm. These Japanese companies in financial trouble then had to look to get overtaken by a non-Japanese firm.

Table 8.6 LP logistic regression

Out-In	Coef.	Std. error	z	$P>\|z\|$	95% conf. interval	
LP2001	0.00	0.00	−1.04	0.30	0.00	0.00
LP2002	0.00	0.00	−0.84	0.40	0.00	0.00
LP2003	0.00	0.00	0.94	0.35	0.00	0.00
LP2004	0.00	0.00	0.56	0.57	0.00	0.00
LP2005	0.00	0.00	−0.43	0.67	0.00	0.00
LP2006	0.00	0.00	1.82	0.07	0.00	0.00
LP2007	0.00	0.00	−1.98	0.05	0.00	−5.73e-06
Industry1	−0.03	0.67	−0.05	0.96	−1.33	1.28
Industry2	0.66	0.54	1.21	0.23	−0.40	1.72
Industry3	0.23	0.64	0.36	0.72	−1.03	1.50
Industry4	−0.34	0.58	−0.58	0.56	−1.47	0.80
Industry5	1.08	0.81	1.33	0.18	−0.51	2.66
Industry6	1.85	0.79	2.33	0.02	0.30	3.40
Industry7	0.36	0.58	0.62	0.54	−0.78	1.49
Cons	−1.12	0.43	−2.60	0.01	−1.96	−0.27

Dependant variable, out-in; Independent variable, Labor productivity (LP) on a yearly basis; Control variable, Industry

Logistic regression: Number of Observations = 217, LR Chi2 (14) = 21.06, Prob > Chi2 = 0.1000, Pseudo R2 = 0.0795

Log likelihood = −121.94118

That fits well with some post-acquisition target performance research using total factor productivity as a measure for performance (Fukao et al. 2005). My idea is that cross-border targets might bounce back to positive financial performance earlier and stronger, as they were in worse financial shape before they got acquired. Bandick and Karpaty find for their Swedish sample, positive employment effects in firms which were taken over by foreign bidders (2007). Girma and Goerg divide employment into skilled and less skilled labor and find for their electronics industry sample that only unskilled labor decreased in cross-border acquisition targets. However, no results of higher downsizing was found for skilled labor (Girma and Goerg 2004).

It is still questionable to the author however, how reliable the results are when measuring the post-acquisition performance of target companies. In the case of an acquisition, the target company's name regularly disappears. For example, after Panasonic finalized the agreement to overtake Sanyo Denki in 2008, no longer can be any reliable information on Sanyo Denki received, as not only their name disappear soon but also several departments of the old Sanyo Denki. Other departments already got restructured, mixed with previous Matsushita departments or even were sold in the form of a business transfer. It is to argue, therefore, that jobs which were eliminated by Panasonic might have been those of previous employees of Sanyo Denki.

Table 8.7 ROE logistic regression

Out-In	Coef.	Std. error	z	P>|z|	95 % conf. interval	
ROE2001	0.002	0.006	0.29	0.775	−0.01	0.14
ROE2002	0.007	0.010	0.65	0.514	−0.01	0.03
ROE2003	0.008	0.009	0.86	0.387	−0.01	0.03
ROE2004	0.001	0.009	0.10	0.920	−0.02	0.02
ROE2005	−0.011	0.006	−1.97	0.049	−0.02	0.00
ROE2006	0.023	0.017	1.34	0.180	−0.01	0.06
ROE2007	−0.031	0.012	−2.60	0.009	−0.05	−0.01
Industry1	0.203	0.637	0.32	0.749	−1.04	1.45
Industry2	0.789	0.545	1.45	0.148	−0.28	1.86
Industry3	0.332	0.644	0.52	0.606	−0.93	1.59
Industry4	−0.186	0.602	−0.31	0.757	−1.36	0.99
Industry5	0.382	0.776	0.49	0.623	−1.14	1.90
Industry6	1.742	0.767	2.27	0.023	0.24	3.25
Industry7	0.154	0.611	0.25	0.801	−1.04	1.35
Cons	−1.252	0.408	−3.07	0.002	−2.05	−0.45

Dependant variable, out-in; Independent variable, Return on equity (ROE) on a yearly basis; Control variable, Industry

Logistic regression: Number of observations = 210, LR Chi2 (14) = 31.30, Prob > Chi2 = 0.0050, Pseudo R2 = 0.1212

Log likelihood = −113.46729

8.9 Conclusion

This research has focused on strategic acquisitions, i.e. acquisitions by companies which had strategic interest in the target companies. In contrast to strategic investors, there are financial investors, so called “vulture” funds. These funds are often times described in Japan as reaping quick profits by taking advantage of troubled target companies (Fukao et al. 2005). To extend this research, it would be promising to compare acquisitions looking at whether the bidder has financial or strategic interests. Another future avenue of research would be to investigate if Japanese financial investors differ in their behavior toward non-Japanese cross-border financial investors. This research is limited to the pre-acquisition period, as the target names regularly disappear. It would be interesting to apply a case study format for investigating changes after the acquisition in target firms with regards to financial performance and downsizing behavior.

This study is not without its limitations. It is to admit that it might not be enough to divide the sample into only two groups, but it does matter where foreign bidders come from. According to Rosenkopf and Almeida, knowledge stock will increase when a geographic similarity is available (2003). That means a Japanese target acquisition by a Korean bidder, for example, might differ from a German bidder.

Another shortcoming might be the fact that Japanese targets could not get classified as keiretsu-grouped companies. Some evidence would suggest that Japanese targets which belong to any keiretsu group might get overtaken by a domestic company more easily.

In spite of its limitations, this work shows alternative explanations for cross-border target acquisitions. I have evidence that foreign companies do not "cherry pick" Japanese targets. There is more a "recovery" from almost ground zero visible. That means, cross border targets are in a more severe situation than their domestically acquired counterparts. This might lead to better performing entities of cross-border targets in the years after the acquisition event.

Questions

1. Why should a government be concerned to attract foreign FDI into the country?
2. What could be a reason that acquisitions are preferably conducted from firms in developed countries?
3. What are reasons why performance research at target firms is difficult to conduct?
4. What can be a challenge for foreign bidders (against domestic ones) overtaking a Japanese firm?
5. Why should performance of a target differ, if overtaken by a foreign or by a domestic bidder?
6. What do you associate under "cherry picking" after studying the chapter?
7. Is there any evidence of "cherry picking", that foreign investors preferable overtake the better (Japanese) targets?
8. What could explain the fact, that foreign firms investing into a Japanese firm, often overtake a weaker firm?
9. How differs the target downsizing of employees by Japanese and foreign investors?
10. Recall some limitations of the study undertaken.

Answers

1. Foreign FDI is linked to many economic benefits. Also Japanese government attracts foreign investors to invest into Japan.
2. Firms from developed countries have the financial capacity and the know how to conduct acquisitions.
3. Normally, target firms get absorbed by bidder firms. They do not exist anymore. Therefore, they can not be investigated. Japan is different especially when foreign firms acquire Japanese firms. These targets often will be left quite independent, so that performance research on these (Japanese) targets is possible.

4. A challenge for foreign bidders overtaking a Japanese firm starts with a lack of information about the target. It is more difficult to negotiate for foreign bidders (than for Japanese firms). Also, the integration of the target into the foreign bidder is difficult because of upcoming cultural misunderstandings.
5. A target should differ in its performance because a foreign firm may support the (Japanese) target more than a domestic bidder in order to enter the Japanese market. Also, foreign bidders are said to be more direct in their approach. That may cause more conflicts, but can also lead to clear results.
6. Cherry Picking is associated to non-Japanese firms overtaking Japanese ones. These foreign firms have higher costs (than comparable Japanese ones) and therefore, would only take the best (Japanese) firms.
7. There is no evidence. The opposite is found out. Japanese targets acquired by foreign investors seem to be the weaker firms.
8. Explanations would be that foreign firms might not be informed compared to Japanese potential bidder firms. Also, foreign investors might generally come late "to the game". In case no other Japanese investor is willing to overtake a target, a foreign firm gets a chance.
9. There is a higher downsizing of the number of employees at Japanese firms overtaken by foreign investors. This leads to a higher labor productivity.
10. The study relies on only a few years of data observations. Also, non-Japanese bidder differ according to their country of origin. A bidder from a developed country may want to enter Japan when overtaking a Japanese target firm. However, if the bidder firm comes from an Emerging Market country, the intention of the acquisition might be rather to absorb famous brand names—for selling the products in their home country.

References

Bandick R, Karpaty P (2007) Foreign acquisition and employment effects in Swedish Manufacturing, Working Paper Series, No. 10, Oerebro University, Sweden. ESI, p 26
Barkema HG, Shijven M (2008) Toward unlocking the full potential of acquisitions: the role of organizational restructuring. Acad Manage J 51(4):696–722
Barkema HG, Bell JHJ, Pennings JM (1996) Foreign entry, cultural barriers and learning. Strateg Manage J 17:151–166
Barnes P (1984) The effect of a merger on the share price of the attacker. Account Bus Res 15(57):45–50
Bebenroth R (2007) In the wave of M&A: Europe and Japan. Iudicium, Munich
Bebenroth R (2010) Inbound M&A to Japan: cherry picking versus rescue mission? Kobe Econ Bus Rev 54:1–16
Buckley PJ, Casson M (1976) The future of the multinational enterprise. MacMillan, London

Dewenter KL (1995) Does the market react differently to domestic and foreign takeover announcements? Evidence from the U.S. chemical and retail industries. J Financial Econ 37:421–441
Eero L, Boeckerman P (2008) Analyzing the employment effects of mergers and acquisitions. J Econ Behav Organ 68:112–124
Fleming G, Johnson RS (2008) How countries are impacted by mergers and acquisitions: a theoretical approach. Virginia Econ J 13:33–40
Fukao K, Amano T (2004) Tainichi chokusetsu toshi to nippon keizai [Direct investment in Japan and the Japanese economy]. Nihon Keizai Shinbunsha
Fukao K, Murakami Y (2005) Do foreign firms bring greater total factor productivity to Japan? J Asia Pac Econ 10(2):237–254
Fukao K, Ito K, Kwon HU (2005) Do out-in M&As bring higher TFP to Japan? An empirical analysis based on micro-data on Japanese manufacturing firms. J Jpn Int Econ 19:272–301
Girma S, Goerg H (2004) Blessing or curse? Domestic plants survival and employment prospects after foreign acquisition. Appl Econ Q 50:89–110
Goehlich R (2009) Make-or-buy decisions in aerospace organizations, Gabler edition. Wissenschaft, Wiesbaden
Gregory A (1997) An examination of the long run performance of UK acquiring firms. J Bus Finance Account 24(7):971–1002
Gugler K, Yurtoglu BB (2004) The effects of mergers on company employment in the US and Europe. Int J Ind Organ 22:481–502
Hebert L, Very P, Beamish P (2005) Expatriation as a bridge over troubled water: a knowledge/based perspective applied to cross-border acquisitions. Organ Stud 26:1455–1476
Iverson RD, Pullman JA (2003) Determinants of voluntary turnover and layoffs in an environment of repeated downsizing following a merger: an event history analysis. J Manage 26(5):977–1003
King DR, Dalton DR, Daily CM, Covin JG (2004) Meta-analyses of post-acquisition performance: indications of unidentified moderators. Strateg Manage J 25:187–200
Kogut B, Singh H (1988) The effect of national culture on the choice of entry mode. J Int Bus Stud 19:411–432
Krug JA, Hegarty WH (2001) Research notes and commentaries: predicting who stays and leaves after an acquisition: a study of top managers in multinational firms. Strateg Manage J 22:185–196
Kruse TA, Park HY, Park K, Suzuki K (2007) Long-term performance following mergers of Japanese companies: the effect of diversification and affiliation. Pac-Basin Finance J 15(2):154–172
Lee PM (1997) A comparative analysis of layoff announcements and stock price reductions in the United States and Japan. Strateg Manage J 18:879–894
Lichtenberg FG, Spiegel S (1990) The effect of ownership changes on the employment and wages of central office and other personnel. J Law Econ 33:383–408
Lin BW, Hung SC, Li PC (2006) Mergers and acquisitions as a human resource strategy—evidence from US banking firms. Int J Manpow 27(2):126–142
Mandelker G (1974) Risk and return: The case of merging firms. J Financial Econ 1:303–335
McGuckin RH, Nguyen SV (2001) The impact of ownership changes: a view from labour markets. Int J Ind Organ 19:739–762
McNamara GM, Haleblian JJ, Dykes BJ (2008) The performance implications of participating in an acquisition wave: early mover advantages, bandwagon effects, and the moderating influence of industry characteristics and acquirer tactics. Acad Manage J 1:113–130
Meshi PX, Metais E (2006) International acquisition performance and experience: a resource-based view. Evidence from French acquisitions in the United States (1988–2004). J Int Manage 12:430–448
Munoz-Bullon F (2008) Who downsizes for longer? A longitudinal analysis, Working Paper 08-28, Business Economic Series, 05 Madrid
Nagashima OT (2008) Inbound direct investment. Int Financial Law Rev 27(7):73–75
Olatunji OR, Uwuigbe U (2009) Psychological effects of mergers and acquisition on employees: case study of some selected banks in Nigeria. World Rev Entrep Manage Sustain Dev 5(1):102–115
Ornaghi C (2009) Positive assortive merging. J Econ Manage Strategy 18(2):323–46

Paprzycki R, Fukao K (2008) Foreign direct investment in Japan. Cambridge University Press, Cambridge

Recof M & A Database, Print Issue, MARR (several issues, latest 2008) Mergers acquisition research report. Recof-data report (in Japanese)

Recof M&A Database, Print Issue, MARR (1995–2009) Mergers acquisition research report. Recof-Data report (in Japanese)

Rhodes-Kropf M, Robinson DT (2008) The market for mergers and the boundaries of the firm. J Finance 63(3):1169–1211

Rosenkopf L, Almeida P (2003) Overcoming local search through alliances and mobility. Manage Sci 49(6):751–766

Rugman A (1981) Inside the multinationals: the economics of international markets. Croom Helm, London

Schaede U (2008) Choose and focus: Japanese business strategies for the 21st century. Cornell, New York

Shimizu K, Hitt MA, Vaidyanath D, Pisano V (2004) Theoretical foundations of cross-border mergers and acquisitions: a review of current research recommendations for the future. J Int Manage 10:307–353

Very P, Lubatkin M, Calori R (1996) A cross-national assessment of acculturative stress in recent European mergers. Int Stud Manage Organ 26:59–88

Wilson BD (1980) The propensity of multinational companies to expand through acquisitions. J Int Bus Stud 11:59–64

WIP Japan (2014) Invest Japan. Foreign direct investment promotion. Cabinet office. http://www.invest-japan.go.jp/en_index.html. Accessed 16 May 2014

Yeh T, Hoshino Y (2001) Productivity and operating performance of Japanese merging firms: keiretsu-related and independent mergers. Jpn World Econ 434:1–20

Zaheer S (1995) Overcoming the liability of foreignness. Acad Manage J 38:341–363

Chapter 9
Unfriendly Takeovers

Abstract This chapter will not only cover theories related to unfriendly takeovers, but will also outline several cases of unfriendly takeovers in Japan within the past 40 years. In recent years the amount of unfriendly takeovers taking place has been increasing in Japan. Furthermore the acquisition of Sanyo Denki by Panasonic and the hostile takeover attempt of Noritz Kitchen by Steel Partners will be presented. Also, the defense measures against unfriendly, also known as "poison pills" will be discussed.

9.1 Introduction

The fact that most acquisitions occur under friendly circumstances is true throughout the world (Bainbridge 2012, p. 25). However, in the case of Japan it was widely known that Japanese managers were very reluctant to overtake another firm; furthermore, unfriendly takeovers were non-existent (Yamagami et al. 2012). This is in sharp contrast to the US, where cash hostile takeovers were very common in the 60s and even regarded as a "potent weapon" in the market for corporate control. However, in the year 1968 the Williams Act was introduced which, required the bidder and the target management a substantial disclosure in order to prevent these deals (Bainbridge 2012, pp. 209–212).

In friendly takeovers a target firm's management endorses the offer. Conversely, in an unfriendly attempt, the target management refuses to be taken over by the bidding firm (Aurora et al. 2011, p. 31). In order to conduct the deal, the bidding firm bypasses the target firm's management and places a tender offer directly to the target's shareholders. The bidder sets a time period and a price for buying shares. It is important to mention that most tender offer bids (TOB) also known as a takeover bids are hostile because the tender will normally be made without endorsement of the target firm's management. However, they can also occur in a friendly attempt as well. In the case of a hostile acquisition, it is important to understand that the management as well as regular employees are usually in opposition to the takeover attempt. In the US, Bainbridge claims that a displacement of managers and changes in the workforce occurs in almost half of all corporate takeovers (Bainbridge 2012, pp. 42–43). The reason is that managers who are taken over unfriendly often get

R. Bebenroth, *International Business Mergers and Acquisitions in Japan*,
DOI 10.1007/978-4-431-54989-5_9

replaced and employees restructured or fired. In every case, unfriendly acquisitions are much more difficult to execute than friendly ones.

In addition to the many difficulties associated with unfriendly takeovers, there are some who benefit from unfriendly takeovers. Shareholders of the target firm as well as banks, who are having a lending relationship with the target firm, may benefit from a deal. In the first case, the shareholders of a target often make a profit from an unfriendly takeover because they receive high premiums for their shares. When unfriendly bidders place a public offer to obtain shares of a firm, they need to set the price far above the price listed on the stock exchange in order to convince shareholders to sell their shares. This means that hostile takeovers are normally more costly for the bidding firm because of this high premium (Campa and Hernando 2006; Goergen and Renneboog 2008). In the second case banks have the opportunity to profit from an unfriendly takeover. In most cases it is safe to assume that the reason a firm is taken over is because it did not perform economically well. Some of the banks affiliated with the target firm will use a takeover as an opportunity to collect outstanding loans because the bidding firm is assumed to be more economically sound. Despite this one advantage, there are also disadvantages for banks affiliated with the target firm. In the case where target firm's bank differs from the bidder's bank, the target firms' bank will lose business to the bidding firm's. In other words, the target firm's bank would lose a customer. Furthermore, banks can play a crucial role in the very lucrative consultation market and act as a "go between" for the target and bidding firm. No firm will expose themselves to the market with the desire to be sold by its shareholders; this is true anywhere in the world. If the stocks of a firm were sold, the value of their stocks would decrease and a "fire sale" may occur. In that case, a firm may even go bankruptcy and be forced to suddenly search for new investors. However, in Japan this issue becomes even more serious because of the anonymity when a target plans to get sold. It is also important to mention that banks may have mixed interests in that they sometimes may act as a shareholders and as well as a source of credit for a firm, which can lead to conflicts of interest (Hasegawa 2007, pp. 87–91).

In short, in a friendly takeover the target management agrees to be taken over, while in an unfriendly (hostile) takeover, the target management as well as the general workforces do not agree to be taken over. The management of the bidding firm sidesteps the market to publically offer to buy the shares of the target firms. It is important to mention, that there are some special legal processes related to unfriendly takeovers. In a friendly attempt, the approval by the Ministry of Finance usually takes 4 weeks; however, in an unfriendly takeover this process can take about 2 months (Ota 2013, p. 367).

After a deal is completed, it can be argued that the target firms of unfriendly acquisitions become streamlined and improve financially. It can also be asumed that a target firm in unfriendly acquitions will become more efficient. In order to improve the target firms' performance and to increase the value of the firms, a hostile bidder may replace inefficient incumbent manager much more easily than a friendly investor (Sudarsanam and Mahate 2006). In an attempt to enhance efficiency, a bidder engaged in a hostile takeover may even breach implicit contracts such as pension obligations (Shleifer and Summers 1988).

9.2 Market Based and Inefficient Management Theory

M&A literature on unfriendly takeovers provides a market based theory and an inefficient management theory which can explain why acquisitions occur. It states that firms are overtaken because they are undervalued. This means, that a given firm has a lower price per share than it should have under normal circumstances. For example, an electronics maker may face financial difficulties; however, the reason may not be because the firm is not selling its products and making profit, but due to bad investments made by managers. Even if these mistakes are not connected to the main business of a firm, it would still lower the price of a firm's share. In other words, the firm would be undervalued. In economic terms, this means that the intrinsic value of a firm is higher than the listing price on the stock exchange. A "healthy firm" may end up with a very low stock price leading them to be taken over by another firm. This means that evaluation of value drives M&A. This is supported by Rhodes-Kropf et al. by decomposing market-to-book ratio into three components (2005). Financially motivated institutional funds, especially, look for firms with low stock prices to invest in. This is also supported for Japan, institutional funds prefer to overtake firms that are facing problems or have high cash reserves.

This theory is expanded by Shleifer and Vishny (1997) who state that target firms are not only inexpensive or undervalued but that bidding firms perceive themselves as worth more or overvalued. This means that bidding firms' managers may perceive their value to be higher than what it actually is, encouraging managers to takeover inexpensive firms. The price of the target firm would then be paid using shares of the bidding firm in a stock swap. In other words, stock swaps are stock-for-stock deals. Than a bidder firm pays a target firm's shareholders not in cash but in their own shares, meaning that the shares of the bidding firm act as a currency. After fixing the purchasing price, the share exchange ratio will be fixed. Technically, the target firms' shareholders are trading their shares for shares of the bidding firm. In some stock swap deals it is sometimes not easy to determine who was taken over by whom. It is important to note that a high stock price of the bidding firm will lead to a smaller number of shares to be paid to the target firm's shareholders. Evidence by Higgins (2013) suggests that Japanese bidder firms will increase their earnings before an acquisition in order to make the acquisition less expensive.

Another theoretical way to explain why M&A, in particular unfriendly takeovers, occur is the "inefficient management theory." The inefficient management theory states that target firms were poorly managed and were, therefore, taken over by another firm, the bidding firm (Mandelker 1974). Therefore, according to this train of thought M&As enhance value because the expertise and financial support of the bidding firm should transform the once weak target firm into a strong firm (Buckley and Casson 1976; Rugman 1981).

The inefficient management theory is somehow closely related to learning. A target will benefit from a bidder through financial help and advances in technology. This means that the transfer of the financial, technical, or management skills of the bidding firm, in other words through education, a target firm will increase its value.

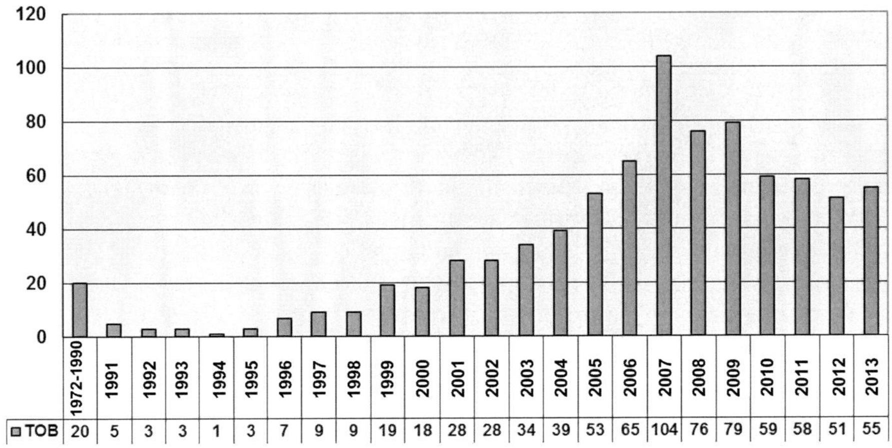

Fig. 9.1 Development of Japanese hostile acquisitions. (Source: Recof M&A Database 1972–2014)

In other words, the target can observe techniques of the bidding firm and learn how to perform better themselves.

9.3 Japanese Market of Unfriendly Acquisitions

The number of unfriendly takeovers in the Japanese market is shown above for roughly the last 40 years. It is evident that unfriendly takeovers in Japan barely existed at all. For example, from the year 1972 to 1990, there was only about one unfriendly takeover per year. Even in the 1990s there were only very few cases of unfriendly takeovers. However, there is a steep increase in the number of unfriendly takeovers in the 2000s. The first time the number of unfriendly takeovers reached more than 20 deals a year was 2001. The peak was seen in the year 2007 with more than 100 unfriendly acquisitions (exactly 104 cases). Even in 2013, there were 55 cases of unfriendly takeovers. It can be said that Japan has experienced a recent increase in unfriendly acquisitions (Fukutani and Dobashi 2008, p. 77). Figure 9.1 shows that unfriendly acquisitions in Japan are much more common nowadays.

There are a few reasons as to why unfriendly takeovers were so rare in the past in Japan. First of all it was ludicrous for Japanese managers' minds to overtake a firm without having the consent of target management. Problems in the integration period—a hot topic recently in worldwide M&A research—was known in Japan in the past. Problems in integrating a target firm into a bidder's strategy increases if the target is against the takeover. This is especially the case when strategic changes need to be implemented.

Japanese firms often have a very strong culture that has developed from their history. In other words, Japanese firms are traditionally focused on their own firm. The relationship between employees and their firm in Japan is much stronger than in other countries. European or US-employees would rather identify with people from their own disciplines. For example, European accountants would probably have a stronger relationship with accountants in another firms rather than a marketing manager from their own firm. It is said that this strong relationship between Japanese employees and their firms enables them to have advantages over other non-Japanese competitors. The management itself enforces this relationship. Japanese firms, tend to develop a strong "firm culture" by having regular in house meetings in which all the managers are present. This "closeness" within a firm is strengthened even further by frequently moving managers to different positions within the firm. This strong relationship between employees often creates problems when a firm is taken over especially in unfriendly takeovers. Due to this "firm culture," unfriendly takeovers are more difficult for Japanese firms to execute than other countries' firms.

Another reason that the number of unfriendly takeovers were relatively low in Japan is the practice of cross-shareholding (Chap. 2), which led to very few outstanding shares. If a presumptive target firm did not want to be taken over, there was often no chance for investors to absorb shares of that firm because all shareholders were so called "stable shareholders." These shareholders would not have sold their shares—no matter how financially attractive the offer was. Several laws also tightly regulated the M&A market making acquisitions difficult. As these laws are either amended or discarded the number of unfriendly takeovers has increased (Fukutani and Dobashi 2008). An example discussed below is the unfriendly (hostile) takeover of Sanyo by Panasonic in the year 2011.

9.4 Examples

9.4.1 Panasonic Takeover of Sanyo (3)

9.4.1.1 Introduction

The takeover of Panasonic over Sanyo started to receive public attention in December, 2008 as it was an unfriendly attempt in its nature (Panasonic News 2014; Kudo 2012). The hostile bid was clearly against the will of the Sanyo Denki managers at that time.

In 2010 Panasonic made a public takeover announcement to acquire Sanyo Denki's shares. The time period for shareholders to decide whether or not to sell their shares was from August 23rd to October 6th 2010. In the end Panasonic absorbed a total of 80 % of all of Sanyo Denki's shares. In 2010 Sanyo Denki became a wholly owned subsidiary of Panasonic, with Panasonic owning 4.9 trillion out of 6.1 trillion outstanding shares (Panasonic Announcement 2010).

9.4.1.2 Panasonic and Sanyo

Panasonic Corporation (in the following just Panasonic) is Japan's largest and well-known electronic corporation and was founded in 1918 in Kadoma, Osaka, Japan. Before the firm was renamed in 2008 to Panasonic, the firm was known as Matsushita Electric Industrial Co., Ltd in Japan (Panasonic History 2014). Konosuke Matshushita founded his firm with the aim to create innovative products at a high technical standard. In the beginning (1918), the firm started up by successfully sellin plugs and double cluster sockets. Soon after its establishment, Matsushita expanded its business to other Asian countries. After WWII, the firm focused on new businesses such as the production of radios and other electrical appliances to participate in the economic boom of post war Japan.

Matsushita first expanded to North America in the 1960s and then to Europe in the late 1970s. For the domestic market and other Asian markets, the firm built many home appliances such as rice cookers. All these factors led to a rapid growth of the company. As a result, Panasonic built manufacturing plants all over the world.

In the year 2008, Matsushita Electric Industrial Co., Ltd. finally changed its name to "Panasonic Corporation". This was a necessary step in order to become a well-known global player in the electronics industry. Previously, the firm faced some trouble because it had three different names. Products sold in Japan were sold under the brand name "national." The same or similar products produced for the USA were sold under the brand name "Panasonic." However, at the same time the name of the firm itself was still Matsushita Electric. In order to simplify things, the firm changed its name to Panasonic and all products were also sold under the brand name Panasonic.

One of the most significant events in recent history of Panasonic was the unfriendly takeover of Sanyo Denki in 2009. In that year, Sanyo Denki became a consolidated subsidiary and finally in 2011 became wholly owned subsidiary of Panasonic (Panasonic History 2014).

Sanyo Electric Co., Ltd (in the following just Sanyo) was founded in 1947 in Moriguchi, Osaka, Japan. This location is geographically located very close to Panasonic (previous Matsushita Electric). The founder of Sanyo, Toshio Iue, was the brother-in-law of Konosuke Matsushita, the founder of Matsushita Electrics. Mr. Iue founded his new firm after ending his career at Matsushita Electrics. "Sanyo" means "three oceans" (三洋)—specifically the Pacific, the Atlantic and the Indian ocean: in other words, the entire world (Panasonic Sanyo 2014). In 1952, Sanyo launched the industry's first plastic radio. One year later, it launched Japan's first pulsator-type washing machine, the SW-53 as well as its first black-and-white television set at the same year.

In 1974, Sanyo was already participating in the "Sunshine Project," with the aim to develop solar/hydrogen energy technologies. This engagement was promoted and actively supported by the Ministry of International Trade and Industry (nowadays the Ministry of Economy, Trade and Industry) (Panasonic Sanyo 2014). This means that Sanyo not only focused on developing its home appliances line, like previous Matsushita Electrics did; but also participated in the development of the renewable energy business. Recently, Sanyo Denki has become famous for their rechargeable lithium-ion battery business, in which they were the world leader before the acquisition took place.

Despite the success of Sanyo, several factors contributed to the problems faced by the Japanese consumer electronics giant. Difficulties started in 2004 when the Chuetsu earthquake hit Niigata prefecture, which caused severe damage to Sanyo's semiconductor plant. As a result, Sanyo recorded a net income loss of 205 billion yen in the 2005 fiscal year (Kudo 2012). In 2006, Sanyo was forced to accept a capital injection by Goldman Sachs, Sumitomo Mitsui Banking and Daiwa Securities. These firms became the major shareholders of Sanyo Denki at that time (McCurry 2009). Furthermore, 5 out of 9 members of the Board of Directors at Sanyo were representatives of these investment banks.

In recent years, Sanyo has also lagged in terms of technological innovation. Sanyo decided to support Toshiba's HD-DVD technology; however, that investment was costly and ultimately unsuccessful. In the end, Sony's Blu-ray Disc triumphed and set the standard for that technology. Sanyo; however, lost all of its investments (Reuters 2008).

The aim of Panasonic's unfriendly takeover of Sanyo was to gain control of its lithium-ion battery business. Even if the founder of Sanyo, Iue san, was a fierce competitor of Konosuke Matsushita for many years, the low stock price of Sanyo triggered Panasonic to overtake Sanyo against their managers will. In the end, Panasonic paid US$ 8.9 billion to absorbing Sanyo (Toyo Keizai 2012).

9.4.1.3 Challenges

As is the case for all unfriendly acquisitions, the managers of Panasonic underestimated the difficulty of integrating Sanyo, the target firm. The bidder underestimated the trouble with the integration of the target. Panasonic believed that by acquiring Sanyo, it could reap the benefits of Sanyo's "green plan development" as well as expand its business and consolidate its position as a leader in the electronics industry. Sanyo was a world leader in the production of many technologies as well as the world's leading producer of rechargeable lithium-ion batteries. Therefore, Panasonic had high hopes for its acquisition of Sanyo. However, many problems arose in the integration of Sanyo's employees into Panasonic. The long and very distant relationship between these two competitors could not be bridged immediately after the deal (Kudo 2012).

Furthermore, the major shareholders of Sanyo were Goldman Sachs, Sumitomo Mitsui Bank and Daiwa Securities, all of whom agreed to sell their shares (McCurry 2009). Panasonic spent 400 billion yen (about US$ 4 billion) to acquire over 50 % of Sanyo's shares (Wakabayashi 2010), but did not face any opposition from investors. However, Sanyo's managers and employees did not agree to the takeover and many resisted by not supporting the new management (of Panasonic). As a result Panasonic's financial performance deteriorated after the deal. In 2012 and 2013, Panasonic recorded a net loss of over US$ 7 billion each years. However, the reasons for this dismal performance is not just the failed integration of Sanyo.

The causes of these challenges for Panasonic are also partly due to the overall economic environment. Not only has the Japanese economy been slowing down due to its deflation spiral, the European and US markets are saturated as well. Even though other markets in East Asia are booming, competitors from China are often able to produce things at a much lower cost than Japanese companies can do such as Panasonic. This is especially true for the renewable energy market in which Chinese firms' solar panels dominate the world markets due to low production costs. Losses were also seen in Panasonic's plasma television business which resulted in the closure of several factories, such as the Amagasaki plant in 2013 (Kondo and Nishimura 2014). The losses in the plasma television business again were caused by strong competition from Chinese and Korean firms. For the 2014 fiscal year, Panasonic recorded a net profit of US$ 1.2 billion after 2 years of heavy losses (Kondo 2014). This positive result; however, is caused mainly by the weakened yen (Kondo and Nishimura 2014). In the end, the Sanyo deal became an economic disaster for Panasonic because despite acquiring Sanyo's leading technologies, Panasonic was unable to stay competitive. In this case a healthy relationship between the bidding firm and the target firm was not established. Even now, more than 4 years after the deal, there are rumors that former Sanyo employees barely work with Panasonic employees. This example illustrates that hostile acquisitions have their limits, especially in a country like Japan.

The following example describes a case of a failed hostile acquisition. The hostile takeover attempt involed the financially driven investment (hedge) fund, Steel Partners and Noritz Kitchen.

9.4.2 Steel Partners Japan Almost Takeover of Noritz Kitchen (4)

9.4.2.1 Introduction

Steel Partners Japan is a well-known institutional buyout fund from the US that operates in Japan. Some of their noteworthy activities include the stock equity participations in the Japanese firm Bulldog Sauce and Sapporo Beer, in which Steel Partners Japan purchased equity stakes in each firm in order to push the management for a better financial performance. These investments were heavily criticized in the Japanese media. Nakata (2008) for example reports the following statement from Roshiji Inagaki, a shareholder of Sapporo Beer: I disagree with any takeover proposal because it gives the impression that a foreign firm is dominating a Japanese company. In 2008, Steel Partners Japan attempted to overtake Noritz Kitchen. In the 12 months prior to the official announcement of Steel Partners' proposal, the stock price of Noritz Kitchen had lost 35 % of its value and had declined from 1476 to 953 yen per share. To Steel Partners, this low price seemed attractive. The stock market responded positively to the announcement, to Steel Partners proposal to unfriendly overtake the firm. The price of Noritz Kitchen's shares rose dramatically because Steel Partners agreed to pay shareholders a premium of 1025 yen per share (Bloomberg 2008).

In the end, the planned takeover by Steel Partners Japan was not completed. However, it is a good example of how opposed a target firm may be to be taken over by an institutional (hedge) fund. In order to understand the event, both firms and their histories are introduced as well challenges will be discussed.

9.4.2.2 Noritz Kitchen and Steel Partners Japan

Noritz Kitchen (with its original name of "Noritsu") was established in 1951 and is based in Kobe. Noritz Kitchen specialized in water heating systems for commercial kitchens general households. The firm had a very modest growth rate in comparison to other Japanese firms in time period of 1951–1970. Many other Japanese firms of the time grew so big that they became global players such as Matsushita (renamed to Panasonic in 2008) or Sony. In contrast to many other Japanese firms, the Kobe-based Noritz Kitchen barely grew in size and only began to grow after the 1970s. The firm can be called a niche player, in that it has excellent technology geared towards a very specific segment of the market. The firm introduced numerous water-heating technologies. These inventions include the tankless water heater, the instantaneous water heater, and the first electronically controlled water heater. In 1993, Noritz went global opening its first foreign branch in China. Twelve years later in 2005, Noritz opened two more branches, one in Germany and another in Australia. The firm also established a business in the USA as well.

Steel Partners is a well-known institutional buyout fund operating in Japan. This type of fund is also called a hedge fund, which overtakes firms in hostile attempts with the aim to increase their market share. The firm was founded in 1980 by CEO Warren Lichtenstein and Lawrence Butler and has its headquarters in New York, USA. The firm has stakes in more than 40 Japanese firms in several different industries such as banking, consumer goods, and restaurants and services. Steel Partners' business in Japan is to stock equity participate in "undervalued" Japanese firms. This means that shares are bought at a time when the price of a company's stock is lower than their estimated "intrinsic value". The difference between the low buying price—and the high selling price, results in profits for the buyout fund. In order to receive the highest dividends, buyout funds like Steel Partners Japan exercise power in the general assembly and try to streamline target firms after their stock equity participation. This means that other, more capable, managers normally replace managers of the target. Employees or whole divisions are also restructured or even separated from the main business of the firm. In order to do this, Steel Partners purchases equity shares of a target firm without the approval of the target management's board of directors. A well-known example of this was the unfriendly tender offer by Steel Partners of the Japanese Bull-Dog Sauce firm. In a 6-year period Steel Partners pressured Bulldog's management to pay higher dividends, restructure the firm, and implement a different corporate governance structure (Hall 2008).

9.4.2.3 Challenges

On September 11th 2008, Steel Partners, which already owned 18.7 % of Noritz's shares, offered to buy (in atender offer) the remaining outstanding shares for 1025 yen each, a total price of 42.3 billion yen (US$ 537 million in 2008). Noritz's average return on equity (ROE) during the period between 1996–2006 was 2.8 %. This is far below the common 8 % rate of return that investors expect nowadays. The Japan Pension Fund Association ("PFA") also agrees that Japanese firms should earn, on average, 8 % ROE. Firms that have a rate of return of less than 8 % for several years will not receive any support for their incumbent directors in the case of an unfriendly takeover (Bloomberg 2008). Steel Partners announced that it would increase Noritz Kitchen's rate of return to 8 %. In order to do so, Steel Partners had a plan for the management of Noritz Kitchen to increase its profits and to trim unprofitable businesses. Under Steal Partners' plan, Noritz's bath systems department should be abolished in order to focus more on the kitchen business. Furthermore, even though Noritz had superior technology, the US market was not adequately served so the volume of sales in this market was much lower than anticipated. It was also suggested that a third party consultant firm should be hired to help improve earnings. Warren Lichtenstein, the CEO of Steel Partners himself accused the board of directors of Noritz of systematically destroying shareholder value. He considered the Japanese firm's management as weak and; therefore, intended to replace the management of Noritz Kitchen in order to turn it back into a profitable business.

The Japanese firm's management vehemently refused the hostile tender offer bid by Steel Partners. There were several reasons for this decision. The official reason given to the (Japanese) media was that Noritz considered the price for their shares too low. Steel Partners proposed to buy Noritz's outstanding shares at a 7.6 % premium, whereas Japanese firms are usually taken over with a 30–40 % premium (Kobayashi 2013, p. 119)[1].

Many Noritz managers were opposed to being taken over because they did not want to streamline the business. Many managers did not want to trim any existing business even if the profitability was low because they were afraid of losing their jobs, and general employees would also be endangered to at least partially get restructured after the unfriendly takeover. There was also no wish to conduct more business abroad, for example in the US. This was not the first time that a US hedge fund tried to overtake Noritz Kitchen. Early in the year 2008, the firm received an unfriendly tender offer bid from another hedge fund, called Fursa. Noritz Kitchen successfully declined the deal, which caused Noritz's stock price to fall about 32 %.

Steel Partners eventually withdrew its proposal to overtake Noritz Kitchen in March 2009. The official reason given to the media was that the price of Noritz's share set by the shareholders was 31 % higher than what Steel Partners' was willing to pay. The price was set at 1347 yen per share, whereas Steel Partners only proposed 1025 yen per share. Steel Partners failed to overtake this Japanese firm.

---

[1] Bainbridge (2012) refers to a premium at 30–50 % for US deals (p. 46) and Inoue (2010) refers only to a premium of 7 % for his Japanese sample (p. 122).

9.5 Defense Measures: Poison Pills

As stated above, sometimes managers at potential target firms oppose a deal because they do not want to get taken over. If this happens, there are strategies that managers can implement to prevent themselves from being taken over. Put differently, how can a target management develop a defense to impede a hostile offer? (Fleischer and Sussman 2012a). Before an unfriendly acquisition occurs, targets often receive information through rumors. Information regarding the unfriendly take over could be leaked through managers of the bidding firm, another player in the industry, or an investment banker.

The market for corporate control argues, that the best defense is to keep a firm's stock price up (Bainbridge 2012, p. 42). In this sense, if managers are able to maintain a high stock price, the agency costs will be minimized and the danger of getting taken over is low. In addition, there are several ways a firm can prevent being taken over. There are advanced warning systems (AWS) as anti-takeover measures (Yamagami et al. 2012, p. 277)

Something called "poison pills" in M&A language, can be implemented by a potential target to prevent an unfriendly takeover attempt (Hasegawa 2007, pp. 185–186; Fleischer and Sussman 2012a, paragraph 5). These measures undertaken by the target firm may prevent an acquisition or at least make it more difficult for a bidder to proceed as planned. Put differently, potential bidders may be persuaded to look for a different target firm. Technically these poison pill strategies must be written in the articles of incorporation or in the bylaws of a firm after being passed by shareholders. Even if most takeover lawyers in the US recommend against the implementation of any defensive measures (Bainbridge 2012, p. 248), a multitude of Japanese firms try to implement defensive measures (Arai 2008). In the US around 10–20 % of all deals are considered hostile (Fleischer and Sussman 2012b, sup. Ex 1–2); however, it is difficult to produce a similar figure for Japan because Japanese firms are reluctant to release such information to the public. However, in 2008, approximately 500 Japanese firms introduced some kind of poison pill measures, in order to prevent an unfriendly takeover. (Okushima and Yan 2009). This is a lucrative business for Japanese lawyers. Hasegawa reports that lawyers may have a conflict of interest and reports much insider trading is conducted by lawyers (Hasegawa 2007, pp. 92–94). The following paragraphs outline several methods to prevent hostile takeovers.

First of all, there is the "shareholder rights plan." With this method, superior or multiple voting rights are issued only to some shareholders. Against the rule of "one share—one vote" some of the shareholders—naturally the ones which are considered as the most trustworthy—would receive multiple voting rights. For example, a trustworthy group of shareholders may receive two votes for each share they hold. A bidder would then have to purchase many more shares in order to gain control over the firm. A so called flip-in, in which all shareholders except the unfriendly bidder would be entitled to purchase additional stock with a 50 % discount in the case of a hostile take over, also exists (Fleischer and Sussman 2012a).

Another form of the poison pill would be that current shareholders could decide to issue new shares in the case anyone attempts to acquire more than 10–20 % of a firm's stock. This increases the number of shares making it more difficult for a bidding firm to acquire a target. Finally, current shareholders could also simply offer to sell their shares at an increased rate of 100 % if there is an unfriendly takeover attempt, as a way to discourage a bidding firm.

This kind of poison pill is in reality difficult to implement because it must be passed by a majority of shareholders in a shareholder meeting. Shareholders without benefits will simply vote against it.

Another way to prevent an unfriendly acquisition is to implement "staggered elections." This strategy is especially useful when the bidding firm is a foreign firm. Under the "staggered elections" strategy, board members at a given target firm cannot be immediately replaced. A staggered election is when a firm elects board members in staggered intervals and not every year. Say a firm had nine board members, then only three board member would be up for election each year with every board member serving for a term of 3 years. If this provision was incorporated into the articles of incorporations or in the bylaws of a firm, the remaining board members of the target firm could block key decisions (such as a full merger agreement or a major asset sale). If a target firm has "staggered elections," an acquirer may not be able to close an acquisition for several years even if it owned a majority of the target's shares. This could discourage potential bidding firms from attempting to takeover a presumptive target firm.

The poison pill called "shark repellent" is the strongest measure a firm can implement to prevent an unfriendly takeover attempt. A potential target firm would take on large debts to make their debt load too high to be an attractive investment for another firm. If an acquirer did acquire a firm that utilized "shark repellant" the acquirer would eventually have to pay back the debt taken on by the target firm. Another way to lower ones own value as a firm would be for a target firm to buy several smaller firms using either cash or a stock swap, which in effect dilutes the value of the target's stock. This measure is like a double edged sword in that the potential target firm may not be handle the amount of debt they took on, which could lead to bankruptcy.

Finally, a potential target firm could implement a poison pills strategy known as the "golden parachute" (Hasegawa 2007, pp. 173–174). This is a poison pill that ensures that managers receive certain financial benefits, which will have to be paid by the bidding firm. A potential target firm would incorporate a clause, to pay their managers a fixed lump sum in the case of a hostile takeover, into their articles of incorporations or bylaws. This poison pill is normally the first measure, managers of a target firm try to implement. It is the most attractive one for Japanese firms attempting to prevent a hostile takeover. It is important to mention that it is standard practice for regular employees of Japanese firms to receive a lump sum for retirement (Kubo 2009). This system has been in place since the Edo period (Nonaka 2013, p. 188). A strategy known as the "silver parachute" also exists. A silver parachute is the same as golden parachute except that it pays benefits to a bigger group of employees.

Another incentive-based preventative measure is based on the thought that managers should not leave the firm, even in the case of an unfriendly takeover. This measure is known as "golden handcuffs". The term "golden handcuffs" is used when a target firm grants its employees a stock option in the case that the firm is involved in an unfriendly takeover. There is then an incentive to keep the old managers at the new firm. Keeping old managers, however, would be detrimental to the new management because members of the old management may try to block decisions made by the new management.

A bidding firm would want to send their own managers into the target firm to implement strategic changes. This is necessary for a bidding firm to align a newly acquired firm with their own strategy. All these measures discourage potential bidder firms from acquiring a potential target firm.

9.6 Conclusion

This chapter covered unfriendly takeovers, which is when managers of the acquired firms opposed the deal. For this, two theories were presented, the market based and the inefficient management theory. The market based theory states, that the target firms are undervalued. It could also be the case that the bidding firm feels overvalued. In this case, there is evidence that stock payment occurs. The second theory is about managers. Incumbent managers get replaced because they did not perform well.

Unfriendly takeovers related to Japan were shown for the last 40 years and it was visible that in recent years the number of unfriendly takeovers in Japan has been increasing. Two examples of unfriendly takeovers were discussed, Panasonic's acquisition of Sanyo Denki and Steel Partners failed acquisition of Noritz Kitchen. Finally, several defense measures, known as poison pills, that potential target firms can implement were discussed.

Questions

1. What is an unfriendly acquisition?
2. What does TOB stands for?
3. Who are the losers when it comes to hostile acquisitions?
4. How has the number of unfriendly acquisitions changed in the last 40 years?
5. Recall reasons why unfriendly acquisitions were previously unknown in Japan.
6. What problems can arise for an unfriendly bidder firm when trying to implement their strategy at the target firm?
7. Give two reasons why Panasonic overtook Sanyo?
8. What is a poison pill in M&A?
9. Recall the different forms of poison pills.
10. What is the heaviest poison pill and how does it work?

Answers

1. Unfriendly acquisition means, the target management is against the will of the bidder to undertake the deal.
2. TOB stands for Tender Offer Bid (or also Take Over Bid) and signifies normally an unfriendly attempt to take over a target against their manager's will. The bidder will bypass the management to place an offer to the target firms' shareholders.
3. Losers when it comes to hostile acquisitions are the managers of the target firm and often also the employees. Managers will probably lose their jobs, or may keep their job the title but without having any more power (as they had before the acquisition). Regular employees may be restructured which may lead to job losses. However, they may also be forced to change the way they did things which can create a sense of anxiety. Banks of a target firm may also be loser because they could potentially lose a client. On the flip side, any outstanding loans will be repaid. There is also financially lucrative M&A consulting business for banks.
4. Previously, unfriendly acquisitions were almost unknown in Japan and hardly ever happened. From the 1970s to the middle of the 1990s, during that period there was only about one deal a year. In the 2000 the number of deals conducted increased to about 20 deals with the peak in 2007 which saw 104 deals.
5. Unfriendly acquisitions were unthinkable for Japanese managers. Previously, it was unthinkable for a firm to take over another without the consent of the target firm's managers. Cross shareholdings and several other legal restrictions prevented unfriendly takeovers.
6. Target managers will oppose the acquisition, which will make it difficult for the bidding firm to implement its strategy. If overtaken unfriendly, there is a high chance that target managers and employees will work against the bidder management in the integration period.
7. Panasonic overtook Sanyo in order to acquire it's leading technology such as its lithium-ion battery business. Sanyo invested in HD DVD technology, but Sony's blue-ray outpaced it. The stock prices of Sanyo, therefore, dramatically decreased making it a very attractive investment for Panasonic.
8. A poison pill is a defense measure that a potential target firm would use in order to discourage bidders from buying them.
9. Forms of poison pills are: shareholder rights plan, staggered elections, shark repellent, golden parachute and golden handcuffs.
10. The shark repellent is the heaviest poison pill to defend against a TOB. The presumptive target firm takes on as much debt as possible to become unattractive for the bidder.

References

Arai T (2008) M & A to shihon shijou—kouritsuteki de kouhei na shihon shijou wo motomete (M & A and financial markets—request for efficient and equal financial markets: 1–18. In: Shadan houjin. M & A jidai no fando to kabunushi rieki. Juridicial person: M & A fund period and shareholders' profits. March, Tokyo

Aurora RS, Shetty K, Kalre SR (2011) Mergers and acquisitions. Oxford University Press, Oxford

Bainbridge SM (2012) Mergers and acquisitions, 3rd edn. Foundation, Eagan

Bloomberg (2008) Steel partners submits proposal to acquire noritz corporation. http://www.bloomberg.com/apps/news?pid=conewsstorytkr=PNSWF:USsid=a.XEaeeM2QTI. Accessed 20 May 2014

Buckley PJ, Casson M (1976) The future of the multinational enterprise. MacMillan, London

Campa JM, Hernando I (2006) M & A performance in the European financial industry. J Banking Finance 30:3367–3392

Fleischer A Jr, Sussman AR (2012a) Takeover defense: mergers and acquisitions, vol 1. Wolters Kluwer, The Netherlands

Fleischer A Jr, Sussman AR (2012b) Takeover defense: mergers and acquisitions, vol 2. Wolters Kluwer, The Netherlands

Fukutani N, Dobashi M (2008) M&A tekitaiteki baishuu bouei kanzen manyuaru (Full manual against unfriendly acquisitions). Chuuo Keizai Sha, Tokyo

Goergen M, Renneboog L (2008) Contractual corporate governance. J Corp Finance 14:166–182

Hall K (2008) Steel partners off the sauce in Japan. April 18th 2008. http://www.businessweek.com/globalbiz/content/apr2008/gb20080418_888202.htm. Accessed 22 June 2011

Hasegawa T (2007) Baishu Boei to M&A hanrei shuu. Casebook on M&A and defense of corporation. LexisNexis, Japan

Higgins NH (2013) Do stock-for-stock merger acquirers manage earnings? Evidence from Japan. J Account Public Policy 32:44–70

Inoue K (2010) Do M & A in Japan increase shareholder value. In: Y Kurokawa (ed) M & A for value creation in Japan, Monden Institute of Management. Japanese Management and International Studies, vol 6. pp 117–132

Kobayashi I (2013) Kaigai M & A ni yaku datsu. Guro-baru senryaku no kandokoro. Usefulness of foreign M & A. Point of global Strategy. Chuo keizai sha

Kondo K (2014) Panasonic juneki 1204 oku en (Panasonic's net profit of 1.2 billion US Dollars) Asahi Shinbun April 29th p. 1

Kondo K, Nishimura K (2014) Pana kuroji keshin no henshin (Panasonic desperate for change). Asahi Shinbun, April 29th, p. 7

Kubo C (2009) Wakariyasui kigyou nenkin. (Company retirement payment system easily explained), (2), Nihon Keizai Shinbunsha

Kudo T (2012) How does a legal department handle a merger review? As an example of Panasonic's acquisition of Sanyo, recent developments and challenges ahead in merger control. Annu Jpn Assoc Econ Law 33:6–114 [Kigyou ketsugo anken ni okeru kigyou no taiou—Panasonikku ni yoru Sanyou denki kogaisha ka anken wo jirei ni. Nihon keizai hou gakkai nenpou, Dai 33 go, 96–114]

Mandelker G (1974) Risk and return: the case of merging firms. J Financ Econ 1:303–335

McCurry J (2009) Panasonic launches Sanyo takeover bid. http://www.guardian.co.uk/business/2009/nov/05/panasonic-launches-sanyo-takeover-bid. Accessed 19 June 2013

Nakata H (2008) Sapporo shareholders vote to keep Steel Partners at bay. March 2008. http://search.japantimes.co.jp/cgi-bin/nb20080329a3.html. Accessed 6 Dec 2010

Nonaka K (2013) M&A no jimu roudou kanri (personnel management of M&A). Chuo Keizai, Tokyo

Ota Y (2013) M&A kigyou soshiki saihen no suki-mu to zeimu (organizational reorganization at M&A and tax), 2nd edn. Omura Zaimu Kyoukai

Okushima T, Yan S (2009) Nikkan no kigyou baishuu boueisaku no riron to genjou [status quo on Japanese-Korean acquisition defense measures], Kinyuu zeisei jijou kenkyuukai. Kinzai
Panasonic Announcement (2010) Announcement to share exchange. http://panasonic.co.jp/corp/news/official.data/data.dir/en101221-5/en101221-5-1.pdf. Accessed 19 June
Panasonic History (2014) Panasonic corporate history: quest for innovation. http://panasonic.net/history/corporate/chronicle/. Accessed on 19 March 2014
Panasonic News (2014) Panasonic announces that it makes SANYO wholly owned subsidiary through share exchange. http://panasonic.net/sanyo/news/2010/12/21-1.pdf. Accessed 25 March 2014
Panasonic Sanyo (2014) Management philosophy. http://panasonic.net/sanyo/corporate/profile/philosophy.html. Accessed 19 March 2014
Reuters (2008) Toshiba to give up on HD DVD, end format war. Reuters 16 Feb
Rhodes-Kropf M, Robinson DT, Viswanathan S (2005) Valuation waves and merger activity: the empirical evidence. J Financial Econ 77:561–603
Rugman A (1981) Inside the multinationals: the economics of international markets. Croom Helm, London
Shleifer A, Summers L (1988) Breach of trust in hostile take-overs. In: Auerbach AJ (ed) Corporate take-overs: causes and consequences. University of Chicago Press, London
Shleifer A, Vishny RW (1997) A survey of corporate governance. J Financ 52(2):737–783
Sudarsanam S, Mahate AA (2006) Are friendly acquisitions too bad for. Shareholders and managers? Long-term. Value creation and top management. Turnover in hostile and friendly acquirers. Br J Manage 17:7–30
Toyo Keizai (2012) Panasonic no daigosan, Sanyo baishu de kyougaku sonshitsu. [Panasonic's big miscalculation. Heavy loss on Sanyo acquisition], Toyo Keizai, Febr. 21st. http://toyokeizai.net/articles/-/8612/. Accessed 19 May 2014
Wakabayashi D (2010) Sanyo deal hits Panasonic results. The wall street journal. Feb 5th. http://online.wsj.com/article/SB10001424052748704533204575046774223872104.html. Accessed 19 June 2013
Yamagami M, Nukada Y, Funakoshi K (2012) Japan. In: Nussbaum AJ, Lipton W, Rosen & Katz, Martin C, Perry S, Macfarlanes LLP (eds) Mergers and acquisitions. Juristical comparisons. First European lawyer reference: pp 263–280

Chapter 10
Evaluation Methods and Market Concentration

Abstract This chapter discusses methods of evaluation of firms; in simple terms, how to determine the price of a target firm. It will be shown that several methods exist such as the book value method, the market value method and the discounted cash flow value method. It will be seen that the market value method is the most popular to use and the discounted cash flow value method is the scientifically most rigorous one to determine the price of a Japanese target firm.

As a secondary topic, market concentration will also be discussed in this chapter. This concerns bigger acquisitions, in which the acquisition will restrain competition because of too much market power. In the case of these "big" acquisitions, the Japanese Fair Trade Commission may prohibit deals from being completed. The mathematical approach of how to define whether a deal will lead to market concentration is the Herfindahl Index, which will also be introduced.

10.1 Introduction

In reality, M&As happen often times out of coincidences, for example, a firm suddenly becomes aware about a competitor who wants to "sell." A reasons could be that the owner of the target firm simply wants to "cash out," for retirement reasons, or it could also be the case that the competition for the target firm is too strong. At bigger firms; however, there are sometimes even specialized M&A departments, which prepare firms for upcoming acquisitions. Regardless of how much preparation a firm undertakes before an acquisition, the evaluation of a target is still very difficult.

Difficulties exist in the access to the target. This can easily be seen by the fact that many firms willing to "sell" cannot openly show their desire to other competing firms. Many firms who want to sell rely on agencies, banks, or investment bankers to introduce them to buyers. These agencies naturally conduct the evaluation of a given target. The theory on this is rather simple; there are three methods by which one can determine the price of a firm[1]. These methods are to be discussed in this

[1] It is important to mention that value is not equal the price for a firm. We will see later that a price depends on certain characteristics not always directly connected to a target firm, but external influences which may change the price of the firm but not it's value.

R. Bebenroth, *International Business Mergers and Acquisitions in Japan*,
DOI 10.1007/978-4-431-54989-5_10

chapter. Furthermore, this chapter will elaborate on market concentration, which is a concern when dealing with rather large transactions where a market concentration may occur that can lead to unnecessarily high prices for consumers.

10.2 M&A Evaluation Methods and Cost of Capital

10.2.1 M&A Evaluation Methods

In order to buy or sell a target firm or a part of it, it is of vital importance to determine a price. In the following paragraphs, three methods to determine an appropriate price for a target firm will be discussed such as the book value method, the market value method and the discounted cash flow value method. It is to mention, that these methodologies are not exclusive to Japan, but are applicable to firms all over the world. Also, M&A firm evaluation is often accomplished by using a combination of all three methods.

The first method is called "book value method," where the value is determined by the target firm's total value of assets minus its liabilities. This method seems to be a viable way to determine a price as its manipulation should be low. Assets such as buildings, land, and equipment are recorded in the books based on their acquisition cost. It is; furthermore, an easy way to come up to a value. However, this method has several weaknesses (Bainbridge 2012, p. 109). First of all, some items may not be recorded as assets. Intellectual property rights, for example, are difficult to give an exact price. Additionally, many other questions arise such as: "How much weight should a patent have for a firm?" or "How can employees be evaluated in financial terms?" Secondly, the value of the assets listed in the books are normally underpriced and the actual market price turns out to be much higher than what is recorded in the books. This is especially a challenge for Japanese firms as the prices of land are normally much higher than what is actually recorded in the books. That means, there is a difference between the high market value of land and a low book value because the market value of land increased compared to the time the firm purchased it. This is also a reason why many firms in Japan are quite rich because of their high land value. Also, some firms are cash rich because they simply save their earnings rather than distribute them to shareholders (Hasegawa 2007).

The most popular method in Japan of evaluating the price of a target firm is called the "market value method." Mathematically it is easy to determine the value of a listed firm by applying the market value method. To calculate the value one must simply multiply the number of shares by the current price per share. The product of these two values is the price to be paid for a given target firm plus or minus some adjustments. Any amount that exceeds this value is considered a premium paid by investors. This premium is meant to entice old shareholders to sell their shares. In the case of Japan, premiums are normally 30 to 40 % of the market price. Kobayashi (2013, p. 119) states that a high premium leads to negative consequences for the start of the new firm because the bidding firm has to save too much money from the beginning. Premiums differ according to the deal. Put differently, when a buyer overpays for the target, the new firm must save more on development costs, which may have negative implications for the target. Cross border acquisitions often require a higher premium, which can be around 80 to 90 %.

However, there are also weaknesses associated with this method. The economic environment in which a firm operates may have a big impact on the firm's value. A firm may be undervalued at certain points in time. For example, in a financial crisis a firm's value might be much lower than in other, more economically stable, times. Conversely, the whole industry may be overvalued because of a boom period. Even if shares can easily be accounted and a price can easily be set, frequent changes in the prices, so called "fluctuations" may lead to conflicts when determining the price of a target.

The market value method can also be used in the case that a firm is not listed on a stock exchange. In this situation direct comparisons to other firms in the industry will be undertaken to determine a price. This method of comparing firms also has several weaknesses. One firm can hardly be compared to another previously sold firm in the market. The challenge, when applying this method, is that every company is unique to some extent and cannot be compared to any other firm. Also, smaller firms hardly announce the price of a deal. Therefore, there are sometimes not enough firms to realistically compare them to receive a trustworthy price. Even if there is this major flaw, this method enjoys a high popularity in Japan.

The most scientific rigorous method to evaluate a firm is the discounted cash flow value method (Abeam 2010, pp. 418–425). In this method, the price for future earnings of the target will be discounted to the present day value (Fig. 8.[2]). This means that a yen earned in a few years has less value than a yen earned today (Ota 2013, pp. 8–12). The assumption is that the value of money is time sensitive. Therefore a lender will charge interest and depositors receive interest for lending/saving their money. Suppose, e.g. Yamamoto san deposits 10,000 yen into Mizuho Bank for 1 year. Out of simplicity, assume Yamamoto san will receive 3 % interest[3]. At the end of 1 year, Yamamoto would receive the 10,000 yen back plus 300 yen in interest. The formula to calculate the future value is:

Model of discounted cash flow

$$FV = A^*(1 + r)n \tag{10.1}$$

[2] Cash flow means the outflow minus the inflow of cash of a firm. Under cash flow there exist three different streams. The first stream is the operational cash flow: Cash out of the company's core business activities (e.g. Toyota: cars). The second stream is the investment cash flow: Cash or costs out of investments or acquisitions. The third stream is the finance cash flow: Cash out of financial activities, such as receiving or paying loans, issuing or repurchasing stock, or paying dividends.

[3] This example is chosen for simplicity to introduce the concept of the present value. In reality, Japanese citizens hardly receive any interest from their banks because the Bank of Japan has maintained a zero interest rate policy for many years.

FV future deposits,
A_i amount of the deposit,
r interest rate,
n number of years, the deposit is in the account.

Suppose Yamamoto san places 10,000 yen to his Mizuho bank receiving interest of yearly 3 %. How much would Yamamoto san receive at the end of 3 years? We can calculate this from the above formula in the following way:

Discounted cash flow value with numbers

$$FV = \text{Yen } 10{,}000\ (1 + 0.03^3) = \text{Yen } 10{,}000 \times 1.092727 = 10{,}927 \quad (10.2)$$

Yamamoto san would receive his initial investment of 10,000 yen plus 927 yen interest, all together 10,927 yen.

The concept of present value is of vital importance to the valuation of corporations and depends on the effect of time on the value for the money. For this, we reverse the question. Instead of asking how much 10,000 yen will be worth in a year, we ask how much has to be invested today in order to receive 10,000 yen in the future.

Present value model

$$PV = \frac{A_k}{(1+k)_n} \quad (10.3)$$

PV present value,
A_k amount to receive,
k interest rate,
n number of years before receiving the amount.

Suppose Tanaka san promises to pay Yamamoto san 10,000 yen in 5 years. What is the value of that 10,000 yen today, with an interest rate of 3 %? The present value would be 8626.1 yen. This is calculated using the following equation.

Present value with numbers

$$PV = \frac{10{,}000 \text{ Yen}}{(1+0.03)^5} = \frac{10{,}000 \text{ Yen}}{(1.03)^5} = \frac{10{,}000 \text{ Yen}}{1.159} = 8626.1 \text{ yen} \quad (10.4)$$

The same formula applies to the discounted cash flow method:

Discounted cash flow value method

$$DCFV = \sum_{t=1}^{N} \frac{FV_t}{(1+d)^t} \quad (10.5)$$

DCFV discounted cash flow value,
FV nominal value of a cash flow amount in a future period,

d discount rate, equals the opportunity cost plus a risk factor (also called the time value of money: "i" in the future-value equation),
N number of periods,
t time.

Each bidding firm has its own strategic interests in a target firm. Each firm has it's own ideas on how to realize synergies with the target firm and its own strategic plan to accomplish this. These strategic approaches focus on creating synergies between the target and bidding firm. Challenges more so than opportunities have to be investigated with due diligence. Many issues regarding the target firm are investigated, especially hidden costs. There are several kinds of due diligence investigations focusing on the given market of a target, on the economic environment, or on intellectual property of the target (Fuchibe 2013; Abeam 2010). It is also common for target firms to carry out their own due diligence investigations on taxes and HR related issues (Nonaka 2013, p. 85–113). This is called "business due diligence." Questions to be raised, for example, are: "In what area and how much value can the target firm offer the bidding firm?" Further questions are: "Does the target firm have any hidden problems, like debts or outstanding loans?" or "How many capable managers will realistically remain at the firm after it is acquired?" These questions will be answered by a due diligence investigation.

10.2.2 Weighted Average Cost of Capital (WACC)

In order to investigate discounted cash flows, it is necessary to estimate the cost of capital. This is done by estimating the discount rate (d). The discount rate (d) is determined by measuring a firm's cost of capital using the weighted average cost of capital (WACC). In other words, how much does a firm have to return to its investors? An investor can theoretically earn interest without taking any risk. A firm pays dividends to its shareholders. Let us assume that a firm pays annual dividends of 3 % and risk is valued at 5 %, the interest a shareholder would hope to receive in addition to the risk free 3 %. In total an investor would receive 8 % what is often the case in reality where institutional investors expect to receive an 8 % return on their investment.

WACC Model

$$d = \frac{E}{K} * y + \frac{D}{K} * b(1 - t_c) \qquad (10.6)$$

K D+E,
d WACC,
y required or expected rate of return on equity, or cost of equity,
b required or expected rate of return on borrowings, or cost of debt,
t_c corporate tax rate,
K total capital invested in the going concern,

D total debt and leases,
E total equity and equity equivalents.

These expectations have several implications especially concerning institutional investors. The implication of these expectations is that it is no longer sufficient for firms to simply stay in the black. They must now perform well enough to offer investors the expected 8 % or run the risk of institutional investors withdrawing their investment. In other words, a good firm nowadays has to offer more to an investor than just not to record any losses.

10.3 Market Concentration and Herfindahl Index

10.3.1 Market Concentration

One of the main motives for firms to acquire another firm is to increase their size. Bigger firms have many advantages and the biggest firms are normally the most profitable ones in their industries (Chap. 6). However, if a firm becomes too big and gains too much power, it might hinder competition. This leads to market concentration. For example, if a firm is too powerful and if there are no serious competitors in that given industry, the prices set by this firm might be too high. This is especially true for horizontal acquisitions, in which there is a fear that firms may create a monopoly due to the increase in their size. Governmental authorities only allow deals to occur when the benefits outweigh the ill effects of market concentration (Fenton 2008).

Governmental authorities in many countries allow acquisitions, but impose ex ante obligations on the merged firms to regulate monopoly power and to protect customers. The role of a given government is not neutral and varies from one country to another. For instance, the US has especially strict authorities. The acquisition of the food retail group Safeway by Morrison was allowed only based under the condition that several of the acquired stores needed to be sold to avoid local monopoly in certain geographic areas. The French are said to have a policy to develop "National Champions." What this means is that a certain level of monopolistic power would be allowed in the home country in order to make firms competitive abroad. In Turkey, the finance industry was encouraged to merge with the aim to withstand competition from international banks (Whittington and Bates 2007).

In Japan as well, M&As are tightly regulated through a complex set of rules to prevent monopolies from forming (Ezaki et al. 2009; Kojima 2005; Igaki and Yamaguchi 2011). This legislation was for many years based upon the Anti-Monopoly Act of 1947. The new Antimonopoly Law was partially amended in 2009 and is effective from January 1st 2010 (Igaki and Yamaguchi 2011). Under this law, firms are not allowed to conduct mergers or acquisitions which would hinder competition to a degree that it negatively affects consumers.

The Act is enforced by Japan's Fair Trade Commission (JFTC), which is an organization that oversees firms to make sure they abide by the law. Larger potential acquisitions, totaling more than 20 billion Yen, are mandated to submit a prior notice to the JFTC for review (Igaki and Yamaguchi 2011). JFTC takes firms' proposals and consults with other regulators and ministries about their influence on market concentration. JFTC has exclusive jurisdiction over the enforcement and control of mergers and acquisitions. If JFTC were to decide that a deal would negatively impact competition, it has complete authority to stop both parties from proceeding any further. Potential M&A firms have to wait for 30 days following the submission of their notification to find out whether or not their deal will be approved. Within that 30 days time period, the JFTC is conducting their review of the impact of market concentration. If the JFTC determined that firms become too powerful after their M&A, then the deal would not be allowed. The JFTC would give the firms a detailed report on what needs to be changed before an approval can be issued. How competition is hindered and which product lines would have to be separated and sold, in order to gain approval, would also be given in the report. If a firm fails the first approval, for the second stage of investigation another 90 days is required (Higgins 2013).

In reality it is not uncommon that firms especially big merger or acquisitions would seek informal consultation regarding their planned deal before going through the official review process. Although these consultations are informal, they use the same review process as governmental review agencies. Therefore, an informal merger review may take as long as the formal ones (Higgins 2013). A measurement of how to test whether a market is too concentrated is the Herfindahl Index.

10.3.2 Measure of Market Concentration: Herfindahl Index

The most popular way for measuring market concentration is the Herfindahl Index. This index is also used by the Japanese Fair Trade Commission (JFTC) to investigate the market concentration of a given product or market share a firm has in Japan. A market is precisely defined in product lines of an industry. Market concentration is defined as the sum of the squares of the market shares each individual firm has at their specific product line. These squares range from approximately 0, which signifies that many companies are in the given market and a full competition exists, to approximately 1, which signifies that only one monopolistic firm exists without any competition. In short, the Herfindahl Index measures the concentration of a given product compared to that of its competitors in the same product line of a given industry. If the added squares are under 0.1, market concentration is not an issue and enough competition left. A value between 0.1 and 0.18 signifies that products of a certain firm are in a moderately concentrated market. A firm with this market concentration can only undertake an acquisition if the new share together is still below 0.18 market concentration. A value above 0.18 means that a firm would restrain competition and would lead to an overly concentrated market. The JFTC would then not allow a takeover. There are other ways to measure a market or product line concentration. However, the Herfindahl index gives more weight to larger firms and is; therefore, also in Japan the preferable tool to measure the market concentration of products. The formula of the Herfindahl Index is as follows:

Herfindahl Index

$$H = \sum_{i=1}^{n} Si^2 \tag{10.7}$$

10.4 Example (5)

10.4.1 Nippon Steel—Sumitomo Metal "Merger"

10.4.1.1 Introduction

To illustrate how market concentration can affect M&A, a recent example of the Nippon Steel —Sumitomo Metal merger is discussed below. This deal between two leading Japanese firms in the steel industry was initially not approved by the JFTC because the new firm would have created an overly concentrated market in several product lines.

Before 1914, the steel industry in Japan grew slowly; however, after the 1923 earthquake, the steel industry flourished as the demand for new construction rose drastically to rebuild the Kanto area. The Japanese steel industry again flourished during WWI and WWII, due to heightened demand for war related steel products. After the war, the industry temporarily waned until the Japanese government began to build up the country's extensive rail network and public-works construction. In 1962, Japan became the 4th largest steel producer in the world. In the 1980's, the steel industry faced difficulties exporting its products because of a stronger Yen-USD exchange rate. After closing many furnaces and sending workers to other businesses or to early retirement, Japanese steelmakers were known as some of the world's most efficient steelmakers.

In 1990, several factors led to a decreased demand in the Japanese steel industry. There was a rise in Japanese raw material prices as well as strong competition from mini-mills and even stronger competition from Chinese, South Korean and Taiwanese steel producers. To adjust to the changing market Japanese steel makers had to cut more jobs; however, the rising costs continue to plague the Japanese steel industry even today.

10.4.1.2 Nippon Steel and Sumitomo Metal

Sumitomo Metal Industries' history starts with the foundation of the Sumitomo group in the late 16th century. Sumitomo began its business with copper mining.

Sumitomo as a modern company began in 1897 in the copper industry. In 1901, Sumitomo Metal began steel production. In 1935, Sumitomo combined the copper and steel divisions to form Sumitomo Metals Industries, Ltd. Before the merger occurred, Sumitomo Metals reported group sales of ¥ 1.29 trillion and had 24,000 workers on its payroll in the fiscal year 2009 (Kyodo News, 4 February 2012).

Nippon Steel (Shin Nippon Seitetsu K.K.) was a firm that was created through a merger back in the 1970s. At that time Yawata Iron & Steel (Yawata Seitetsu) and Fuji Iron & Steel (Fuji Seitetsu) merged to become Nippon Steel. The firm owns steel mills in several locations all over Japan including Hokkaido, Iwate, Chiba, Tokyo, Aichi, Osaka, Hyogo, Yamaguchi, Fukuoka, Oita, and Kyushu. Before the merger between Sumitomo Metal and Nippon Steel took place, Nippon Steel was listed as the 6th largest steel-producing company in the world with ¥ 3.5 trillion turnover for the 2010 fiscal year. Nippon Steel's employees numbered 52,205 at the end of the year. In November 2011, Nippon Steel entered the Indonesian steel market with a joint venture with three local Indonesian steel companies to produce steel for the local automotive industry (Yulisman 2012). In the latter years, there is argumentation that Nippon Steel became a target of Indian Mittal group. Under this constellation, it is argued that the merger was a response to a potential takeover by a foreign (non-Japanese) firm. In 2012 Nippon Steel Corporation and Sumitomo Metal Industries merged to establish Nippon Steel & Sumitomo Metal Corporation (Sugimoto 2014).

In recent years, the steel industry has faced worldwide pressure due to higher material costs and new, stronger competition from China, India, and South Korea. As a result the Japanese steel industry struggled in the 1980's. Between the 1980's and 1990's, Nippon Steel annual profits declined. Only throught cost-cutting methods and product diversification was the company able to compete against competitors. In 2005, Nippon Steel began various programs to improve their facilities to produce more environmentally friendly products. For example, a high tensile strength steel allowed shipping containers to be larger and lighter. This would improve the fuel efficiency of the ships carrying the containers.

10.4.1.3 Challenges

The deal between Nippon Steel and Sumitomo Metal faced serious challenges due to a market dominance that the merger would have created in several product lines. Initially, the JFTC did not approve the proposed "merger," because the market dominance of the new firm in several product lines was so high that it would have threatened other firms in the industry. The new firm was given 30 days to change the clauses of the deal in order to separate some of their product lines into a different firm. There was an order by the JFTC to drop 10 steel products out of the new firm's portfolio. After splitting up some of their products into other independent firms, the threat of market dominance was reduced to an acceptable level. In December 2011, after the firm changed their portfolio, the JFTC approved the merger of Nippon Steel and Sumitomo Metal, making Japan's 1st and 3rd biggest steelmakers the world's 2nd largest steelmaker (Kyodo News, 15 December 2011). The ratios of shares of the new firm consisted of 1 Sumitomo Metal share to 0.735 Nippon Steel shares.

In order to survive the fierce competition of foreign steel producers, these two companies publicly declared to merge with each other. The goals of the new firm were to globalize the steel business, to utilize advanced technologies, to improve cost competitiveness, and to reinforce non-steel business segments. The arrangement was that the former president of Nippon Steel, Shoji Muneoka, would be appointed as the new chairman and the former president of Sumitomo Metal, Hiroshi Tomono would be appointed as the president of the new firm (Company Brochure 2012). However, in May 2014, Muneoka continues to be chairman even though Shindo Kosei, who also comes from Nippon Steel, was appointed the new president (Nikkei 2014). After the deal was completed, the new firm still needed to perform cost cutting activities because of the strong yen and new competition from other countries (Kanashima 2012). In 2011, Nippon Steel had a profit rate of 3.5 % and Sumitomo Metal of 4.1 %. In contrast to this, Posko, a South Korean competitor, had a profit rate of 6.9 %. The better financial performance of the Korean firm was a result of the high Japanese Yen and the low Korean Won despite the fact that Japanese firms' products, technological advancement and their services etc. was rated higher—than that e.g. of Posko (Kobayashi 2013, p. 96).

The market outlook was uncertain due to a large supply-and-demand gap in Asia (Inoue 2012). Rating agencies such as Fitch downgraded the new firm on November 26, 2012 one notch from BBB+to BBB with a negative outlook. This downgrade; however, was not a result of the merger itself but by the uncertainty of the future of the Japanese steel industry as a whole (SteelGuru 2013). The reported problem was that Japan consumes only 60 million t of the 110–120 million t of steel that it produces. Therefore, Japan is highly dependent on exporting their steel to other countries (Ernst and Young 2013). A problem for Japanese steel makers is that firms in emerging market countries have at least two advantages over Japanese firms. First of all, the cost of employment is much lower in emerging market countries. Secondly, the steel market normally takes place in these emerging market countries, so Japanese steel makers face higher costs to export their steel to these locations. These higher costs were associated with transportation or import taxes. Even further barriers existed. For example, after the incident at the Fukushima atomic power plant offer the Great East Japan Earthquake in March 2011, steel firms had to issue special certifications for all of their exported products certifying that the steel was not contaminated with radiation. These expenses of higher costs let steel makers experience disadvantages against other countries' steel firms.

Recently, however, there are signs that the Japanese steel industry has recovered. Toyota, for example, had historic earnings of about US$ 20 billion in 2014 and aims to sell 10 million cars this year. Toyota has its steel products produced by the new firm. The yen also weakened recently against the US dollar which has lead to a more favorable exchange ratio, put differently to higher earnings in exports. On February 19th 2014, Moody's investors raised the grade of the newly formed firm from "negative" to "stable" and the firm received an A3 (Moody's 2014).

Cost cutting activities were seen as successful and a high earning was expected. Indeed, in the 2014 fiscal year, the new firm increased their profit four fold against the previous year to 3500 oku en, which is equivalent to $ 3.5 billion (Sugimoto 2014).

10.5 Conclusion

This chapter dealt with evaluation methods and market concentration. It was shown that there are three different techniques available, to evaluate a potential target firm. The book value is the easiest one but not reliable. The market valuation method is widely used in Japan but also has many shortcomings especially the fluctuation of stock prices. Also external circumstances, such as recessions can cause price fluctuations. The scientifically most solid method used to evaluate a target firm is the discounted cash flow method. In this method, future cash received by the new firm is discounted to the present day. For this, synergies and possible pittfalls are investigated by so called due diligence investigation.

Market concentration was also discussed in this chapter. If market concentration is too high, competition becomes too weak what results in monopoly position for the remaining firm. That leads at the end to higher prices to be paid by consumers. Japan tends to allow a higher market concentration than the governments of many other countries. This is to support bigger firms internationally. Even if the market concentration in Japan leads to higher prices for consumers in Japan, it would lead to a higher level of competitiveness against international competitors on the world market. In a small case study, it was also shown how profitable the merged firm Nippon Steel Sumitomo Metals became.

Questions

1. Describe shortly the three existing valuation methods used to estimate the value of a target firm
2. What are weaknesses of the book value method?
3. Describe weakpoints of the market value method.
4. Which authority deals with market concentration in Japan?
5. Why does the Japanese government allow a rather higher market concentration?
6. What does the Herfindahl Index estimate?
7. Recall a “merger” in the Japanese steel industry, which failed to receive approval in the first round because of an overly concentrated market in several product lines.
8. Recall reasons for mergers in the Japanese Steel industry

Questions for the Herfindahl Index

9. In case 1, we assume that six firms in the same industry each produce 15 % of output and 10 other firms each equally 1 %. What would be the market concentration as measured by the Herfindahl Index? In case 2, we assume only one firm produces 90 % of output and 10 others each equally 1 %. What would the market concentration be measured as by the Herfindahl Index now?
10. In the first case, the six firms have a concentration rate equal to 90 % for both, case 1 and case 2. However, in the first case there is fierce competition as there are six equally strong competitors, in the second case we approach a situation of a monopoly. What would be the market concentration be measured by the Herfindahl Index at both cases?

Answers

1. Book value method, market value method and discounted cash flow value method. The market value method is by far most often used to evaluate a target firm, in Japan. Scientifically most solid is the discounted cash flow method.
2. A weak point for the book value is that market value and book value differ. Machines are recorded in the books at lower prices because of depreciation. Land is recorded at the books to much lower prices because the price paid many years ago was much lower than nowadays caused by inflation. Also, only tangible assets can be counted. Intangible assets such as the quality of employees cannot be expressed by financial figures in the books.
3. Market value method underlies fluctuations (for example seasonal changes). The value will differ, therefore, not because the firm is better or worse, but because of external changes. Also, there is often a very limited market, so that a comparison of firms is difficult to undertake.
4. Market concentration is a subject for the Japan Fair Trade Commission. This is the Japanese institution having the authority to reject an acquisition if market power gets restrained. A Fair Trade Commission can be found in many other countries as well.
5. Normally governments aim to prevent market concentration. However, Japanese governmental authorities allow a rather higher market concentration in Japan (than for example the US) for the sake of having stronger (Japanese) firms to compete against international rivals.
6. The Herfindahl Index measures the market concentration of product lines of given industries. If the Herfindahl Index value is higher than 0.18, the market is too concentrated and a new acquisition (or merger) will be forbidden by the Japanese Fair Trade Commission (JFTC).

7. JFTC did not initially give approval for the merger between Nippon Steel and Sumitomo Metal in the year 2012. After the second round (which took another 90 days), the firms received an approval but needed to separate several steel product lines in order to operatate as a new firm.
8. Several reasons lead to M&A in the Japanese steel industry. There is pressure to get taken over from foreign firms (like the attempt by Mittal to overtake Nippon Steel). Also, the Japanese domestic demand for steel shrinks and exports become; therefore, more important. Also, foreign Asian competitors become stronger. This leads Japanese firms joining forces with each other to become more efficient to compete against foreign firms, to sell their steel to foreign markets.
9. (Case of applying Herfindahl Index, Case 1)
   Herfindahl Index = 6 * 0.15 + 10 * 0.01
10. (Case of applying Herfindahl Index, Case 2)
    Herfindahl Index = 1 * 0.90 + 10 * 0.01

Two additional cases
Case 3: Herfindahl Index = 10 * 0.05 + 20 * 0.025
Case 4: Herfindahl Index = 1 * 0.80 + 5 * 0.02 + 10 * 0.01

(Case of applying Herfindahl Index, case 1:)
Herfindahl Index = 6 * 0.15 + 10 * 0.01 = 0.136 (moderate concentrated)

(Case of applying Herfindahl Index, case 2:)
Case 2: Herfindahl Index = 1 * 0.90 + 10 * 0.01 = 0.811 (concentrated)
Two additional cases
Case 3: Herfindahl Index = 10 * 0.05 + 20 * 0.025 = 0.013 (not concentrated)
Case 4: Herfindahl Index = 1 * 0.80 + 5 * 0.02 + 10 * 0.01 = ???? 0.643 (concentrated)

References

Abeam (2010) bijinesu due diligence no jimu. Business of due diligence, 2nd edn. Abeam M & A Consulting, Chuo Keizai

Bainbridge SM (2012) Mergers and acquisitions, 3nd edition, Thomson Reuters, New York USA ISBN 978-1-60930-132-3

Company Brochure (2012) Nippon Steel & Sumitomo Metal Corporation. http://www.nssmc.com/en/company/pdf/nssmc_brochure_en.pdf. Accessed 18 June 2013

Ernst and Young (2013) Global steel 2013: a new world, a new strategy. http://www.ey.com/Publication/vwLUAssets/Global_steel_2013/$FILE/Global_Steel_Report_India_conference_Feb_2013.pdf. Accessed 18 June 2013

Ezaki S, Hara A, Moussis V (2009) Japan: merger control. The Asia-Pacific Antitrust Review 2009. Anderson Mori and Tomotsune

Fenton K (2008) Mergers and acquisitions. Understanding the Antitrust Issues, 3rd edn. American Bar Association, Sect. Antitrust Law, Chicago, February Issue

Fuchibe Y (2013) Chiteki zaisan Dyuu diligence no jitsumu [Practice of Due Diligence on intellectual property], 2nd edn. Chuuou Keizaisha
Hasegawa T (2007) Baishu Boei to M & A hanrei shuu. Casebook on M & A and Defense of Corporation. LexisNexis Japan
Higgins NH (2013) Do stock-for-stock merger acquirers manage earnings? Evidence from Japan. J Acc Public Policy 32:44–70
Igaki T, Yamaguchi Y (2011) Japan. In: Campbell D (ed) Mergers and Acquisitions in North America, Latin America, Asia and the Pacific Selected Issues and Jurisdictions, Center for International Legal Studies. Wolter, Kluwer, pp 359–393
Inoue K (2010) Do M&A in Japan increase shareholder value. In: Kurokawa Y (ed) M&A for value creation in Japan, monden institute of management. Jpn Manage Int Studies 6:117 -132
Inoue Y (2012) Nippon Steel & Sumitomo eyes more cost cuts as debuts in weak market, Reuters, http://www.reuters.com/article/2012/09/30/nipponsteelsumitomo-merger-idUSL4E-8KO60520120930. Accessed 18 June 2013
Kanashima H (2012) Sour ties hurt Japan's exports to China, Asia one, The Yomiuri Shimbun. http://news.asiaone.com/A1Business/News/Story/A1Story20121217-389944.html. Accessed 18 June 2013
Kobayashi I (2013) Kaigai M & A ni yaku datsu. Guro-baru senryaku no kandokoro. Usefulness of foreign M & A. Point of global Strategy. Chuo keizai sha
Kojima A (2005) Merger control in Japan: its history, realities, and future. Deputy Secretary General for Economic Affairs. Fair Trade Commission of Japan
Kyodo News (4 February 2011) Huge steel merger planned for 2012. The Japan Times Online, http://www.japantimes.co.jp/text/nb20110204a1.html. Accessed 18 June 2013
Kyodo News (15 December 2012) FTC gives steel giants approval for merger, The Japan Times Online, http://www.japantimes.co.jp/text/nb20111215a9.html. Accessed 18 June 2013
Lok J (2010) Institutional logics as identity projects. Acad Manage J 53(6):1305–1335
Moody's (2014) Moodies Japan, Shintetsu sumitomo to JFE henkou. [Moody's Japan, Nippon Steel Sumitomo Metals and JFE Change]. Nikkei Shinbun, Febr 19th, p 15
Nikkei (2014) Shinnitetsu sumitomo shachou ni shindo shi [Newly appointed president of Nippon Steel is Mr. Shindo.] Nihon Keizai Shinbun, Jan. 16th p. 1 (Nikkei (Jan. 16th) Shinnitetsu sumitomo shachou ni shindo shi. [Mr. Shindo Newly Appointed President of Nippon Steel]. Nihon Keizai Shinbun, Jan. 16th p 1)
Nonaka K (2013) M & A no jimu roudou kanri (Personnel Management of M & A). Chuo Keizai
Ota Y (2013) M & A kigyou soshiki saihen no suki-mu to zeimu (Organizational reorganization at M & A and Tax.), 2nd edn. Omura Zaimu Kyoukai
SteelGuru (2013) Stainless steel suppliers. Fitch downgrade. http://www.steelguru.com/international_news/Fitch_cuts_Nippon_Steel_and_Sumitomo_Metal_to_BBB%252B_outlook_negative/293175.html. Accessed 18 June 2013
Sugimoto T (2014) Shinnitetsu juukin, beikouryaku he shuunen, [Japan Steel Sumitomo Metal and Obsession for American Strategy]. Business Today, Nikkei May 2nd p 13
Whittington M, Bates K (2007) M & A as success. In: Angwin D (ed) Mergers and acquisitions. Blackwell Publishing, Oxford, pp 27–62
Yulisman L (2012) Nippon Steel sets up joint venture with local firms, The Jakarta Post, http://www.thejakartapost.com/news/2011/11/04/nippon-steel-sets-joint-venture-with-local-firms.html. Accessed 18 June 2013

Chapter 11
Institutional Investors

Abstract Equity stake purchases by institutional investors is a phenomenon that has become increasingly common in Japan. This chapter investigates how the post-acquisition performance of target firms differs across domestic versus cross border and friendly versus unfriendly equity stake purchases. Two contrasting concepts, the arms-length principle and geographic-proximity theory are applied. Results partly confirm that Japanese equity stake purchased target firms in an unfriendly attempt performed better right after the deal. Subsequently, the performance was significantly higher for equity stake purchased target firms by cross border institutional investors compared to domestic ones. The number of employees after the purchase decreased significantly for Japanese and for friendly attempts but increased for cross border and unfriendly ones. Implications are discussed.

11.1 Introduction

In recent years, governments around the world have understandably come to appreciate the economic benefits associated with inward cross border direct investment (FDI) by global acting institutional investors. FDI, inter-alia, increases competition among firms and creates jobs in the local economy (Fleming and Johnson 2008). Japan's seriousness for, and interest in attracting FDI is demonstrated by the setting up of an Expert Committee on FDI Promotion as an advisory group to the Minister of State on Economic and Fiscal Policy (WIP Japan 2014). This development is in line with an increasing inbound M&A market to Japan and early support for more globalization of Japanese firms (Ohno 1999). While inward FDI and inbound M&A to Japan are relatively low compared to other countries (see Chap. 2), equity stake purchases by cross border institutional investors to Japan is increasing rapidly. For instance, from 1991 to 2009, the proportion of Japanese stocks held by cross bor-

---

This chapter is an updated version of Bebenroth and Kshetri (2013) Post-acquisition performance of Japanese firms: domestic vs. cross-border equity stake purchases. Journal of Knowledge Globalization Vol. 6, No. 1, pp. 1–22

R. Bebenroth, *International Business Mergers and Acquisitions in Japan*,
DOI 10.1007/978-4-431-54989-5_11

der institutional investors increased from 6 to 26% (MacDonald 2007; TSE 2009). In terms of the total institutional investors' assets, Japan ranks second only to the United States holding 18% of the world's assets (Gonnard et al. 2009).

The spectrum of institutional investors includes mutual funds, pension funds, hedge funds, banks and insurance firms, where more strategically oriented funds tend to have a long term perspective (Koh 2007). The economic power of these institutional investors has increased tremendously in recent years. It is suggested that more than 70% of U.S. equity is purchased by institutional investors (Gillan and Starks 2007). These high stakes in firms reflect a high bargaining power of institutional investors in having access to research and information not available to other investors (Gillan and Starks 2007). Ferreira et al. (2010) find evidence that cross border institutions facilitate more cross-border M&As in countries with less developed stock markets.

While inbound FDI to Japan has some staunch supporters, it also has strong critics. There has been a shift in the role of institutional investors which involves increased monitoring (Anderson et al. 2007). Institutional investors are able to pressure executives by threatening to take their investment out of the firm in case the management is not willing to follow the institutional investor's way (Filatotchev and Toms 2006). In an analysis of U.K. corporate governance reports, Lok (2010) found that institutional investors actively engage with company management as part of an effective corporate governance system, which leads to macroeconomic benefits such as improved productivity, wealth creation, efficient capital allocation, and economic growth. Also for other Asian countries, there is evidence that foreigners and institutional investors drive the equity market. A study on South Korea revealed that both foreigners and institutional investors performed well in the sample period, whereas individual investors performed poorly (Hong and Lee 2011). Institutional investors may be more aggressive in its attempt to get a better performance out of their invested firms. For a long term development; however, that could also be interpreted in a negative way. The better the performance for the institutional investors the more pressure for profits the firms face in the short term. Choe et al. argue that cross border institutional investors contribute to the destabilization of the whole financial market (2005).

Most prior research on institutional investors and financially motivated equity stake purchases has focused on the U.S. (Connelly et al. 2010; Gillan and Starks 2007; Bundo 2000). This is not surprising given the fact that the U.S. accounts for 50% of the world's institutional investors' assets (Gonnard et al. 2009). In this chapter, all non-Japanese institutional investors are put together as cross border institutional investors as they should face similar problems no matter whether they are from the U.S or from a country such as, for example, Germany.

Institutional investors also differ according to their behavior. They have in common to consider shareholders as the owners—and that a financial profit should be the result of their activities (Fukutani and Dobashi 2008, pp. 80–82). There are so called activist hedge funds such as the Japan-based Steel Partners or Aderans, which always purchase equity stake of firms in unfriendly attempts (Nakahara 2008). Also some of the Japanese funds stock participate preferable in unfriendly attempts. One of these funds is the Murakami fund. Most of the institutional investors, however, are friendly in their equity stock participation behavior so as to reach an agreement with the target management before shares are acquired (Chap. 8).

This chapter concerns about differences of cross border versus domestic (Japanese) institutional investors. Our research also focuses on contrasting friendly to unfriendly institutional investors. Two questions are to be answered. First, do Japanese targets' performances differ across the bidder's origin (Japan versus foreign)? Do Japanese targets perform differently when an institutional investor purchases equity stake in a friendly or unfriendly manner?

This empirical chapter is structured as follows. The next section provides a theory and formulates some hypotheses. It is followed by a section on results and a discussion. The final section provides a conclusion and implications.

11.2 Theory Discussion and Hypotheses Formulation

This theory discussion section focuses on how institutional investors' origin and characteristics may affect the efficiency and profitability of the targets they invest in. For this, the arms-length principle and geographic-proximity theory will be applied to formulate some testable, contrary hypotheses.

11.2.1 Arms-Length Principle Versus Geographic-Proximity Theory

There is reason to believe that equity stake purchases by cross-border and domestic acquirers lead to different outcomes. Arms-length principle (ALP) can be understood as a condition where the parties to a transaction are independent of each other and on equal footing. This principle is based on transaction cost theory and widely discussed in the area of income distribution (e.g. Kaplan and Rauh 2009). In the context of this chapter, we use ALP to refer to non-Japanese institutional investors since they should differ from Japanese in their information gathering, functioning and decision taking. In regard to cross border (non-Japanese) investors, Institutional Investor Magazine noted in September 2007, "These [foreign] investors are more outspoken than their Japanese counterparts in demanding growth, prodding managements to do more deals…" (MacDonald 2007). Similarly, Lok (2010, p. 1317) argues that "institutional investors should actively and openly pressure and discipline management to ensure shareholder value maximization, and they should seek to replace management teams with poor shareholder value creation track records".

Geographic-proximity theory (GPT) provide explanations that institutional investors enjoy advantages from being close to a given target firm. This theory has been widely used in Marketing (e.g. Ganesan et al. 2005) and in economics (Krugman 1991). It suggests that closeness is associated with strong(er) performance.

In light of the two different approaches discussed above, differences in the performance of target firms are discussed whether equity stake was purchased by domestic (Japanese) or by cross border (non-Japanese) institutional investors.

11.2.2 Hypothesis Development

11.2.2.1 Domestic Versus Cross Border Investors

It is to investigate if there is a difference in the performance of the target whether the institutional investor is Japanese or not. There is some evidence that cross border institutional investors contribute to a better performance of targets. Ferreira and Matos (2008) argue that cross-border investors play a crucial role in corporate governance as they improve firm performance and reduce capital expenditures (also see Ferreira et al. 2010). According to the ALP, non-Japanese institutional investors might be more willing to downsize a Japanese target rather than rescuing it. Japanese institutional investors could be seen as mentally closer to their target firms. Cross border investors are said to have a strong voice as to how things are to be done at the equity stake purchased Japanese firms. It is also likely that cross border institutional investors may work more professionally than domestic investors. In line with arms-length principle arguments, they may know better how to deal with a given target.

However, critics claim that cross border investors enter a market by increasing their market shares in the form of equity and bond investments in financially distressed firms during crises to earn enormous profits. After that they tend to exit the market by selling their shares at higher prices. One reason why domestic institutional investors might end up purchasing equity stake at weaker performing targets is that they have less of an arms-length relation with local corporations. Domestic institutional managers are more sympathetic to incumbent management (Ferreira et al. 2010; Davis and Kim 2007) whereas cross border institutions are less encumbered by ties with the management of target firms.

There are opposing arguments that can be derived from geographic–proximity theory. According to this approach domestic institutional investors outperform cross border ones. Domestic institutional investors possess private information about the future prospects of a given firm, which allows them to have an informational advantage against cross border institutional investors (Baik et al. 2010). Geographic-proximity can serve as a good proxy for the extent of private information held by investors. For example, Baik et al. (2010) found that geographically close institutional owners predict a higher future stock return. Also, geographically close institutional investors are better able to observe firms through local media reports (Baik et al. 2010). Furthermore, they can have conversations more easily with closely related stakeholders. Finally, domestic investors can easily visit geographically close firms and meet chief executive officers (CEOs) face-to-face at lower cost. Choi et al. (2010) found that bondholders of cross-border bank M&As perceive an increased risk compared to domestic bank mergers. In their research, the yield spread increased by about four basis points following the announcement of a transaction. These aspects are important especially for a country such as Japan, where cross border institutional investors face higher cultural difficulties. The above discussion leads to the following two contrasting hypotheses:

H 1.1: Japanese firms in which an equity stake is purchased by cross border institutional investors are likely to demonstrate a better post acquisition performance (ALP).

H 1.2: Japanese firms in which an equity stake is purchased by domestic institutional investors are likely to demonstrate a better post acquisition performance (GPT).

Similar to financial performance, changes of the number of employees at the target after the takeover are investigated. There is evidence from the US that employees are significantly worse off (Bainbridge 2012, p. 47). From an ALP standpoint, cross border institutional investors are not socially influenced in their decision making process. That means that according to ALP, a cross border investor would more easily be able to downsize a workforce if it is necessary.

In contrast, it is more difficult for a domestic institutional investor to downsize a target. One reason could be that the Japanese investor is mentally closer to the target connected and can hardly introduce changes. The local media would be more effective against a local institutional investor than against a cross-domestic one. The reason for this is that only local ones would fear a negative critics.

However, there are also opposing arguments to GLP, that closeness and better information could lead to a situation that an investor would rather introduce changes the better the investor is familiar with a target. That could lead to the result that domestic institutional investors would downsize a given target even more than a cross border investor. The close familiarity with a target could lead to more substantial changes implemented by a domestic institutional investor. Geographic-proximity theory would deliver arguments that a cross border investor would leave the target as it is because the investor has a limited knowledge about the target. There are again two contrasting hypotheses:

H 1.3: J Japanese firms in which an equity stake is purchased by cross border institutional investors are likely to have a higher employee downsizing (ALP).

H 1.4: Japanese firms in which an equity stake is purchased by domestic institutional investors are likely to have a higher employee downsizing (GPT).

11.2.2.2 Friendly Vs. Unfriendly Takeovers

In a friendly takeover, a target company's management and board of directors agree to an equity stake purchase by the institutional investor. In an unfriendly attempt, the participating institutional investor publicly demands stock but the target firms' management refuses the deal.

That means in contrast to friendly types of institutional investors, institutional investors would purchase equity stake at targets in hostile attempts. Steel Partners, a so-called vulture fund, is an example of this kind of firm. It purchases equity stake at other firms without the approval of the target management or their board of directors (as discussed at Chap. 9).

Most activities are likely to be centered around efficiency and profitably. In order to improve performance and to create higher value, a hostile bidder may replace the inefficient incumbent management more easily than a friendly investor (Sudarsanam and Mahate 2006). In an attempt to enhance efficiency, a bidder engaged in a hostile takeover may even breach implicit contracts such as pension obligations (Shleifer and Summers 1988).

At strategically driven hostile takeovers, shareholders of the acquiring firms are normally negatively impacted. That results out of high prices to be paid for the targets. The prices will even increase (the premium) paid to the target shareholders at unfriendly attempts (Campa and Hernando 2006; Goergen and Renneboog 2008). Sirower (1997) stated “The level of the acquisition premium has a strong negative effect on performance across all 28 measures of shareholder performance: the higher the premium, the larger the losses” (p. 82).

On the opposite, the expectation regarding an improved efficiency in the target firm after a hostile M&A could be seen as more favorable. For the US, there is some evidence that block holdings of unfriendly takeovers by activists are linked to higher profits to be taken out of the target firms (Helwege et al. 2012). Other researchers state that there is not yet clear empirical evidence available if friendly or unfriendly financial investors lead to a better target firms’ performance (Feito-Ruiz and Menéndez-Requejo 2011).

According to the arms-length principle, unfriendly equity stake purchases should be more successful than friendly ones. One reason for this is that institutional investors see the potential of a given firm and participate at it even if managers at the target firm refuse it. To accept the difficulties of realizing synergies in the integration period, the institutional investor must be strongly convinced that the stock equity purchase is still favorable for the fund at the end. Put differently, there is a high chance that the investment, in the end, is financially rewarding; therefore, the investor decides to purchase equity stake on it—against the managements’ refusal. However, an unfriendly equity stake purchase should lead to a higher payment for the transaction. It is clear that the performance of that target has to outweigh the higher initial price. Also, it might be more challenging to have a successful integration period, especially in case strategic changes are intended to be implemented at the firm.

In regard to geographic-proximity theory, it could be argued that friendly equity stake purchases should preferably lead to a higher post acquisition performance. The reason is that the target management agrees to the deal and with the financial help of the institutional investor, the performance should increase. Synergies can be realized with a higher level of trust from the institutional investor. The above discussion leads to the following two contrasting hypotheses:

H2.1: Japanese firms in which an equity stake is purchased in an unfriendly attempt should have a higher post acquisition performance (ALP).

H2.2: Japanese firms in which an equity stake is purchased in a friendly attempt should have a higher post acquisition performance (GPT).

Again, also changes in the number of employees are investigated because the type of equity stake purchase might also affect the workforce. An unfriendly equity stake purchase should cause higher employee fluctuation as the target obviously disagreed to the takeover. Our arms-length principle approach can explain that managers are under serious pressure in firms in which an equity stake is purchased in an unfriendly attempt. The target managers might also downsize the workforce in an unfriendly attempt as they feel higher pressure to send positive messages to the (unfriendly) institutional investors. All arguments may lead rather to serious problems at a given target with a high restructuring activity.

In contrast, arguing from the GPT, a friendly takeover might lead to a higher employee fluctuation. A reason for this could be that an unfriendly investor might stay out of the operative business more than a friendly investor. The friendly investor is in line with our GPT more involved with the target, which might lead to a higher target employees downsizing than for unfriendly ones. Again there are two contrasting theories:

H 2.3: Japanese firms in which an equity stake is purchased in an unfriendly attempt are likely to have a higher employee downsizing (ALP).

H 2.4: Japanese firms in which an equity stake is purchased in a friendly attempt are likely to have a higher employee downsizing (GPT).

11.3 Methods

This section describes the data and the statistical analysis we employed in the empirical investigation. First, the sources of the data and how the variables were measured are presented. Second, the statistical analysis used to examine the effects of the independent variables on the performance of target firms is discussed.

11.3.1 Data and Measures

The target firms used in this chapter for the two years of 2007 and 2008 derived from Recof M&A Database, Print Issue, MARR, (Febr. 2008 and Febr. 2009 issues). All firms were located under the rubric "sonota kinyu" ("equity stake purchased by other financial institutions"). Our whole data set consists of 174 institutional investments in 2007 and of 85 institutional investments in 2008. Only a part of these 259 firms were listed at the Stock Exchange, so that we could only retrieve data for a part of our firms.

Data for 105 firm observations in 2007 and for 52 observations in 2008 were retrieved. Firms in the following categories were deleted from our analyses: real estate, services, and securities. Also a cut off-point at 10% stock equity purchase was set. In other words, under that threshold the influence of the institutional investor we supposed was too low. Therefore, firms with participation lower than 10% equity purchase were not included at this analysis. This study is based on a sample of 115 observations for a 2 year period (Recof M&A Database, Print Issue, MARR, Febr. 2007 and 2008). Financial data in form of ROA and number of employees were collected from Nikkei Needs Financial Quest (electronic data base). Furthermore, industry average data were collected to use as control variables.

11.3.1.1 Dependent Variables

The Return on Assets (ROA) is used to measure the performances of target firms. Note that ROA measures the efficiency with which a company manages its investment and is stated as a robust number not easily to influence (Wu 2010). ROA is given for year $t-1$ and for the years of $t+1$ and $t+2$. The ratio of ROA one year before and one and two years after the equity stake purchase was taken (ΔROA1 and ΔROA2). That is, $\Delta ROA1 = ROAt+1 - ROAt-1$ and $\Delta ROA2 = ROAt+2 - ROAt-1$. As for the second variable, the difference of employment (EMP) was used. That means, there is EMP for the years $t+1$ and $t+2$ (ΔEMP1 and ΔEMP2) compared to the EMP for year $t-1$. That is, $\Delta EMP1 = EMPt+1 - EMPt-1$ and $\Delta EMP2 = EMPt+2 - EMPt-1$.

11.3.1.2 Independent Variables

The first independent variable was a categorical measure of the bidder origin. When the bidder was a cross border institutional investor, we assigned the value of 1 (non-Japanese) and 0 otherwise. For the second variable, the value of 1 was assigned for unfriendly bidder and 0 for a friendly one.

11.3.1.3 Control Variables

As in prior research (Asaba 2005), also this research relied on the change in industry level ROA and employment level for the corresponding year as control variables. That is, the control variable used for the year $t+1$ as $\Delta ROAIND1 = ROAINDt+1 - ROAINDt-1$ (and $\Delta EMPIND1 = EMPINDt+1 - EMPINDt-1$). The control variable used for the year $t+2$ was $\Delta ROAIND2 = ROAINDt+2 - ROAINDt-1$ and alternatively $\Delta EMPIND2 = EMPINDt+2 - EMPINDt-1$ for the ratio of employees.

11.3.2 Statistical Analysis

Two multiple regression analyses were performed with differences of ROA and changes of employment as dependent variables for two years of data.

$$\Delta ROA = \beta_0 + \beta_1(\text{cross border}) + \beta_2(\text{friendly}) + \beta_3(\text{industry}) + \varepsilon$$

$$\Delta EMP = \beta_0 + \beta_1(\text{cross border}) + \beta_2(\text{friendly}) + \beta_3(\text{industry}) + \varepsilon$$

11.4 Results

The means of the dependent and control variables are presented in Table 11.1. Targets of Japanese institutional investors show a decrease in ROA of up to 8.8 % in the first year and 8 % in the second year observation. Targets equity stock purchased by cross border institutional investors only decrease by 1.5 % in the first year and 0.9 % in the second year observation. That means there is a big gap between well-performing "foreign" targets and relatively weak performing "domestic" targets.

The change in ratio of employees is opposite of what is expected. The employee ratio has been downsized in targets equity stake purchased by Japanese institutional investors as suggested by our theory. However, the employee ratio of targets equity stake purchased by cross border institutional investors even increased. That means after a cross border institutional investor purchased equity stake at a Japanese target, the number of employees went up. Similar unexpected results are evident for friendly and unfriendly equity stake purchased targets. Unfriendly equity stake purchased targets end up having a higher employee ratio in both years after the transaction with 2.3 % for the first and 3.8 % at the second year data observation. Targets equity stake purchased in a friendly attempt decrease their number of employees to 98 % in the first-year and to 92 % in the second-year data.

The regression analysis shows that the performance of targets is significantly positive for the second-year data when targets were purchased by cross border institutional bidders. An independent sample t-test supports the assumptions and partly provides supportive evidence for our hypothesis 1.1 (for the second year with $p<0.1$). Unfriendly equity stock purchases significantly outperformed friendly ones in the first-year data ($p<0.1$). That is supported by conducting an independent sample t-test (Table 11.2). That means that targets equity stock purchased unfriendly at least performed better in the first-year data, partly supporting our hypothesis 2.1.

Also the employee ratio was significantly different for friendly and unfriendly equity stake purchases. Also this is supported by the independent sample t-test (Table 11.3). Support for the hypothesis 2.3 for the second-year data was received, that unfriendly purchases lead to a higher rate of employees, which even increased after the transaction ($p<0.05$).

Table 11.1 Mean values for some of the variables in the sample

	$\varDelta ROA_1$	$\varDelta ROA_2$	$\varDelta ROAIND_1$	$\varDelta ROAIND_2$	⊿EMP1	⊿EMP1	⊿EMP-IND1	⊿EMP-IND2
Total sample	−0.04443 (109)	−0.0370 (110)	−0.0054 (113)	−0.0135 (109)	1.0062 (111)	1.0003 (111)	0.9707 (113)	0.9573 (109)
Japanese	−0.0884 (43)	−0.0805 (43)	−0.0024 (47)	−0.0100 (44)	0.9961 (44)	0.9606 (44)	0.9543 (47)	0.9649 (44)
Non-Japanese	−0.0156 (66)	−0.0091 (67)	−0.0074 (66)	−0.0159 (65)	1.0126 (67)	1.0264 (67)	0.9825 (66)	0.9521 (65)
Friendly	−0.1175 (32)	−0.0632 (32)	−0.0023 (33)	−0.0092 (30)	0.9811 (31)	0.9239 (31)	0.9644 (33)	0.9644 (30)
Unfriendly	−0.0174 (75)	−0.0283 (76)	−0.0066 (80)	−0.0151 (79)	1.0233 (78)	1.0383 (78)	0.9734 (80)	0.9545 (79)

The numbers in the parentheses are the number of companies

$\varDelta ROA_1$ = ROA one year after the participation minus ROA one year before

$\varDelta ROA_2$ = ROA two years after the participation minus ROA one year before

$\varDelta ROAIND_1 = _{\text{Industry adjusted}}$ ROA one year after the participation minus ROA one year before

$\varDelta ROAIND_2 = _{\text{Industry adjusted}}$ ROA two years after the participation minus ROA one year before

$\varDelta EMP_1$ = No. of employees one year after the participation minus no. of employees one year before

$\varDelta EMP_2$ = No. of employees two years after the participation minus no. of employees one year before

$\varDelta EMPIND_1$ = Industry adjusted no. of employees one year after the participation minus no. of employees one year before

$\varDelta EMPIND_2$ = Industry adjusted no. of employees two years after the participation minus no. of employees one year before

Table 11.2 Minimum and maximum values and standard deviations

Descriptive statistics for ROA and EMP						
	N	Min	Max	Mean	Std. deviation	
ROA1all	109	−2.22	0.28	−0.04	0.23	
ROA2all	109	−0.07	0.04	−0.01	0.02	
EMP1all	111	0.35	1.56	1.00	0.15	
EMP2all	111	0.32	1.95	1.00	0.25	
Friendly versus unfriendly participation						t-test
ROA1friendly	32	−2.22	0.02	−0.11	0.40	5 %
ROA1unfriendly	75	−0.82	0.28	−0.01	0.11	
ROA2friendly	32	−1.26	0.23	−0.06	0.23	Not sign
ROA2unfriendly	76	−0.69	0.25	−0.02	0.12	
EMP1friendly	31	0.35	1.34	0.98	0.17	Not sign
EMP1unfriendly	78	0.52	1.56	1.02	0.13	
EMP2friendly	31	0.32	1.28	0.92	0.21	5 %
EMP2unfriendly	78	0.4	1.95	1.03	0.26	
Domestic versus cross border participation						t-test
ROA1domestic	43	−2.22	0.2	−0.08	0.36	Not sign
ROA1cross border	66	−0.61	0.28	−0.01	0.09	
ROA2domestic	43	−1.26	0.25	−0.08	0.24	5 %
ROA2cross border	67	−0.21	0.24	−0.00	0.07	
EMP1domestic	44	0.35	1.56	0.99	0.18	Not sign
EMP1cross Border	67	0.5	1.4	1.01	0.13	
EMP2domestic	44	0.32	1.95	0.96	0.32	Not sign
EMP2cross Border	67	0.47	1.64	1.02	0.19	

Table 11.3 Regression results

	Dependent variable=⊿ROA$_1$	Dependent variable=⊿ROA$_2$	Dependent variable=⊿EMP1	Dependent variable=⊿EMP2
Constant	*−0.150[c] (−3.069)*	*−0.109[c] (−2.980)*	*0.727[a] (4.212)*	*0.832[c] (2.651)*
Country classification	0.062 (1.288)	*0.063[a] (1.859)*	0.16 (0.561)	0.49 (1.006)
Friendly/unfriendly	*0.095[a] (1.871)*	0.30 (0.832)	0.40 (1.276)	*0.114[b] (2.153)*
⊿ROAIND$_1$	0.249 (0.128)			
⊿ROAIND$_2$		−0.783 (1.165)		
⊿EMPIND$_1$			0.253 (1.423)	
⊿EMPIND$_2$				0.074 (0.816)
R^2	0.052	0.060	0.41	0.55
Adj. R^2	0.025	0.032	0.13	0.27
F-value	1.891	2.139	1.484	1.969
N	107	104	104	106

The numbers in the parentheses are the t-values.
[a] Significant at 0.01 level.
[b] Significant at 0.05 level
[c] Significant at 0.01 level
Legend of variables:
Dependent variables:
⊿ROA$_{1,}$ ⊿ROA$_{2,}$ ⊿EMP1, ⊿EMP2
Independent variables:
Country classification (domestic or cross border)
Friendly/unfriendly
Control variables:
⊿ROAIND$_{1,}$ ⊿ROAIND$_{2,}$ ⊿EMPIND$_{1,}$ ⊿EMPIND$_2$

11.5 Discussion

In this chapter, an integrative organizational framework to explain differences in characteristics and the structure of target firms was developed and empirically tested. For this, geographic-proximity theory against arms-length principle was used as theoretical concepts to explain differences in performances when a firm is equity stake purchased by a cross border versus a domestic (Japanese) and by a friendly versus an unfriendly bidder.

At the second year data observation, it was found that cross border institutional investors outperformed local (Japanese) institutional investors. There are several reasons that could explain these findings. In a time horizon longer than a year, the direction of a target might be implemented better by more experienced cross border institutional investors than by Japanese ones. Cross border institutional investors which participate at a given target take longer time to realize synergies and payoffs.

These results mainly support the arms-length principle hypothesis (at least for the second year observation), that equity stake purchased targets perform better at cross border investors.

The first hypothesis 1.1 was supported for the second-year data, indicating that arms-length principle is more applicable than geographic-proximity theory. It was found that cross border institutional investors were more successful in managing their targets than their domestic counterparts.

Also the hypothesis 2.1, which stated that unfriendly institutional investors outperform friendly ones, was partly supported, at least for the first-year data. Again ALP has a higher level of prediction than GPT, which means that unfriendly institutional investors might be better able to articulate their understanding of the future direction of a given target. These results confirm the arguments of Yamamoto that unfriendly investors to Japan might better align the management and please the employees of the target (2009). In this sample, the new direction implemented immediately after an unfriendly participation leads to an increase in the number of employees. That might lead, at least for the shorter term, to a better performance.

At the observation of the number of employees, hypothesis 2.4 confirms an increased downsizing at targets which were equity stake purchased in a friendly attempt at a higher rate than when taken over in an unfriendly manner. This result is, to some extent, opposite of what was expected. One could try to explain this with the GPT that unfriendly investors might be more careful after the deal in regard to the employees of the target than friendly ones.

11.6 Conclusion

The chapter found empirical evidence that not Japanese but international institutional investors lead to a better performance at Japanese firms they stock equity purchased. Also, unfriendly bidder were more successfully turn around their targets than friendly ones. This empirical research is not without limitations. First, due to time constraints finding firms, this project relies on firm data for only a 2 year time period. Second, this study relies only on ROA and on accounting measures. An interesting avenue for future research would be to explore a more precise segmentation of corporate governance models for institutional investors from different countries of origin. There exists a considerable body of literature on the varieties of capitalism as a model, whereas the USA and Great Britain belong to the neo-liberal, market oriented Anglo/Saxon model. From the standpoint of exerting influence on the management, U.K. institutional investors are found to have less aggressive and more informal approaches compared to those in the U.S. (Lok 2010; Mallin 1996). In contrast to the market oriented Anglo-Saxon version, there is the organization-oriented "coordinated market economy" system available in countries such as Japan and Germany. While this analysis lumped together all cross border firms, an analysis of behavioral differences of cross border institutional investors in Japan coming from countries with various characteristics (e.g., types of capitalism) might be worthwhile target of study. Even the Anglo Sachs system could be divided into single countries. Also, it would be worthwhile to investigate stock market changes of the targets in a future study. Furthermore, management turnover at the targets would be an interesting avenue to investigate.

It is also to mention that the years of 2007 and 2008 were around the Lehman shock. In other, more normal years, the result may be different. With all its limitations, this research investigates an important area dealing with institutional investors which equity stake purchased Japanese target firms.

Questions

1. Why do governments appreciate FDI to their countries?
2. Recall a Japanese buyout fund.
3. What does it mean to equity purchase a target?
4. According to the study in this chapter, do Japanese targets' performances differ by the bidder's origin (Japan versus foreign). If so, which origin of the institutional investor leads to a higher performance?
5. What might be reasons that foreign equity purchased Japanese firms performed better?
6. How can you explain with Arms-Length-Theory that foreign institutional investors might be for a Japanese firm the better investors?
7. Give an explanation using Geographic-proximity Theory that Japanese institutional investors would participate at the better performing targets.
8. Besides geographical closeness of the investment fund to the target firms, how would you think about personal closeness?
9. Does it matter for a Japanese target firms' performance if an institutional investor purchases equity stake in a friendly or in an unfriendly manner? Which target firms performed better?
10. Does it matter for a Japanese target firms' performance if an institutional investor is a domestic one or a cross-border one? Which target firms performed better?

Answers

1. FDI to a country leads to many positive economic effects. Directly comes new techniques into a country and more people will be employed. Besides, own country firms' may be able to use indirect spill over effects and learn from foreign investors
2. A famous Japanese buyout fund is for example Murakami Fund. Mr. Murakami went to jail because of insider trading.

3. Shares are bought by institutional investors. These investors can raise their voice to introduce changes if the volume of shares bought is high enough to do so. There are two different types to mention. In case they are long term oriented investors, such as pension funds, they normally do not conduct operational changes at the target firm. However, short term oriented hedge funds try to implement strategic changes at the target. These latter investors try to increase their performance by selling shares often rapidly.
4. The better performing targets were the ones equity purchased by foreign funds.
5. The voice of foreign funds might be harsher. To give Japanese firms clear instruction but also a clear guideline which might help Japanese firms to become more successful in business.
6. Arms-Length-Theory states that direct approach is more efficient. Foreign investors might not be influenced in their decision making as it may be a problem at some Japanese funds.
7. Geographic-proximity theory states that funds which are geographically closer have access to information of the target firms. Therefore, they would have an advantage to choose the better performing firms (against foreign funds without insider information).
8. Also personnel closeness would give Japanese funds advantages (against foreign ones). They can share better information with the firms, as they are on the spot and especially because the fund managers speak the same (in this case Japanese) language what leads to a smoother communication.
9. Yes, targets perform differently, according to whether they are purchased friendly or unfriendly. Unfriendly equity stock purchased Japanese firms performed better after the deal. Unfriendly purchased targets may have had a higher potential. That could have been a reason why they got stock equity purchased even in an unfriendly attempt.
10. Yes, cross-domestic institutional investors overtook the better performing targets. The better performance might have relied on a clearer articulation of foreign institutional investors to the target management (Arms-Length-Theory). Another explanation would be that non-Japanese investors might be more experienced. The target can then gain profit out of their investor's experience.

References

Anderson DW, Melanson SJ, Maly J (2007) The evolution of corporate governance: power redistribution brings boards to life. Corp Gov Int Rev 15(5):780–797

Asaba S (2005) Do foreign shareholders change Japanese firms? Working paper presented at the 65th academy of management, annual meeting; 5–10 August 2005; Hawaii, USA

Baik B, Kang J-K, Kim J-M (2010) Local institutional investors, information asymmetries, and equity returns. J Financ Econ 97:81–106

Bainbridge SM (2012) Mergers and acquisitions, 3rd edn. Foundation Press, New York

Bebenroth R, Kshetri N (2013) Post-acquisition performance of Japanese firms: domestic vs. cross-border equity stake purchases. J Knowl Glob 6(1):1–22

Bundo H (2000) 1980 nendai shoukenshijou to M&A undou –kikan toushika niokeru hoyuu kabushiki no baibai undou. (M&A movements of institutional investors in the 1980's—M&A movement and stock selling behavior of institutional investors [in Japanese]. Jpn Financ Manage Assoc 3:39–46

Campa JM, Hernando I (2006) M&A performance in the European financial industry. J Bank Financ 30:3367–3392

Choe H, Bong-Chan K, Stulz RM (2005) Do domestic investors have an edge? The trading experience of foreign investors in Korea. Rev Financ Stud 18(3):795–829

Choi S, Francis BB, Hasan I (2010) Cross-border bank M&As and risk: evidence from the bond market. J Money Credit Bank 42(4):615–645

Connelly BL, Tihanyi L, Certo ST, Hitt MA (2010) Marching to the beat of different drummers: the influence of institutional owners on competitive actions. Acad Manage J 53(4):723–742

Davis G, Kim EH (2007) Business ties and proxy voting by mutual funds. J Financ Econ 85:552–570

Feito-Ruiz I, Menéndez-Requejo S (2011) Cross-border mergers and acquisitions in different legal environments. Int Rev Law Econ 31(3):169–187

Ferreira MA, Matos P (2008) The colors of investors' money: the role of institutional investors around the world? J Financ Econ 88:499–533

Ferreira MA, Massa M, Matos P (2010) Shareholders at the gate? Institutional investors and cross-border mergers and acquisitions. Rev Financ Stud 23:601–644

Filatotchev I, Toms S (2006) Corporate governance and financial constraints. J Manage Stud 43:407–433

Fleming G, Johnson RS (2008) How countries are impacted by mergers and acquisitions: a theoretical approach. Va Econ J 13:33–40

Fukutani N, Dobashi M (2008) M&A tekitaiteki baishuu bouei kanzen manyuaru (Full manual against unfriendly acquisitions) Chuuo Keizai Sha, Tokyo

Ganesan S, Malter AJ, Rindfleisch A (2005) Does distance still matter? Geographic proximity and new product development. J Mark 69(4):44–60

Gillan SL, Starks LT (2007) The evolution of shareholder activism in the United States. J Appl Corp Financ 19:55–73

Goergen M, Renneboog L (2008) Contractual corporate governance. J Corp Financ 14:166–182

Gonnard E, Eun JK, Ynesta I (2009) Recent trends in institutional investors statistics. OECD J Financ Mark Trend 2008(2):299–320

Helwege J, Intintoli VJ, Zhang A (2012) Voting with their feet or activism? Institutional investors' impact on CEO turnover. J Corp Financ 18(1):22–37

Hong G, Lee BS (2011) The trading behavior and price impact of foreign, institutional, individual investors and government: evidence from Korean equity market. Jpn World Econ 23(4):273–287

Kaplan SN, Rauh J (2009) Wall street and main street: what contributes to the rise in the highest incomes? Rev Financ Stud 23:1004–1050

Koh PS (2007) Institutional investor type, earnings management and benchmark beaters. J Account Public Policy 26:267–299

Krugman P (1991) Geography and trade. MIT Press, Cambridge

Lok J (2010) Institutional logics as identity projects. Acad Manage J 53(6):1305–1335

MacDonald SB (2007) Japanese M&A—the surf's up. http://www.atimes.com/atimes/Japan/IA11Dh01.html. Accessed 25 March 2014

Mallin CA (1996) The voting framework: a comparative study of voting behaviour of institutional investors in the U.S. and the U.K. Corp Gov 4(2):107–122

Nakahara K (2008) It's best not to stand out. Nikkei business online. June 9th 2008. http://business.nikkeibp.co.jp/article/eng/20080609/161053/. Accessed 22 June 2011

Ohno K (1999) Nihon kigyou no guro-baruka ni motomerareru kigyousha ishiki ni kan suru: M&A no jimu kara no shisa [in Japanese] A study on management focus required to globalize Japanese corporations: a suggestion from M & A affairs [in Japanese]. Nippon Acad Manage 40:47–51

Shleifer A, Summers L (1988) Breach of trust in hostile takeovers'. In: Auerbach A (ed) Corporate takeovers: causes and consequences. University of Chicago Press, Chicago

Sirower MC (1997) The synergy trap: how companies lose the acquisition game. Free Press, New York

Sudarsanam S, Mahate AA (2006) Are friendly acquisitions too bad for. Shareholders and managers? Long-term. Value creation and top management. Turnover in hostile and friendly acquirers. Br J Manage 17:7–30

TSE (2009) Tokyo stock exchange share ownership survey. http://www.tse.or.jp/english/market/data/shareownership/b7gje60000003t0u-att/English2009.pdf. Accessed 12 April 2011

WIP Japan (2014) Invest Japan. Foreign direct investment promotion. Cabinet office. http://www.invest-japan.go.jp/en_index.html. Accessed 16 May 2014

Wu C (2010) Liquidity discount in valuing unlisted targets–Japanese M&A market evidence. http://bai-conference.org/files/BAI2010%20Proceeding/ISFA2010/Papers/9130.pdf. Accessed Feb 2012

Yamamoto T (2009) shijou no hikouritsusei to TOB zenryaku-Nihon ni okeru riron to kesu) (The impact of market inefficiency on TOB strategies in Japan: a theory and a case in Japan) [in Japanese]. J Manage Account Jpn 17(2):49–64

Part III
Human Resources in Mergers and Acquisitions Processes

Chapter 12
Organizational Identification at Cross-Border Mergers and Acquisitions: A Theoretical Concept

Abstract This chapter proposes a theoretical framework for organizational identification of target employees at cross-border Mergers and Acquisitions (M&A) on communication, training and consulting. Against the literature stating that all target employees will generally identify less with the new firm, it will be shown on Japan as a country of example that this is not automatically true. It depends on certain characteristics whether or not employees identify with their new bidder firm. For example it matters whether employees are in regularly employed positions. Possibly, non-regular employees might feel afraid of getting replaced. However, it is also thinkable that they may even stronger identify with their organization. Younger regular employees might see an acquisition more as a chance, to more fully use their talents effectively. This should count especially when taken over in a cross border deal where young talents may get more international exposure.

12.1 Introduction

Merger and Acquisitions increasingly occur in all over the world and there is also a sharp increase of transactions in Japan visible. In this vein, Japan had its peak of Mergers and Acquisitions (M&A) in 2006 with almost 2800 transactions and still in 2013, there is a level of over 2000 transactions reported (see Chap. 7; Recof M&A Database, Print Issue, MARR, Febr. 2014). Academic research about M&A is traditionally a domain of finance majors, highly concentrated on studies conducted about US and UK firms (Larsson and Finkelstein 1999). In contrast to this, research on psychological aspects of employees at M&As have been neglected (Aguilera and Dencker 2004). There is only very limited research carried out so far in the field of M&A concerning HRM aspects at Asian countries.

It is frequently reported that most of the takeovers end in failure. According to Schoenberg (2006) M&As are successfully to only 56 %. Other researchers are far more pessimistic in their studies. If failures cover ineffective organizational cultures what lead to problems in the aftermath of an M&A, there is a level of failure reported to be around 70 % (Styhre et al. 2006).

Winners at M&A are the shareholders of the targets because they sell their shares over the actual price on the stock exchange. This is based on the premiums bidder

R. Bebenroth, *International Business Mergers and Acquisitions in Japan*,
DOI 10.1007/978-4-431-54989-5_12

firms pay in order to receive the shares. Less clear are benefits for the acquirer side. There exist studies which compare cultural differences between firms in different countries at cross-border M&A. There is; however, the call for studies in more depth, preferably to analyze all employees at only one single firm instead of relying on key informants at many firms (Stahl et al. 2005). This way of research focusing on employees at a single target firm has been done by Gerpott and Neubauer, who investigated this issue on a domestic German deal (2011).

This chapter theorizes about organizational identification of Japanese target employees and their effects in regard to communication, training and consulting at the M&A integration period. In this way, this research aims to entangle the black box of employee issues at M&A to bring more successful acquisitions to Japan. This chapter comes up with propositions for communication, training and consulting issues. Two research questions are to be addressed. First, how differ regular employees and non-regular employees in their organizational identification at the target firm? Second, to which extent should communication, training and consulting cover both types of employees in the M&A integration period for having a successful M&A integration?

12.2 M &A Integration

Anecdotal evidence suggests that a smoother integration predicts a better performance at M&A, even if there is not yet clear evidence in the literature that organizational integration leads to a successful takeover at all. Even worse, there is still no agreement on how performance should be measured (Stahl and Voight 2008; Zollo and Meier 2008).

Capron (1999) shows in his study that the transfer of resources improves the post-merger performance. Some other research suggests that executives of acquired cross border firms are more likely to quit their job as when being acquired by a domestic firm (Krug and Hegarty 2001). In this sense, cross border acquisitions, so the theory, are more challenging to handle than domestic acquisitions. King et al. (2004) analyzed 93 prior empirical studies in their meta-analyses and found out that they did not know more than before they conducted their study (Weber and Tarba 2010). M&A research up to date is hardly able to answer even basic questions, for example, about the drivers of a successful acquisition. Several of their proposed variables, such as the method of payment or the degree of relatedness between firms were not statistically significantly linked to the performance of the acquisition. As a result, the King study suggests to integrate other (not yet considered) factors which have not been studied yet in order to find factors that matter for a success in the integration period of an acquisition (King et al. 2004). This attempt is followed by investigating organizational identification of target employees in Japan.

This chapter argues that employees at a Japanese target firm are not a homogeneous group and that different types of employees exist at the target firms. These types of employees have to be distinguished. Depending on the type of employees, there is a different organizational identification and a different attitude prevalent when getting taken over by a foreign investor. That means, there is resistance of some individuals at the target firm which may cause major problems leading to unsuccessful takeovers. Other types of employees might be even in favor of getting taken over, for example, to become a part of a new international firm and to be able to use their talents even better.

12.3 Knowledge-Based View in M&A Context

The knowledge-based view of the firm considers knowledge as the most important resource a firm holds as it is difficult to imitate and as it is a socially complex phenomena. The knowledge-based view is embedded in culture, systems and in employees, which are significant determinants for a competitive advantage of a given firm. The knowledge-based view is based on the resource-based view first proposed by Penrose (1959). In the following, the knowledge-based view of the firm as proposed by Kogut and Zander (1992) will be discussed for the M&A integration period. To achieve strategic goals, the organizational identification of employees is of detrimental value.

There is a dominant line of cultural studies, which depart from the Hofstede research for investigating different countries' cultures. As a result they demonstrate that a centralized control is associated with a higher level of uncertainty avoidance and a higher level of acceptance of power distance among acquirers (Kirkmann et al. 2006). These capabilities can be transferred through expatriations. In this vein, headquarter send employees to transfer knowledge to the target firm (see Chap. 15; Lubatkin et al. 1998). Child et al. found in their British sample that there were differences in the level of autonomy during the integration process (2001).

The integration of two organizations or more precisely, the annexation of a Japanese target firm to a non-Japanese bidder firm addresses various HR related issues. Cultural and institutional differences between the bidder and target employees may lead to difficulties that create conflicts in form of a low organizational identification. These conflicts could lead to employee resistance against the bidder firm (as seen at the Panasonic—Sanyo Denki case in Chap. 9).

Also in Japan, M&A research focuses predominantly on the financial side including domestic transactions, where a decline in productivity, Return on Equity and Return on Assets was found at the acquirer side (Yeh and Hoshino 2001). Research about foreign entrants into Japan via acquisitions remains still limited in numbers. Fukao et al. (2005) report, that foreign companies overtake comparatively profitable targets when entering Japan. Domestic acquisitions, however, are seen as "rescue missions" where Japanese bidders overtake weak firms in order to help them. In contrast to these results, Bebenroth (2009) finds opposite ones. According to his data, foreigners overtake the comparably weaker Japanese targets and concludes that the reason for this might be that other Japanese bidders did not want to overtake them (Bebenroth 2009; Chap. 8).

As far as the author is aware, there is hardly any research published in English about target employee's attitudes at cross border M&A at the Japanese context. It is conventional wisdom that foreigners hesitate to overtake Japanese firms as they fear hidden problems, especially at the Japanese target employee side (Bebenroth 2003). As most M&A have to be seen more than merely financial transactions, it is rather a process which significantly affects all employees in a given target firm. It is well documented in the literature that downsizing leaves employees in stress, fear and anxiety about their career (McBain 1999). This naturally reduces productivity of the target company and leads to an increase of absenteeism and probably to a lower organizational identification of the employees to their new firm.

Japanese employees can be categorized into regular and non-regular employees. In the traditional Japanese employment practices, regular employees are usually allowed to stay in the same organization until mandatory retirement age. That is called in Japanese "seishain", what is often interpreted as lifetime employed. To be correct, regular employment does not juristically ensure employment for a whole lifetime in Japan. These employees are on a "gentlemen agreement" of not having a fix term contract. This counts even for civil servants. In contrast to the bureaucratic system of the West, where civil servants have a life time employment ensured by the government until a certain age (what is written with a fixed year in their contract), employees in a bigger Japanese firm have their contract until retirement only assumed. That is, in Japan, it has been a social norm especially for large firms that regular employees are hardly dismissed until they become mandatory retirement age.

Non-regular employees, on the other hand, lack job security and are employed on a temporary or part-time basis. There is a wide range of non-regular employees, which can be divided into several different employment types. Employees could be sent from temporary work agencies. This case is called *haken shain* in the rest of the chapter. *Haken* is characterized as "triangular employment relationship" where *haken shains* are legally employed by temporary service agencies but work in the client firms away from these agencies. This type is also known as dispatched workers. A different type of non-regulars is the contracted worker, so called *keiyaku shain.* They are employed on fixed-term contracts often on a yearly basis. Also, *Keiyaku shains* usually work for many years at the same firm; however, they do not receive bonuses or any other benefits all regular employees receive. It should be mentioned that the Japanese bonus system is not to compare with the one in Western societies. The bonus is not based on individual performance; rather on the whole group (firm), so that everyone receives the same amount of bonus. In this, the amount of the bonus is rather high with about 4.4 monthly salaries, given out twice a year. Another type of non-regular employees is the part-timer. This employee type is in Japan called *pato-taimu or arubaito* (derived from German language of *Arbeit*, meaning work). They all have in common that their firm endurance is limited to the day where the firm faces hardship. In other words, they will leave the firm before any regular employed would get laid-off.

12.4 Organizational Identification

The concept of organizational identification can be described in three criteria: central, enduring and distinctive (CED). This concept "who we are, as an organization" was first specified by the work of Albert and Whetten (1985). It is the sense of oneness individuals have with an organization and the degree to which individuals define themselves as organization members (Ashforth and Mael 1989). Organizational identification, as well as other forms of employee attitudes such as organizational commitment, is a type of employee attachment to the organization. Employees get attracted to organizations that share similar characteristics and that they admire (Pratt 1998). In addition, employees will increase organizational identification when there are threats from an outgroup, for example from competing organizations or from a bidder firm (Riketta 2005).

This chapter theorizes on possible changes in the identification of target employees. Organizational identification has been found to be associated with various individual and organizational outcomes such as cooperation effort, participation, organizationally beneficial decision making, intrinsic motivation, task performance, information sharing, turnover intentions, job satisfaction, work adjustment and organizational citizenship behaviors (Ashforth et al. 2008).

In the case of M&A, there is evidence that fear and anxiety of Japanese employees might be even more important to consider than in firms of other industrialized countries (Fukutani and Dobashi 2008, p. 69). This is because the mental distance of Japanese employees to foreign bidders should be considered rather high compared to people at other countries (Pease et al. 2006). Also, the labor market for experienced, mid-career workers in Japan is relatively immature compared to relatively easy employable school graduates. Therefore, it is more difficult for mid-career workers to find a new position in another firm if they have to leave their current employers. Also, there might be a danger for a regular who switches to other firms to become a non-regular employee at the new firm. However, it should be given weight to the idea that some of the target employees, especially younger ones or the whole range of non-regular, such as *haken shain*, *keiyaku shain or part-timer/ arubaito* might take a takeover as a chance rather than a threat for themselves.

In this chapter it is assumed that organizational identification differs between regular and non-regular employees. Regular employed tend to identify themselves strongly with their "old" organizations. This is because regular employees normally come to the firm after graduating from university. These employees will change positions and the departments; however, always remain staying at the same firm. Therefore, friendships will be established with co-workers which go beyond professional connections and even include families and the housing. This will lead to a stronger organizational identification of regular employed. In contrast, as non-regular employees are not included into this system, they tend to identify themselves less with their employing organization but may tend to identify themselves more with other industrial or occupational categories such as professional associations. In the case of *haken shains* it could be even more complex because dispatched employees are under the triangular employment relationship. They may identify themselves to their agency where they got dispatched from, to the client firm, or to their occupation (e.g. programmers).

The utmost concern for a regular employee would be that the new foreign investor stops the whole setting of lifetime employment as exercised in the target firm and puts every job at disposition. As regular employees are firm educated and closely bound to their firm with the given atmosphere, a change of culture to another firm for them is difficult to understand. The network of regular employees at a given target can be considered as strong, so that they would support each other remaining at the firm. Because senior regular employees are more imbedded to their firm, at the time of an acquisition they should have a lower organizational identification with their new firm.

Non-regular employees identify themselves more with their own strength; it might be easier for them to get adjusted to the new firm.

Propositions 1.1
Regular employees have a higher organizational identification with the older firm than non-regular employees.

Proposition 1.2
Senior regular employees have a higher organizational identification with their older firm but less organizational identification with the new firm.

Proposition 1.3
Non-regular employees are more open for changes because of bidder influences. It would be easier to integrate them into the new firm.
In the following, it is to shed some light on communication (inclusive knowledge transfer), on training and the influence of consulting in order to come up with some propositions.

12.5 Communication and Knowledge Transfer

There is evidence in the literature that communication and knowledge transfer (in the following just referred as communication) is crucial for a successful integration (Szulansky 1996) for both regular as well as for non-regular employees. It is said that uncertainty rather than change bears a stressful element for employees and managers at target firms. Freud stated it as "unheimlich", etymologically "unfamiliar", or "uncanny", having the notion of not being in the "Heim", home (Freud 1955). This does not suggest that managers and employees are not capable of grasping the strategies of the foreign investors but that anxiety emphasizes predominantly the changes as an emotional experience, where any kind of employee does not feel save. To cope with these anxieties of Japanese employees, immediate and honest information has to be communicated from the bidder firm. The cost for additional communication has to be lower than the profit earned for an increase in performance. The appropriate communication stream to all employees can be done through different channels. Leading managers of the bidder firm can have single talks with target employees, or seminars can be offered where advantages and possible disadvantages can be communicated and reactions observed. This might be a preferred method for regular employees, which stay with the firm after the acquisition. Also workshops seem to be a successful channel to reduce regular employee stress and uncertainty (Leroy and Ramanantsoa 1997).

For non-regular employees, personnel meetings as well as workshops could be considered as too costly, even if there is evidence that the communication program is a vital tool for all kinds of employees for a better organizational identification to the success of the M&A (Bryson 2003).

We distinguish employees merely into two groups, with regular employees as the steam of the Japanese target. It is supposed that regular employees have an easier communication acceptance. Especially for Japan it is said, that Japanese have an "implicit understanding" of not outspoken words. Non-regular employees like time contracted, *haken shain* or part-time workers do not fit into this concept and stay out of closer information circles. This leads to the following propositions.

Proposition 2.1
Higher investment in communication to regular employees of the target firm at the M&A integration period will lead to a better organizational identification what will lead to a higher M&A performance.

Proposition 2.2
Higher investment in communication to non-regular employees of the target firm at the M&A integration period will be hard to justify at the headquarter but will lead to a better organizational identification what will lead to a higher M&A performance.

Proposition 2.3
A changed status from non-regular employees to regular employees moderates the relationship between communication and organizational identification, in such a way that organizational identification increases what will lead to a higher M&A performance.

12.6 Training

The training specifically at the target firm is of outmost importance for a successful integration. It is of conventional wisdom that in order to integrate a target firm, the training must include more than rarely technical skills and new work processes but also has to deal with conflict solving techniques in order to deepen cultural understanding between the two firms. Training also improves knowledge integration. Bresman et al. (1999) show that training programs at M&A had a positive impact to knowledge transfer. Training involves additional costs; therefore, it may be sanctioned only if it outbalances these costs.

It is to focus on the question who should be trained and to which extend, clustering employees again in regular vs. non-regular employees. As globalization continues it becomes important for employees to develop special and unique skills. In this sense, relatively universal Japanese educated regular employees might feel the need to get more specifically educated in a given field. Therefore, especially younger regular employees could end up being more motivated after the acquisition than they were before, as these target firm employees see a takeover as a good chance to receive better training opportunities. Younger employees are more favorable to specific training. In contrast to this, senior regular employees are used to get exchanged to other units to become stronger involved with their firms' culture. Therefore, organizational identification should preferably increase at younger regular employees.

Non-regular employees might see an acquisition out of various angles. As some of them are equipped with necessary skills for the foreign investor, they might even applaud to be "a new member" of the foreign firm. There is some evidence that especially *haken shain* sent employees have higher skills in English language and more experiences at other firms. That makes them easier to get acquainted to the new situation after the acquisition. Also, some of the non-regular employees might receive a fair chance of getting switched to a regular position after the acquisition as they have skills required by the bidder firm.

There also appear negative aspects in regard to non-regular employees. Non-regular employees are considered to have a short time orientation at a given firm. It can be expected that this is countering an increased training as it might not be worthwhile for an investor to train people which might leave soon afterwards the firm (and sometimes even join the competitors). Hence, the bidding firms would be reluctant to spend the training investment that does not contribute to the long term wealth of the firm. Regular employees on the opposite, give a wider planning horizon and probably more reason for staff training. It is because organization oriented HR practices are the norm in Japanese firms to develop organization-specific human resources from a long-term perspective. Because of the tradition to hold regular employees, these employees in Japanese target firms appreciate the training investment from the bidding firms. These arguments lead to the following propositions:

Proposition 3.1
Investment of training for regular employees at the Japanese target firm will lead to a higher organizational identification, which will lead to a better M&A performance.

Proposition 3.2
Training to non-regular employees will be hard to justify at the headquarter but a worthwhile investment for a higher organizational identification, which will lead to a better M&A performance.

Proposition 3.4
A changed status from non-regular employees to regular employees moderates the relationship between training and organizational identification, in such a way that organizational identification increases, which will lead to a better M&A performance.

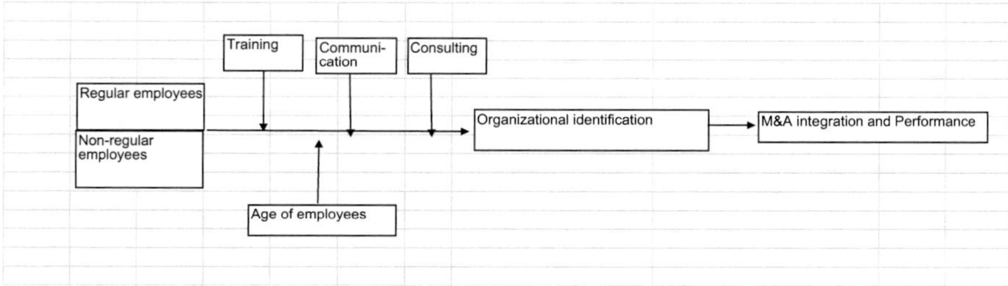

Fig. 12.1 Model. (Model by the author)

12.7 External Consulting

As acquisitions occur relatively unpredictably and infrequently it leads bidder firms to rely on external consulting services for ensuring an adequate integration period of procedures and systems. Even if bigger firms with worldwide operations encounter acquisitions frequently, it is not to expect that this happened more often in Japan. In this vein, all firms undertaking M&A in Japan can be considered as being without experience. As Japan is very different from the Western world and from other neighboring Asian countries as well, logically it would be advisable to incorporate external consultancy at the M&A integration process. According to the knowledge-based view of the firm, external experts already in Japan could be considered as a fruitful source to train local employees as well as to increase the communication level between target employees and the staff in charge at the foreign headquarters. Both of these efforts should lead to a better organizational identification.

In terms of the consulting, regular employees should preferably be included to participate in these activities. Especially younger regular employees might be better equipped for being included into projects with external consultants than non-regular employees. This is because regular employees are more knowledgeable about the firm in order to take advantage of their organizational identification and to promote performance. This leads us to the following two propositions. (Fig. 12.1)

Proposition 4.1
Regular employees should be more actively involved with external consulting services than non-regular employees for having a higher organizational identification, which leads to a better M&A performance.

Proposition 4.2
External consulting moderates the relationship between training/communication and organizational identification, in such a way that an increase in external consulting has positive effects on organizational identification, which leads to a better M&A performance.

12.8 Discussion

Studies on M&A and HRM in Japan are still in its infancy. This theoretical approach makes an attempt to shed some light on this issue. This chapter discussed effects of communication, training and consulting on the organizational identification of Japanese target employees. It is stated that a company is advised to increase both in order to have a higher organizational identification which leads to a more successful integration. Communication has to be increased at the level of regular employees, and training should be provided to those regular employed. Also, external consulting is proposed to moderate positively the effects of training and communication to a higher organizational identification which will lead to a better M&A integration performance. In short, organizational identification depends on the type of employees, whether regular or not will influence the organizational identification which will influence the performance of the M&A. For senior regular employees there might be on the one hand a decrease of organizational identification because of unknown changes at the new firm. This could also be caused by the fact that the so called life time employment system could be abolished by the new bidder firm. On the other hand, all regular employees should feel safer at the new firm in contrast to non-regular employees, as they will be the first ones getting out of the job in case of economic hardship. Besides, it is suggested that the age of regular employees has an effect on their organizational identification. Rather younger regular employees should be motivated to get involved with the integration of the target into the bidder firms.

12.9 Conclusion

This study aimed to provide a framework for organizational identification and performance implications of employees at an acquisition. The research has some limitations, however. First, it is a theoretically driven paper and the proposed ideas in this paper need to be transformed into hypotheses and tested in order to understand the effects of communication, training and consulting to the organizational identification of the employees, as well as the performance drivers. These propositions might be tested in the future by conducting empirical research. This chapter shed some light on three areas, as on communication, training and on consulting knowing that there are still other untouched areas like the autonomy of the target firm etc. (Zhou et al. Shin and Canella 2008). The autonomy given to the target firm after the acquisition, might influence organizational identity as well. Concrete, if a target maintains widely autonomous then communication, training and consulting might not be even a necessary tool to be implemented. Also, it could be too expensive and not worthwhile for an investor. Finally, our theoretical framework applies to only two different groups. The first group is quite homogeneous; however, the second one is rather heterogeneous in its nature. Non-regular employees differ in their professionalism, for example *haken shain* have higher skills compared to classical part-time workers. In this vein, it would be more exacte to separately analyse non-regulars at each type. These issues may be pursued in a future research project. With all its weaknesses, this chapter sheds light on two different contrasting types of Japanese employees in connection to their organizational identification at an M&A process.

Questions

1. What is an advantage of doing research on a single firm case, in contrast of a many firm case design?
2. Recall a practical reason why researcher but also practical oriented people, for example, consultants focus preferably on the monetary side on M&A.
3. What is the difference between regular and non-regular employed?
4. Recall different types of non-regular employees in Japan.
5. How differ regular employees and non-regular employees in their organizational identification when taken over by a foreign firm?
6. To which extent may communication, training and consulting differ between both types of employees at the M&A integration period?
7. Why should the investment of training in regular employees be more profitable than in non-regular employees?
8. Have senior regular employees a higher or a lower organizational identification with the new firm?
9. Where is the advantage for a foreign bidder firm also to include non-regulars into the new firm?
10. What are disadvantages when a firm provides training for its employees?

Answers

1. Researchers are able to focus on questions in a more depth approach. It may be more reliable to ask every employee at one single firm, than to rely on key informants at many firms. Because these key informants might not be the adequate information source. Also, especially questionnaires often do not arrive at these intended key informants. There is a high chance that not the intended informants but younger (and uninformed) employees answer questionnaires at the targeted firms.
2. Monetary side is relatively easy to research. Consultants are preferably interested in making money, this comes when the deal is signed. After that, even if many firms report about problems at their post integration period, they are often led alone.
3. Regulars are normally out of the group of university graduates, which joined the firm as so called "life time employed" or "permanently

employed". That means, this type of employee is considered to stay at the firm until retirement. In contrast, non-regular employed are all others. They only have a time contract, or not even that. There is no secure future for them and they also do not receive any bonuses (what makes a substantial part of a salary in Japan).

4. Haken Shain (dispatched workers), Contract workers with a fix term, Part timer (pato taimu) which are normally working fulltime but without having any contract (or might be issued for a two month period, upon renewal each time).
5. Regulars may feel afraid for atmosphere change at the new firm. Especially at a foreign bidder, there might be danger that the existing life time concept will be abolished. Non-regulars, are the first group what gets restricted in cases of economic difficulties. However, some non-regulars, for example dispatched workers, might even see it as a chance (for example to get into a regular position at the new firm).
6. Communication, training and consulting will focus normally much more on regular employed than on non-regulars.
7. Because regular employees stay permanent at the firm. In contrast, non-regular employees may leave the firm easier so that training investment might be lost (especially if non-regular leave to the competitor firm)
8. Senior employees are supposed to have a lower organizational identification to the new firm. The reason is that they were culturally trained to be very different to other firms' culture. In case the firm is taken over by another firm, these senior employees should face bigger problems to adjust to the new culture.
9. Non-regulars have talent, especially dispatched workers often even speak English. Also, their open cultural attitude may be easier to handle for a foreign investor than regular employed.
10. Disadvantages could be that a firm normally cannot provide training by themselves. It is rather expensive to hire specialized external consultancies. Also, employees are needed especially in a time of organizational change, to have them send to a training brings a lack at the business lines. Also, several of the trained employees may leave the firm after the training. Finally, it is difficult to provide training for all employees, some of the left out may feel even jealous.

References

Aguilera RV, Dencker JC (2004) The role of human resource management in cross-border mergers and acquisitions. Int J Hum Resour Manage 15(8):1355–1370

Albert S, Whetten DA (1985) Organizational identity. In: Cummings LL, Staw MM (eds) Research in organizational behavior, vol 7. JAI, Greenwich, pp 263–295

Ashforth BE, Mael FA (1989) Social identity theory and the organization. Acad Manage Rev 14:20–39

Ashforth B, Harrison S, Corley K (2008) Identification in organizations: an examination of four fundamental questions. J Manage 34:325–74

Bebenroth R (2003) Bewertung bei Akquisitionen japanischer Targetunternehmen—aus Sicht deutscher Industrieunternehmen

Bebenroth R (2009) Inbound M&A to Japan: cherry picking versus rescue mission? Kobe Econ Bus Rev 54:1–19

Bresman H, Birkenshaw J, Nobel R (1999) Knowledge transfer in international acquisitions. J Int Bus Stud 30:439–462

Bryson J (2003) Managing HRM risk in a merger. Empl Relat 31:347–353

Capron L (1999) The long-term performance of horizontal acquisitions. Strateg Manage J 20(11):987–1018

Child J, Faulkner D, Pitkethly R (2001) The management of international acquisitions. Oxford University Press, New York

Freud S (1955) The uncanny. In: Strachey J (ed) The standard edition of the complete psychological works of sigmund freud, 17, an infantile neurosis and other works. Vintage, London, pp 218–256

Fukao K, Ito K, Kwon HU (2005) Do out-in M&As bring higher TFP to Japan? An empirical analysis based on micro-data on Japanese manufacturing firms. J Jpn Int Econ 19:272–301

Fukutani N, Dobashi M (2008) M&A tekitaiteki baishuu bouei kanzen manyuaru (Full manual against unfriendly acquisitions). Chuuo Keizai Sha, Tokyo

Gerpott TJ, Neubauer FB (2011) Integrationsgestaltung und Zusammenschlusserfolg nach einer Unternehmensakquisition—Eine empirische Studie aus Mitarbeitersicht. Z fuer Betriebswirtschaftliche Forschung (ZfBf) 63:118–154

King DR, Dalton DR, Daily CM, Covin JG (2004) Meta-analyses of post-acquisition performance: indications of unidentified moderators. Strateg Manage J 25:187–200

Kirkmann BL, Lowe KB, Gibson CB (2006) A quarter century of culture's consequences: a review of empirical research incorporating Hofstede's cultural values framework. J Int Bus Stud 37:285–320

Kogut B, Zander U (1992) Knowledge of the firm, cominative capabilities and the replication of technology. Organ Sci 3:383–397

Krug JA, Hegarty WH (2001) Research notes and commentaries: predicting who stays and leaves after an acquisition: a study of top managers in multinational firms. Strateg Manage J 22:185–196

Larsson R, Finkelstein S (1999) Integrating strategic, organizational, and human resource perspectives on mergers and acquisitions: A case study of synergy realization, Organ Sci 10:1–26

Leroy F, Ramanantsoa B (1997) The cognitive and behavioral dimensions of organizational learning in a merger: an empirical study. J Manage Stud 34:871–894

Lubatkin M, Calori R, Very P, Veiga JF (1998) Managing mergers across borders: a two-nation exploration of a nationally bound administrative heritage. Organ Sci 9:670–684

McBain R (1999) Human resource management. Manage Update 11(1):22–30

Pease S, Paliwoda S, Slater J (2006) The erosion of stable shareholder practice in Japan ("Anteikabunushi Kosaku"). Int Bus Rev 15:618–640

Penrose ET (1959) The theory of the growth of the firm. Wiley, New York

Pratt MG (1998) To be or not to be: central questions in organizational identification. In: Whetten DA, Godfrey PC (eds) Identity in organizations: building theory through conversation. Sage, Thousand Oaks, pp 171–207

Recof M&A Database, Print Issue, MARR, Febr. (2014) Mergers acquisition research report. Recof-data report (in Japanese language)

Riketta M (2005) Organizational identification: a meta-analysis. J Vocat Behav 66:358–384

Schoenberg R (2006) Measuring the performance of corporate acquisitions: an empirical comparison of alternative metrics. Br J Manage 17:361–370

Stahl KG, Voight A (2008) Do cultural differences matter in mergers and acquisitions? A tentative model for examination. Organ Sci 19(1):160–176
Stahl KG, Mendenhall ME, Weber Y (2005) Research on sociocultural integration in mergers and acquisitions: points of agreement, paradoxes, and avenues for future research. In Stahl GK, Mendenhall ME (eds) Mergers and acquisitions: managing culture and human resources. Stanford Business Books, Stanford
Styhre A, Boerjesson S, Wickenberg J (2006) Managed by the other: cultural anxieties in two Anglo-Americanized Swedish firms. Int J Hum Resour Manage 17(7):1293–1306
Szulansky G (1996) Exploring internal stickiness: impediments to the transfer of best practice within the firm. Strateg Manage J 17:27–44
Weber Y, Tarba SY (2010) Human resource practices and performance of mergers and acquisitions in Israel. Hum Resour Manage Rev 20:203–211
Yeh T, Hoshino Y (2001) Productivity and operating performance of Japanese merging firms: keiretsu-related and independent mergers, Jpn World Econ 434:1–20
Zhou J, Shin SJ, Canella AA (2008) Employee self-perceived creativity after mergers and acquisitions: Interactive effects of threat opportunity perception, access to resources, and support for creativity. J Appl Behav Sci 44(4):397–421
Zollo M, Meier D (2008) What is M&A performance? Acad Manage Perspect 22(3):55–77

Chapter 13
Identification and Job Satisfaction at Mergers and Acquisitions

Abstract This chapter sheds light on Japanese target firm employees' perceptions after being taken over by a German firm. Specifically, it was tested how target firm employees' perception of procedural justice and their cultural openness influence two variables: job satisfaction and organizational identification. It is found that the perceived procedural justice leads to a higher level of job satisfaction and to a better organizational identification. Fair treatment matters more for the satisfaction of employee's with a higher cultural openness. Implications and future research directions are discussed.

13.1 Introduction

Cross border mergers and acquisitions (M&As) are a common way of firms to enter foreign markets even if the failure rate remains high (Moeller and Schlingemann 2005). After the deal is signed, the integration period shows to what extent synergies can be realized and whether or not the deal will be a successful one at the end (Fried et al. 1996). The most important element for realizing synergies is to successfully include human resource issues as a major trigger (Aguilera and Dencker 2004). For doing this, it is important that employees at both firms are positively exposed to the deal and that they feel to be treated in a fair way. Acquisition literature suggests that the successful combination of resources between the bidder firm and the target firm leads to an increase in a firm value (Weber and Tarba 2010; Grimpe 2005; Haspeslagh and Jeminson 1991). In this sense, material resources e.g. computer centers are easily transferable but also easily to imitate by competitors. A successful transfer of material resources, therefore, will only have a marginal gain and might lead to a short term profit. Immaterial resources are more difficult to successfully transfer and to combine. However, if done successfully, this leads to advantages which are then difficult to imitate by competitors (Barney 1991).

After an acquisition, a successful integration should include personnel transfers. Normally, managers from the bidder firm will move into the target firm for several plausible reasons. They could help to coordinate between the bidder and the target, or they could be in charge to control the target firm. Research suggests that personnel transfers have a positive effect on the success of the new firm (Fugate et al. 2002).

R. Bebenroth, *International Business Mergers and Acquisitions in Japan*,
DOI 10.1007/978-4-431-54989-5_13

However, this evidence is based on expert's information from single key informants at the firms. These results might look different, when employees at the targets themselves are contacted (Gerpott and Neubauer 2011; Gerpott 2009).

There are studies conducted about perceptions of employees at target firms, even with German firms being the acquirer (Gerpott and Neubauer 2011; Gerpott 2009; Mueller-Stewens 2010; Becker 2005; Grimpe 2005; Hoyningen-Huene 2004) However, as far as the author is aware, there is no study concerning an Asian target with a German acquirer. In this vein, this chapter constellation is that the bidder firm is a (German) subsidiary which overtakes a local (Japanese) firm. That means, even if this study belongs to the field of cross domestic acquisitions, not only the managers of the bidder firm are much more familiar with the host country than at other studies. Also the employees of the bidder firm are familiar with the target country as they live there already. In fact, many are local nationals (Japanese) which can more easily deal with employees of the target firm than in other studies undertaken (e.g. Melkonian et al. 2011). Specifically, this study examines a Japan-based German subsidiary which overtook a Japanese target firm.

This is a single firm study, compensating the disadvantage of having only one single firm source with the advantage of receiving in depth knowledge of the employee perceptions. There is recent evidence in the literature, that this kind of study is superior than to rely on key informants at different firms (Gerpott and Neubauer 2011; Homburg and Klarmann 2009; Glaum and Hutzschenreuter 2010; Hurrle and Kieser 2005). This research is in line to investigate employee perceptions at two points in time at the integration period (see for a similar approach at: Gerpott and Neubauer 2011; Meglio and Risberg 2010).

This chapter builds on constructs taken from psychological research arena. Specifically, it is to examine how justice and cultural openness correlate with individual psychological variables such as job satisfaction and organizational identification (Berthold 2005; Grewe 2005; Piske et al. 2006). Therefore, in this empirical chapter employees' perceptions are to be investigated. Questions to be answered in this research are (1) How fair do employees feel to be treated and how culturally open are the employees? (2) How do these factors impact individual psychological outcomes such as job satisfaction and organizational identification?

The paper is structured as follows. The chapter proceeds by first providing a theoretical background and then comes up with some hypotheses. Next, methods are described and then the results are discussed. The final section provides discussion and implications for future research.

13.2 Theoretical Background

13.2.1 Effect on Procedural Justice

The term justice (in the literature also called: fairness) refers to the idea that an action or decision is morally right (Tabibnia et al. 2008). Organizational justice is then the applied form to organizations. It is a topic of recent interest in industrial and organizational psychology. Organizational justice refers to how morally right employees feel to be treated (Eberlin and Tatum 2008).

Organizational justice can be divided into distributive justice, defined as outcome oriented as well as in a procedural one, defined as decision making process (McFarlin and Sweeney 1992; Colquitt 2001; Melkonian et al. 2011).

Procedural justice is concerned with formal aspects (Folger and Dies 1989) and can be defined as a process oriented justice (Konovsky and Cropanzano 1991; Phillips et al. 2001). This construct measures how much individuals feel that they have a voice in a given process (Leventhal 1980). Recently, procedural justice has received increasing attention from strategy scholars (Ellis et al. 2009; Luo 2007) and also this chapter focuses solely on procedural justice.

Two other variables investigated at this chapter are job satisfaction and organizational identification. Job satisfaction refers to the feeling of employees as a mental state and can be described as "how satisfied are employees at the target firm". Organizational identification measures how much an employee identifies with their new firm. Job satisfaction reflects a rather current situation while identification is long term based. To put different, the difference between these two variables is that even if employees are not happy with their current situation (job satisfaction), they may still identify with their firm (organizational identification).

Previous research conducted at other firms shows that procedural justice is positively related to the success of individual psychological outcome criteria (Klendauer and Deller 2009). For example, Tyler and Blader (2000) find evidence that procedural justice positively affects the satisfaction of employees and their commitment to the firm (Tyler and Blader 2000). This positive correlation becomes even stronger especially at uncertain environments, when employees for example feel unsafe about their future (Van Den Bos 2001). Taken all together, employees which feel to be treated in a rather fair manner by the top management of the bidder firm at the M&A process should have a higher job satisfaction. Also, these employees should have a higher organizational identification with their firm (Lind 2001). The above leads to the following two hypotheses:

Hypothesis 1.1: Higher perceived procedural justice will be positively related to job satisfaction of employees at a cross border acquisition.

Hypothesis 1.2: Higher perceived procedural justice will be positively related to organizational identification of employees at a cross border acquisition.

13.2.2 Effect on Cultural Openness

Literature about cultural openness of employees on acquisitions has been conceptionelly and empirically validated (Stahl and Voigt 2008; Teerikangas 2007; Teerikangas and Very 2006; Earley and Ang 2003). Culture can be basically divided into a national and a firm level culture. There is evidence that even when coming from the same country the bidder and the target employees may culturally differ. There is some evidence suggesting that domestic acquisitions can be as challenging as cross border ones (Sarala and Vaara 2010; Weber et al. 2009; Weber and Drori 2008).

There is a long research stream on cultural change, focusing on how successfully two firms are able to merge their previous cultures into a new one (Earley and Mosakowski 2004). In negative terms, a cultural clash can exist if the firms are not able to overcome the cultural changes and the whole acquisition will result in failure (Weber and Drori 2008; Weber et al. 2009). On the other side, there is some evidence that different cultures of target and bidder firms can also have its advantages. In this case creative resources and learning processes could be established (Sarala and Vaara 2010; Goulet and Schweiger 2006; Reus and Lamont 2009).

Cultural openness in its way is an attitude of employees to cope with new cultures (Peterson 2004; Ng and Earley 2006). This refers to a mental openness of employees (Thomas 2006). That means, more cultural intelligent employees are more flexible to adapt at new circumstances. It is therefore investigated to which degree the cultural openness influences employees' job satisfaction and their organizational identification. It is suggested that culturally more open employees are more likely to favor M&A transactions as they might benefit more from such activities. For example, culturally more open employees at the target firm could take the acquisition rather as a chance to learn from the bidder side new techniques. Especially at our cross border acquisition, culturally more open employees can more easily communicate with the bidder firm employees. Also, some may even want to get more internationalized. There would be more chances to practice English and also traveling could increase.

There are also for employees at the bidder side arguments that the culturally more open employees should feel more job satisfied and better identified. More culturally open minded bidder firm employees' can easier communicate with their new target firm colleagues. To sum up, a higher cultural openness for employees at both sides of the new firm should lead to a higher job satisfaction and a higher organizational identification. In line with these arguments, the following hypotheses are presented:

Hypothesis 2.1: Cultural openness will be positively related to job satisfaction at a cross border acquisition.

Hypothesis 2.2: Cultural openness will be positively related to organizational identification at a cross border acquisition.

13.2.3 Effect of Cultural Openness on Procedural Justice

Besides our main hypotheses that procedural justice and cultural openness should matter for employees in order to have more job satisfaction and a better organizational identification, it is proposed that employees with a higher cultural openness should also be more sensitive to be treated fairly in order to be satisfied and integrated to their job. That means, the management might focus especially on culturally more open minded employees, to treat them in a fair manner. In contrast, culturally not open minded employees do not care as much about a favorable perceived fair treatment. The impact of fair treatment for them is; therefore, rather low. The arguments above lead to two interaction term hypotheses: (Fig. 13.1)

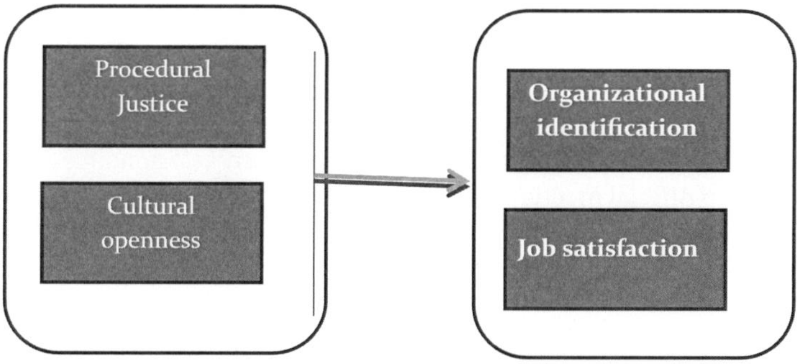

Fig. 13.1 Model

Hypothesis 3.1: Employee perceptions of procedural justice will be more positively related to job satisfaction when cultural openness is rather high than low.

Hypothesis 3.2: Employee perceptions of procedural justice will be more positively related to organizational identification when cultural openness is rather high than low.

13.3 Methods

13.3.1 Sample and Procedure

This research investigates employee perceptions at a cross border acquisition in Japan. Specifically, it is investigated of how fair they perceived to be treated and of how culturally open they are. The bidder firm is a Japan-based German subsidiary in the technical testing device industry. The top management of the German subsidiary was already in Japan long before the takeover was announced. The leading executive of the Japan based German subsidiary is a German but living in Japan for many years, which speaks fluent Japanese. Some other managers at the bidder firm are non-Japanese but also with a good knowledge about Japan. In contrast, the Japanese managers at the bidder firm can be considered as German influenced as they work at the German subsidiary. Having this constellation of a knowledgeable bidder firm about the host country but still different to a local (Japanese) firm, this study is a unique attempt of investigation because both firm employees' will be affected by the acquisition. Therefore, a study of employee perceptions and their changes seems to be a fruitful attempt.

The questionnaire was administered in two rounds. It was first distributed in July 2012, shortly after the official announcement of the takeover. The second round of distribution took place half a year later, in December 2012. That was the time some strategic changes were implemented at the target firm. The leader of the German subsidiary personally requested all employees in a special meeting to participate at the survey. Then, a link to the internet based questionnaire was sent out from the subsidiary management to all of its 72 employees of the target firm and to about 120 employees in its own subsidiary. In all, 102 employees followed the announcement after the second reminder and responded to the survey. The second round of the questionnaire was sent out 6 month after the first official announcement of the deal. Again, in an official meeting the leader proposed the second round and the link was sent to all of the employees. A total of 99 employees participated at the second round.

13.3.2 Measures

The construct "procedural justice" of "how much the employees still have to say" was measured with 7 items. The construct "organizational identification" was measured with 12 items as revised from the Organizational Identification Questionnaire (Cheney 1983), including the eight items used by Gautam et al. (2004) but changed to M&A content. The construct "job satisfaction" was measured with six items closely related to the short version of the Minnesota Satisfaction Questionnaire by Igalens and Roussel (1999) but also adapted to M&A and target firms. The construct "cultural openness" was composed of five items, measuring openness to change (Wanberg and Banas 2000).

The organizational tenure "firm years" were measured in five groups. First group was "under 1 year" and the fifth group was "over 16 years employed at the firm". Therefore, the term three e.g. means the group "under 10 years employed at the firm". That grouping was done as the bidder firm management did not want the participants to fear that their responses could be traced back to them. Because of this type of categorization, a moderator analysis taking the variable related to firm years was not performed.

13.4 Results

First, descriptive statistics are discussed. The average of the employees' response to the items related to justice was just above the neutral point of 3, which indicates that employees perceived that they were treated fairly. The average response to items related to cultural openness was 3.70 for the first round and 3.58 for the second round. This means that employees at the new firm are rather open minded. The mean of the respondents' job satisfaction level was 2.87 in both rounds, which is well below the neutral point. Organizational Identification has values above mean such as 3.43 (for the first round) and 3.31 (for the second round).

To interpret these results, employees at the new firm feel more or less to be treated fairly having employees with a rather high cultural openness. As the subsidiary employees were exposed to the German headquarter before the acquisition, the results for our explanatory variables are reasonable.

Table 13.1 Descriptive statistics and correlation matrix (round 1)

	M	SD	[1]	[2]	[3]	[4]
Procedural justice [1]	3.272	0.839				
Cultural openness [2]	3.7	0.727	0.09			
Firm years [3]	2.96	1.238	−0.164	0.034		
Organizational identification [4]	3.43	0.65	0.461***	0.078	−0.075	
Job satisfaction [5]	2.867	0.663	0.518***	−0.057	−0.183*	0.295***

*=10%; ***=1%

Table 13.2 Descriptive statistics and correlation matrix (round 2)

	M	SD	[1]	[2]	[3]	[4]
Procedural justice [1]	3.112	0.716				
Cultural openness [2]	3.582	0.759	−0.051			
Firm years [3]	2.9	1.165	0.026	−0.111		
Organizational identification [4]	3.315	0.64263	0.592***	0.105	0.04	
Job satisfaction [5]	2.866	0.675	0.637***	0.018	−0.223**	0.438***

*=10%; ***=1%

Our dependent variables such as job satisfaction shows that employees are rather less satisfied with their jobs but that the organizational identification still tends to be more to the positive side. That can be interpreted as follows: even the employees are not as happy in a given moment, they still identify with their firm. The correlation analyses (Tables 13.1 and 13.2) show that job satisfaction and organizational identification loads positively with justice. Also, job satisfaction loads positively with organizational identification. Job satisfaction has a negative correlation to firm years. That means, younger employees with a shorter tenure at the firm have a higher job satisfaction than the ones with a longer tenure. This last result is reasonable as employees with a longer tenure at the firm might face more trouble with the new setting than younger employees. For example, younger employees at the target firm might hope to become more international. They could have a chance to practice more English and be equipped with non-Japanese management methods. Therefore, a takeover should have different impact at a given tenure at the firm.

In the first round data of our regression analyses (Table 13.3), the perception of procedural justice was found to have significant effects on both job satisfaction and organizational identification related variables (Table 13.3 model 1 and 3). However, when including the interaction effects there was not anymore a significance visible (Table 13.3 model 2 and 4).

In the second round data (Table 13.4), having organizational identification as the dependent variable, procedural justice has a significant positive effect (Table 13.4, model 3 and 4). In the regression models with job satisfaction as the dependent

Table 13.3 Regression analyses results for round 1 data

	Job satisfaction model 1	Job satisfaction model 2	Organizational identification model 1	Organizational identification model 2
Constant	1.883***	3.584	2.195***	2.712
Firm years	−0.047	−0.05	−0.024	−0.025
Procedural justice	0.414***	−0.086	0.342***	0.191
Cultural openness	−0.062	−0.496	0.048	−0.083
Procedural justice* cultural openness		0.128		0.039
R^2	0.281	0.29	0.207	0.208
Adj.R^2	0.252	0.252	0.175	0.165
F	*9.771****	*7.568****	*6.446*^{c}	*4.796****
N	79	79	78	78

*=10%; ***=1%

Table 13.4 Regression analyses results for round 2 data

	Job satisfaction model 1	Job satisfaction model 2	Organizational identification model 1	Organizational identification model 2
Constant	1.367***	3.829***	1.221***	−0.187
Firm years	−0.164***	−0.171***	0.018	0.021
Procedural justice	0.645***	−0.146	0.531***	0.983**
Cultural openness	−0.015	−0.661**	0.113	0.483
Procedural justice*cultural openness		0.21**		−0.12
R^2	0.486	0.51	0.332	0.341
Adj.R^2	0.469	0.487	0.309	0.31
F	*27.151****	*22.13****	*14.258****	*11.001****
N	90	90	90	90

*=10%; **=5%; ***=1%

variable, procedural justice has only a significant positive effect when not putting in interaction effects. However, when including the interaction effects of this variable, no significant results were received (Table 13.4).

The effects are more significant with the second round data than with the first round data. Hypothesis 1.1 and 1.2 are thus mainly supported by the data. For both rounds of data, cultural openness has no direct significant effect on organizational identification ($p>0.10$ in all models in Tables 13.3 and 13.4). Hypotheses 2.1 and 2.2 are not supported by the results. There is mixed results for the moderating variable of cultural openness and procedural justice on job satisfaction as the dependent variable. At least at the second round, a significant interaction effect of procedural justice and cultural openness was found (Table 13.4, model 2). This means that among employees that perceive higher level of procedural justice, job satisfaction is higher among more culturally open employees than those with lower level of cultural openness. Besides, the findings do not provide support for hypothesis 3.2. The findings thus suggest that employees with a higher level of cultural openness are no different from those with a lower level of cultural openness in terms of organizational identification in cross-cultural M&A.

13.5 Discussion

The above findings show that the post-integration success of cross border M&A hinges strongly on the ability of the acquirer to create a perception of fairness (justice) within the newly created organization. The higher proportions of variance explained at the variable job satisfaction compared with organizational identification imply that employees with different levels of perceptions of procedural justice and different levels of cultural openness show a higher variability in terms of job satisfaction than to organizational identification. Moreover, corresponding values of R^2 are higher for the second round data than for the first round, which indicated a temporal effect in the relationship between the independent and dependent variables. These observations indicate that it had advantages to have a time lag in the response of employees' perception of justice.

Also, employees with longer organizational tenure are more dissatisfied than those with a shorter tenure in the post-acquisition integration stage (Time 2). This result suggests that employees with shorter organizational tenure are more flexible and generous even when their employer is taken over in a cross border deal.

In the post-acquisition stage at time 2, employees higher in cultural openness are more likely to be generous and accept ongoing changes when they are treated in a procedurally fair manner. The reason might be that those employees have a higher ability to understand management practices which have different cultural perspectives.

13.6 Conclusion

The results of this study extend the literature on organizational justice by providing evidence that perception of justice has distinct contributions in affecting job satisfaction and organizational identification in cross border acquisitions. A further contribution of this study is in examining how the relationships changes over time. From the comparison of the magnitudes of regression coefficients (and correlation coefficients) between round 1 and 2, it is clear that the effect of procedural justice on satisfaction and organizational identification becomes stronger as time goes by.

Despite the above contributions, this study has its own limitations. The focus of this analysis was laid on procedural justice as done in many other studies (Lipponen et al. 2004). Therefore, other justice criteria, like distributive justice was excluded. Against Adams, a workplace and behavioral psychologist, it is not investigated about employees and their fair treatment which might cause them to be (or not to be) motivated. In future studies, input of employees could be measured to their outcomes that they receive from it or, alternatively, measured against other members of the organizations (Adams 1965). Because even it is based on the deprivation theory by Stouffer et al. (1949) and then developed to the equity theory by Adams (1965), it does not fit into investigating employees' perception at our setting. Furthermore, it was not possible to connect both rounds of the questionnaires. Therefore, only two cross sectional studies were possible to conduct without being able to sort out whether e.g. justice influenced identification or the other way around. Also, it would have been helpful to cluster employees in regular and in a group of non-regular ones, for example in dispatched employees (as discussed in Chap. 12). As it was not possible to implement this question at the questionnaire; employees had to be put together into one single group. However, at both of the participating firms, there was a rather low portion of non-regulars, so that it should not matter to treat all employees the same.

In spite of its limitations, this investigation is based on real firm data, placed in a unique setting and it is my hope to enrich the strategic literature with it.

Questionnaire (English Version, Distributed to the BIDDER Firm)

Procedural Justice

1. How do you agree to the following statements in regard to (TARGET) participation?
   - I have been able to express my views and feelings
   - I have had influence over the outcome
   - The decision-making processes have been applied consistently
   - The decision-making processes have been free of bias
   - The decisions have been based on accurate information
   - I have been able to appeal the outcomes
   - The decision-making processes have upheld ethical and moral standards

Cultural Openness

2. How do you agree to the following statements about other cultures?
   - I enjoy interacting with people from other cultures
   - I am confident that I can socialize with locals in a culture that is unfamiliar to me

- I am sure I can deal with the stresses of adjusting to a culture that is new to me
- I enjoy living in cultures that are unfamiliar to me
- I am confident that I can get accustomed to the shopping conditions in a different culture

Organizational Identification

3. How do you agree to the following statements?
   - When I talk about (BIDDER), I usually say 'we' rather than 'they'
   - TSJ successes are my success
   - When someone praises (BIDDER), it feels like a personal compliment
   - If a story in the media criticizes (BIDDER), I would feel embarrassed
   - When someone criticizes (BIDDER), it feels like a personal insult
   - I am very interested in what other think about (BIDDER)
   - When I talk about (TARGET), I usually say 'we' rather than 'they'
   - (TARGET)' successes are my success
   - When someone praises (TARGET), it feel like a personal compliment
   - If a story in the media criticizes (TARGET), I would feel embarrassed
   - When someone criticizes (TARGET), it feels like a personal insult
   - I am very interested in what others think about (TARGET)

Job Satisfaction

4. How would you answer the following questions?
   - I am satisfied with the company
   - I am satisfied with my job security at the company
   - I am satisfied with the overall communication in the company
   - I am satisfied with the facilities provided by the company
   - I am satisfied with my job
   - I am satisfied with my salary in the company
   - I am satisfied with the opportunities to advance in the company
   - I am satisfied with the training & development provided by the company

Questions

1. How do you describe the term "procedural justice"?
2. Why is organizational identification of employees of detrimental importance to a successful M&A post integration?
3. Why does it make sense that job satisfaction and organizational identification have a positive relationship?
4. According to this study outcome, do fair treated employees have a higher job satisfaction

5. According to this study outcome, do fair treated employees have a higher organizational identification?
6. Do culturally more open employees feel a higher job satisfaction?
7. Do culturally more open employees feel a higher organizational identification?
8. Do culturally more open employees with a fairer treatment (higher procedural justice) have a higher job satisfaction?
9. Do culturally more open employees with a fairer treatment (higher procedural justice) have a higher organizations identification?
10. Why should culturally more open employees have a higher job satisfaction but not a higher organizational identification?

Answers

1. "Procedural Justice" is a construct in psychology what measures how fair an employee feels to be treated. Precisely, how much saying an employee has and to what extent he/she is a part of the whole process. This measure in M&A research is normally positive to organizational identification, meaning the higher the perception to be treated in a fair way leads to a higher organizational identification.
2. Only employees which identify with their organization will give the new firm the chance to outperform other competitors. To put different, when employees do not identify themselves with the new organizations, a performance increase can not be expected.
3. That makes sense and means, that satisfied employees do preferably also have a better organizational identification with their firm.
4. Yes, fair treated employees have a higher job satisfaction.
5. Yes, fair treated employees have a higher organizational identification.
6. No, there was no correlation found between these two constructs.
7. No, also at these two constructs there was no correlation found.
8. Yes, there are at least mixed results, with a significance for the second year.
9. No, there was no significance found.
10. Organizational identification is a long term process, while job satisfaction is a merely short period. Employees might feel shortly happy but that does not mean that their identification to the firm changed at the long term.

References

Adams JS (1965) Inequity in social exchange. In: Berkowitz L (ed) Advances in experimental social psychology, vol 2. Elsevier, San Diego, pp 267–299

Aguilera RV, Dencker JC (2004) The role of human resource management in cross-border mergers and acquisitions. Int J Hum Resour Manage 15(8):1355–1370

Barney JB (1991) Firm resources and sustained competitive advantage. J Manage 17(1):99–120

Becker DR (2005) Der Ressourcen-Fit bei M&A-Transaktionen. Deutscher Universitats-Verlag, Wiesbaden

Berthold C (2005) Unternehmenskultur, strukturelle Voraussetzungen und Erfolg von Unternechmenszusammenschluessen. Shaker, Aachen

Cheney C (1983) The rhetoric of identification and the study of organizational communication. Q J Speech 69(2):143–158

Colquitt JA (2001) On the dimensionality of organizational justice: a construct validation of a measure. J Appl Psychol 86:386–400

Earley PC, Ang S (2003) Cultural intelligence: individual interactions across cultures. Stanford Business Books, Stanford

Earley PC, Mosakowski E (2004) Cultural intelligence. Harvard Bus Rev 82(10):139–146

Eberlin RJ, Tatum BC (2008) Making just decisions: organizational justice, decision making, and leadership. Manage Decis 46(2):310–329

Ellis KM, Reus TH, Lamont BT (2009) The effects of procedural and informational justice in the integration of related acquisitions. Strateg Manage J 30:137–161

Folger K, Dies KJ (1989) Managerial responsibilities and procedural justice. Empl Responsib Rights J 2:79–90

Fried Y, Tiegs R, Naughton T, Ashforth B (1996) Managers' reactions to a corporate acquisition: a test of an integrative model. J Organ Behav 17:401–427

Fugate M, Kinicki AJ, Scheck C (2002) Coping with an organizational merger over four stages. Pers Psychol 55(4):905–928

Gautam T, Van Dick R, Wagner U (2004) Organizational identification and organizational commitment: distinct aspects of two related concepts. Asian J Soc Psychol 7(3):301–315

Gerpott TJ (2009) Forschung & Entwicklung und technologieorientierte Unternehmensakquisitionen. Z Planung Unternehmenssteuerung 20:9–41

Gerpott TJ, Neubauer FB (2011) Integrationsgestaltung und Zusammenschlusserfolg nach einer Unternehmensakquisition—Eine empirische Studie aus Mitarbeitersicht. Z fuer Betriebswirtschaftliche Forschung, ZfBf 63:118–154

Glaum M, Hutzschenreuter T (2010) Merger & acquisitions. Stuttgart, p 94

Goulet PK, Schweiger DM (2006) Managing culture and human resources in merger and acquisitions. In: Stahl Guenter K, Bjorkman I (eds) Handbook of research in international human research management. Edward Elgar Publishing, Northampton, pp 405–429

Grewe A (2005) Integration akquirierter Unternehmen. Peter Lang, Frankfurt a. M.

Grimpe C (2005) Post-merger integration der forschung und entwicklung. Deutscher Universitätsvlg, Wiesbaden, pp 82–102

Haspeslagh P, Jemison DB (1991) Managing acquisitions: creating value through corporate renewal. Free Press, New York

Homburg F, Klarmann M (2009) Multi Informant-Designs in der empirischen betriebswirtschaftlichen Forschung. Die Betriebswirtschaft 69:151–157

Hoyningen-Huene J (2004) Integration nach Unternehmensakquisitionen. Deutscher Universitätsverlag, Wiesbaden, pp 371–373

Hurrle B, Kieser A (2005) Sind key informants verlässliche datenlieferanten? Die Betriebswirtschaft 65:586–598

Igalens J, Roussel P (1999) A study of the relationships between compensation package, work motivation and job satisfaction. J Organ Behav 20(7):1003–1025

Klendauer R, Deller J (2009) Organizational justice and managerial commitment in corporate mergers. J Managerial Psychol 24(1):29–45
Konovsky MA, Cropanzano R (1991) The perceived fairness of employee drug testing as a predictor of employee attitudes and job performance. J Appl Psychol 76:689–707
Leventhal GS (1980) What should be done with equity theory? New approaches to the study of fairness in social relationship. In: Gergen K, Greenberg M, Willis R (eds) Social exchange: advances in theory and research. Plenum Press, New York, pp 27–55
Lind EA (2001) Fairness heuristic theory: justice judgements as pivotal cognitions in organizational relations. In: Greenberg J, Cropanzano R (eds) Advances in organizational justice. Stanford University Press, Stanford, pp 56–88
Lipponen J, Olkkonen ME, Moilanen M (2004) Perceived procedural justice and employee responses to an organizational merger. Eur J Work Organ Psychol 13(3):391–413
Luo Y (2007) The independent and interactive roles of procedural, distributive and interactional justice in strategic alliances. Acad Manage J 50(3):644–664
McFarlin DB, Sweeney PD (1992) Distributive and procedural justice as predictors of satisfaction with personal and organizational outcomes. Acad Manage J 35(3):626–637
Meglio O, Risberg A (2010) Merger and acquisitions: time for a methodological rejuvenation of the field? Scand J Manage 26:87–95
Melkonian T, Monin P, Noorderhaven NG (2011) Distributive justice, procedural justice, exemplarity, and employees' willingness to cooperate in M&A integration processes: an analysis of the Air France-KLM merger. Hum Res Manage 50(6):809–837
Moeller SB, Schlingemann FP (2005) Global diversification and bidder gains: a comparison between cross-border and domestic acquisitions. J Bank Finance 29:533–564
Mueller-Stewens G (2010) Post merger integration: Zum Stand des Wissens. In: Mueller-Stewens G, Kusnich S, Binder A (eds) Merger & acquisitions: analysen, trends und best practices. Poeschel, Stuttgart, pp 198–228
Ng KY, Earley PC (2006) Culture and intelligence: old constructs, new frontiers. Group Organ Manage 31(1):4–19
Peterson B (2004) Cultural intelligence: a guide to working with people from other cultures. Intercultural Press, Yarmouth
Phillips JM, Douthitt EA, Hyland MAM (2001) The role of justice in team member satisfaction with the leader and attachment to the team. J Appl Psychol 86(2):316–324
Piske R, Gebert D, Lahnwehr R (2006) Wann vertraut ein akquiriertes Unternehmen dem Akquisiteur? Die Betriebwirtschaft 66:54–68
Reus TH, Lamont BT (2009) The double-edged sword of cultural distance in international acquisitions. J Int Bus Stud 40:1298–1316
Sarala RM, Vaara E (2010) Cultural differences, convergence, and crossvergence as explanations of knowledge transfer in international acquisitions. J Int Bus Stud 41:1365–1390
Stahl GK, Voigt A (2008) Do cultural differences on merger and acquisitions performance: a critical research review and an integrative model. In: Cooper C, Finkelstein S (eds) Advances in mergers & acquisitions, vol 4. Emerald Group, Bingley, pp 51–82
Stouffer S, Suchman EA, DeVinney LC, Star SA, Williams RM (1949) Adjustment during army life. Princeton University Press, Princeton
Tabibnia G, Satpute AB, Lieberman MD (2008) The sunny side of fairness: preference for fairness activates reward circuitry. Psychol Sci 19:339–347
Teerikangas S (2007) A comparative overview of the impact of cultural diversity on inter-organisational encounters. In: Cooper C, Finkelstein S (eds) Advances in mergers & acquisitions, vol 6. Emerald Group, Bingley, pp 37–75
Teerikangas S, Very P (2006) The culture-performance relationship in M&A: from yes/no to how. Br J Manage 17:31–48
Thomas DC (2006) Domain and development of cultural intelligence: the importance of mindfulness. Group Organ Manage 31(1):78–99
Tyler TR, Blader SL (2000) Cooperation in groups. Procedural justice, social identity, and behavioral engagement. Psychology Press, Philadelphia

Van den Bos K (2001) Uncertainty management: the influence of uncertainty salience on reactions to perceived procedural fairness. J Personal Soc Psychol 80:931–941
Wanberg CR, Banas JT (2000) Predictors and outcomes of openness to changes in a reorganizing workplace. J Appl Psychol 85:132–142
Weber Y, Drori I (2008) The linkages between cultural differences, psychological states, and performance in international mergers and acquisitions. In: Cooper C, Finkelstein S (eds) Advances in mergers & acquisitions. Emerald Group, Bingley, pp 119–142
Weber Y, Tarba SY (2010) Human resource practices and performance of mergers and acquisitions in Israel. Hum Resour Manage Rev 20:203–211
Weber Y, Tarba SY, Reichel A (2009) International mergers and acquisitions performance revisited- the role of cultural distance and post-acquisition integration approach. In: Cooper C, Finkelstein S (eds) Advances in mergers & acquisitions. Emerald Group, Bingley, pp 1–17

Chapter 14
Cultural Concepts

Abstract This chapter deals with culture because an understanding of the impact of culture on one's behavior is critical to the study of international business. If Managers are not aware of cultural differences, e.g. hardly understand the Japanese culture, problems may occur due to misunderstandings.

This chapter discusses the roots of cultures and the dimensions of those cultures by introducing one of the most often cited studies conducted by Hofstede. Data from its dimension model for several countries will be reported. Additionally, the Global Leadership and Organisational Behavior Effectiveness project as well as the cultural dimensions by Trompenaars will be presented.

14.1 Introduction

The word culture derives from the Latin word "cultura" and is related to worship and cult. The term refers in its broadest sense to human interaction (Joynt and Warner 1996). Culture is acquired knowledge that people generate through social interactions. Although cultural norms, customs, and practices change, they do not change easily nor do they change at the same rate. Changes occur in response to the economic environment and technical demands. Put differently, culture is embedded in a social structure that is quite resistant to change (Robinson 2003). Besides the national culture, firm specific cultures is also important to consider. In this chapter, however, only the national culture will be analyzed. From one's national culture, values will be formed, attitudes created, and behaviors influenced. The following characteristics are generally used to describe the concept of a culture (Luthans 1995). A culture is:

- Learned: Culture is not biologically based or inherited; rather, it is acquired by learning and experience.
- Shared: Culture consists of people as members of a group or organization; it is not specific to single individuals.
- Trans generational: Culture is cumulative; it is passed down from one generation to the next one.

R. Bebenroth, *International Business Mergers and Acquisitions in Japan*,
DOI 10.1007/978-4-431-54989-5_14

- Symbolic: Culture is based on the human capacity to comprehend symbolism; or using one thing to represent the other.
- Patterned: Culture exists within a structure and is fully integrated; a change in one part of the culture will bring changes to other parts.
- Adaptive: Culture is based on changes and adaption; This is different than the genetic adaption that occurs in human beings.

The national culture can serve as an explanation as well as a prediction of how organizations are formed. A national culture is based on cultural perceptions, attitudes, values and goals of the people within that culture (Hostede 1980, 2001; Trompenaars 1994). To analyze a national culture, characteristics of it are grouped into dimensions.

14.2 Studies of Cultural Dimensions

To cover the most important concepts discussed in the literature, we will discuss the concepts of Hofstede (Hofstede 2010), the GLOBE project (House et al. 2002), and the research done by Trompenaars (Trompenaars 1994).

14.2.1 Cultural Dimension Research by Hofstede

The dimensions described by Hofstede in the early 1980s, is one of most widely recognised methods to measure country specific cultures; however it is also strongly criticized (1980, 2001). The original study by Hofstede (1980) was based on a survey of 88,000 IBM managers and employees in 66 countries. The aim of this study was to find out how people differ in their behaviour according to the country they live in. For example, how do the behaviours of the Japanese differ to those of the French? Through his study, Hofstede originally identified four cultural dimensions (Hofstede Centre 2014). The scores for each of the four dimensions start as low as 0 points and go as high as 100 points. Recently, Hofstede has added several new dimensions. In 2001, Hofstede added a fifth dimension, short-term vs. long term, which increases the maximum score to 120 points. Furthermore, in collaboration with Minkow (Hofstede et al. 2010), two more dimensions were added, "indulgence vs. constraint" and "pragmatic vs. normativistic" societies. These dimensions are briefly explained below, in regard to Japan.

Table below shows the seven dimensions:

1. Power Distance Index (autocratic v. democratic management style)
2. Uncertainty Avoidance Index (tolerance of uncertainty v. certainty)
3. Individuality (individualism v. collectivism)
4. Masculinity v. Femininity (degree of masculine assertiveness v. feminine)
5. Long-term Index (long term v. short term)
6. Pragmatism Index (pragmatism v. normativism)
7. Indulgence Index (indulgent v. constraint)

14.2.1.1 Power Distance Index (PDI)

The Power Distance Index (PDI) is the extent to which the less powerful members of organizations and institutions accept and expect that power is unequally distributed. This represents more versus less inequality, but defined from the perspective of those not in power, not from those in power. This suggests that the followers as much as the leaders, endorse a society's level of inequality. Power and inequality are fundamental to any society and anybody with some international experience will be aware that "all societies are unequal, but some are more unequal than others" (Hofstede 2001). Japan receives a middle range score of 54 points for this dimension.

14.2.1.2 Uncertainty Avoidance Index (UAI)

The Uncertainty Avoidance Index (UAI) deals with a society's tolerance for uncertainty and ambiguity. It indicates to what extent a culture programs its members to feel either uncomfortable or comfortable in unstructured situations. Unstructured situations are situations which are novel, unknown, surprising, and different from usual. People in countries that try to avoid uncertainty do this by enacting strict laws and rules, safety regulations, security measures; and on the philosophical and religious level, by a belief in absolute truth. People in countries that try to avoid uncertainty are on the one hand also more emotional, and motivated by one's nervousness. On the other hand, countries that accept uncertainty, are more tolerant of opinions different from what they are used to; they try to have as few rules as possible, and on the philosophical and religious level they are relativist and allow many currents to flow side by side. People within these cultures are more phlegmatic and contemplative, and not expected by their environment to express emotions.

Japan scores the highest in this category out of all participating countries, with a score of 92 points, which means that the Japanese are extremely concerned about avoiding uncertainty. This fact can be observed every day in train stations when people board a train. People will stand exactly at the marked signs where the train doors will open. The load speaker voice informs passengers exactly about what to do and what not to do. For example, passengers are informed to stand in two lines, not to stand out of it—and not to move forward before the train has finally arrived.

14.2.1.3 Individuality (IDV)

Individuality (IDV), is the range between individualism on one side, and collectivism, the degree to which individuals are integrated into groups, on the other. In individualistic societies ties between individuals are loose: everyone is expected to look after him/herself and his/her immediate family. Collectivistic societies have people integrated into strong, cohesive in-groups from birth onwards. Collectivistic societies are often characterized by extended families, which include uncles, aunts and grandparents, and unquestioning loyalty. The word 'collectivism' in this sense has no political meaning: it refers to the group, not the state. The issue addressed by this dimension is according to Hofstede rather a fundamental one.

In this dimension Japan has a mid-low score with 46 points, whereas the USA has a relatively high score of 91 points. This means that the US culture is extremely individualistic. The rather low score for Japan can be traced to the childhood of every Japanese. In Japanese schools it is always more important to blend into the group, rather than to stand out with unusual, but possibly interesting, ideas. Recently, it is very common for young Japanese women to have an expensive Gucci designer bag. These designer bags are visible all over the city; however, the popularity of these bags stems not necessarily from quality, but from the fact that almost everyone seems to have one. This creates pressure for the minority group to buy one, so as to not stand out.

14.2.1.4 Masculinity (MAS)

Masculinity (MAS) versus femininity refers to the distribution of roles between the genders, which is another fundamental issue for every society to which a range of solutions can be found. This dimension encompasses more than a simple distinction between men and women. According to Hofstede, masculinity is described as, "a situation in which the dominant values in society are success, money and things" (Hofstede 1980, pp. 419–420). On the other hand, femininity is described as "a situation in which the dominant values in society are caring for others and the quality of life" (Hofstede 1980, p. 420). Women in feminine countries have the same modest, caring values as men. In contrast, masculine countries are rather assertive and competitive.

In this dimension, Japan has the highest score (95 points), whereas Sweden has the lowest score with only 5 points. This means that Japan is an extremely masculine country in contrast to Sweden, which is very feminine. This extremely masculine culture can be easily seen in the Japanese business world. Hard work is highly appreciated and there are high levels of competition between rivals. Many employees do overtime at work because it has a positive connotation. Additionally, women are hardly seen in the Japanese business world, which is significant even though the masculinity measure is not merely the difference between women and men.

14.2.1.5 Long-Term Orientation (LTO)

Long-Term Orientation (LTO) versus short-term orientation is the fifth dimension, which was introduced in 2001. This dimension is based on a study conducted by Chinese scholars about students in 23 countries around the world. Values associated with long term orientation are respect for tradition, fulfilling one's social obligations, and protecting one's 'face'. The values defined by this dimension can be found throughout the teachings of Confucius, the most influential Chinese philosopher who lived around 500 B.C. However, this dimension also applies to countries without a Confucian heritage.

After China and Hong Kong, Japan scores third highest with 80 points in long-term orientation. This is significant especially at the business world. Contracts for Japanese managers, for example, are often seen as future investments. For many Japanese, the aim of business transaction is not immediate profit, but rather the formation of a long-term relationship. This dimension causes major problems when it comes to international joint projects, for example, when joint ventures involving western firms. Joint ventures between Japanese and US firms, especially, tend to be ridden with misunderstandings, which cause friction between both firms. Usually, the US firms are more focused on making immediate profit out of the joint venture while Japanese firms are looking to increase profits in the long-run.

14.2.1.6 Pragmatism (PRA)

Pragmatism is a dimension, which was introduced in 2010 (Hofstede et al. 2010). It describes how people relate to what happens around them, and how this can or cannot be explained. The opposite of pragmatism is normativism. Societies with a normativistic orientation are characterized by people that have a strong desire to explain as much as possible. In contrast, societies with a pragmatic orientation are characterized by people that feel little need to explain everything. Pragmatic societies believe that it is impossible to fully understand the complexity of life, which means "The challenge is not to know the truth but to live a virtuous life" (Hofstede Centre 2014).

Japan is considered one of the most pragmatic oriented societies with 88 points. To Japanese, life is seen as a short moment compared to a long history of mankind. Hofstede points out that some kind of fatalism is not strange to this culture. "You do your best in your life time and that is all that you can do" (Hostede Centre 2014). The notion of single god does not exist to most Japanese. Instead their lives are guided by virtues and the good examples set by others. For example, the founder of Matsushita Denki (now: Panasonic Corporation) Konozuke Matsushita, was a role model for many employees. In corporate Japan, R&D is also long term orientated and is largely regarded as an investment in the future and is undertaken even in economically difficult times. Rather than focus on higher quarterly profits, Japanese firms place a higher priority on the growth of market share and the number of employees. The idea behind this pragmatic approach is that firms do not serve their shareholders, but their stakeholders, which in most cases are normal Japanese (Hofstede Center 2014).

14.2.1.7 Indulgence (IND)

Indulgence is "the extent to which people try to control their desires and impulses" (Hofstede centre 2014). A challenge of humanity nowadays is the degree to which little children are socialized to fit into society in later life. Without socialization there is no route to become "human." This means, desires and impulses are based on the way children are raised. A society that weakly controls children, is called an "indulgent" society; while a society that strongly control for children, is called a "restraint" society. Cultures can therefore, be described as indulgent or as restrained, depending on their control when raising children.

Societies with a low score in this dimension, according to Hofstede, have a tendency towards cynicism and pessimism. In contrast to indulgent societies, leisure time has a high value in restrained societies. As a result, people in restrained societies place a high value on efforts and achievements. People with a restrained orientation also have positive feeling towards small amounts of pressure.

In this category Japan, scores relatively low with only 42 points. This means that Japan is a relatively restrained culture and that children are rather strongly socialized to fit into Japanese society. Translated into business world, employees that are transferred to a new location, usually within the same firm, would not complain about the transfer, even if it meant being separated from one's friends and family, because they would consider it as a need to support the firm.

Table 14.1 shows scores for several countries of PDI, UAI, IDV, MAS and the three extended dimensions LTO, PRA and IND.

14.2.2 GLOBE Project

The GLOBE (Global Leadership and Organisational Behavior Effectiveness) project is a multi-phase, multi-method project examining the interrelationships between societal culture, organizational culture, leadership, and societal achievements. At the first official GLOBE conference, held in Calgary, Canada in 1994, organizational leadership was defined as: "the ability of an individual to influence, motivate, and enable others to contribute toward the effectiveness and success of the organizations of which they are members" (House et al. 2002, p. 5). The term culture was defined as "shared motives, values, beliefs, identities, and interpretations or meanings of significant events that result from common experiences of members of collectives and are transmitted across age generations" (House 2002, p. 5). More than 170 researchers jointly combined collected information on more than 17,000 managers from 62 countries in industries such as food processing, finance, and telecommunications (House et al. 2002, 2004).

Information on nine cultural and six leadership dimensions were investigated (Javidan and Dastmalchian 2009). Compared to other studies in the field of organizational behaviour, the GLOBE research is particularly closely connected to leadership (House et al. 2002).

Cultural dimensions by the GLOBE project can be regarded as a further development of the Hofstede study dimensions in 1980. House et al. states this as follows: "We have a very adequate dataset to replicate Hofstede's (1980) landmark study and extend that study to test hypotheses relevant to relationships among societal level

Table 14.1 Hofstede's cultural dimensions. (Source: Hofstede: Internet: http://geert-hofstede.com/japan.html, accessed 31 July 2013 and 2 March 2014)

Country	Power distance index (PDI)	Uncertainty avoidance index (UAI)	Individualism (IDV)	Masculinity (MAS)	Long-term-orientation (LTO)	Pragmatism (PRA)	Indulgence (IND)
USA	40	46	91	62	29	26	68
UK	35	35	89	66	25	51	69
Italy	50	75	76	70	–	61	30
Australia	36	51	90	61	31	21	71
Netherlands	38	53	80	14	44	67	68
Canada	39	48	80	52	23	36	68
Switzerland	34	58	68	70	–	74	66
Sweden	31	29	71	5	33	53	78
German	35	65	76	66	31	83	40
France	68	86	71	43	–	63	48
Korean	60	85	18	39	75	100	29
Hong Kong	68	29	25	57	96	61	17
Taiwan	58	69	17	45	87	93	49
China	80	30	20	66	118	87	24
Denmark	18	23	74	16	–	35	70
Singapore	74	8	20	48	48	72	46
Finland	33	59	63	26	–	38	57
Japan	54	92	46	95	80	88	42

variables, organizational practices, and leader attributes and behaviour (2004, preface XXV). Put differently, the Globe project replicated the Hofstede study but with two amendments. First of all, It did not ask employees and managers at one single firm, like Hofstede did by only surveying IBM employees. Instead, only managers were asked at different firms in several industries. Secondly, even thought the dimensions are similar to those seen in the Hofstede study, those found in the GLOBE project differed to some extent from the Hofstede study.

The first six dimensions have their origins in the cultural dimensions of the Hofstede study. The dimension "collectivism I" measures societal emphasis on collectivism. By means of laws, social programs, or institutional practices, low scores reflect individualism, and high scores reflect a collectivistic emphasis. The dimension "Collectivism II" measures in-group collectivism as family or loyalty. This also integrates pride to organizations or to families. Based on Hofstede's masculinity dimension, GLOBE researcher developed two separate dimensions "gender egalitarianism" as well as "assertiveness." Furthermore, the last two dimensions, "performance orientation" and "humane orientation" were also developed based on past models by Hofstede and Bond (1988).

The GLOBE dimensions (House et al. 2004, p. 743) are as follows:

1. Uncertainty avoidance: defined as the extent to which members of an organization or society strive to avoid uncertainty by reliance on social norms, rituals, and bureaucratic practices to alleviate the unpredictability of future events. Japan scores surprisingly low in that dimension with a score of 4.07, even lower than, for example, the Netherlands, which scored 4.81.
2. Power Distance: defined as the degree to which members of an organization or society in general expect and agree that power should be unequally shared. Japan has a score of 5.23, lower than, for example, Germany which scored 5.48 points.
3. Collectivism I: defined as "Societal Collectivism" which reflects the degree to which organizational and societal institutional practices encourage and reward collective distribution of resources and collective actions. Japan receives relatively high scores (5.23). This is in contrast to e.g, Italy, which only scored 3.75.
4. Collectivism II: defined as "In-Group Collectivism" reflects the degree to which individuals express pride, loyalty and cohesiveness in their organizations or in their families. In this category Japan had a score of 4.72, lower than, for example, Italy (4.99).
5. Gender Egalitarianism: defined as the extent to which an organization or a society minimizes gender role differences and gender discrimination. Japan scored a 3.17, lower than, for example, Germany which scored 3.25.
6. Assertiveness: defined as the degree to which individuals in organizations or societies are assertive, confrontational, and aggressive in their social relationships. Japan again, scored rather low (3.69) in comparison to Germany (4.66).
7. Future Orientation: defined as the degree to which individuals in organizations or societies engage in future-oriented behaviours such as planning, investing in the future, and in delaying gratification. In this dimension Japan scores rather high (4.29) in contrast to the USA (4.13).

8. Performance Orientation: defined as the extent to which an organization or society encourages and rewards group members for improvements in performance and excellence. This dimension is based on the Confucian Dynamism dimension by Hofstede and Bond (1988). Here Japan has lower scores (4.22) compared to the USA (4.45).
9. Humane Orientation: defined as the degree to which individuals in organizations or societies encourage and reward individuals for being fair, altruistic, friendly, generous, caring, and kind to their other fellows. This dimension is based on the dimension Heartedness by Hofstede and Bond (1988) and shows high scores for Japan (4.34) in contrast to, for example, the Netherlands (4.02) or Germany (3.30).

14.2.3 Cultural Dimension Research by Trompenaars

Both the Hofstede cultural dimensions and the GLOBE leadership and organizational behavioral studies are widely recognized and accepted in the literature of International Business. Another Dutch researcher, Fons Trompenaars, also did research on, "cultural differences and how they affect the process of doing business and management" (1994, p. 1). Surveys were administered to over 15,000 managers from 28 countries; at least 500 usable responses were collected for each country.

Trompenaars created five relationship orientations that address the way people treat each other. Two additional factors: time and environment were also investigated. This research is similar to both of the aforementioned studies of Hofstede and the GLOBE project. Like the Hofstede study, scores range from 0 to 100. Furthermore, it builds on studies done by the well-known sociologist Talcott Parsons (1951).

Each of the five relationship orientations as well as attitudes toward time and environment will be discussed:

14.2.3.1 Universalism Versus Particularism

Universalism is the belief that ideas and practices can be applied everywhere in the world without modification. Particularism, on the other hand, is the belief that circumstances dictate how certain ideas and practices should be applied. Highly universalistic cultures pay more attention to formal rules than on relationships. For example, people in business believe that "a deal is a deal". Highly particularistic cultures pay more attention to relationships and trust than on formal rules. This leads to the fact that in highly particularistic cultures legal contacts often are modified, and the way in which deals are executed can change according to how well people know each other.

Trompenaars and Hampden-Turner analyze the universalism vs. particularism aspect of culture by presenting respondents with a dilemma and asking them to make a decision. For clarification, here is one of the dilemmas introduced:

"You are riding in a car driven by a close friend. He hits a pedestrian. You know he was going at least 35 miles per hour in an area of the city where the maximum allowed speed is only 20 miles per hour. There are no witnesses. His lawyer says that if you testify under oath that he was driving 20 miles per hour it may save him from serious consequences. What right has your friend to expect you to protect him?

a. My friend has a definite right as a friend to expect me to testify to the lower figure.
b. He has some right as a friend to expect me to testify to the lower figure.
c. He has no right as a friend to expect me to testify to the lower figure".

Japan scores 67 points in this category, which is in the mid-range of scores. Canada received the highest score (96 points) and South Korea scored the lowest (26 points) (Trompenaars 1994, p. 37).

14.2.3.2 Individualism Versus Collectivism

This aspect of culture is similar to the dimension used in Hofstede's study; however, Trompenaars approaches it slightly different. For Trompenaars, individualism refers to people regarding themselves as individuals; while collectivism refers to people regarding themselves as a part of a group. To illustrate how respondents believe in individual decision making, Trompenaars asked the two questions to which respondents can choose one of two answers:

a. The person causing the defect by negligence is the one responsible
b. Due to the fact that he or she happens to work in a team, the responsibility should be carried out by the group.

In this category Japan scores rather low with only 24 points (Trompenaars 1994, p. 57). This means that Japanese prefer decisions and responsibilities to be spread out among members of a group.

Trompenaars recommends that when managers from cultures with high individualism deal with those from collectivistic cultures, time and patience should be taken to consult with each other in order to find a common ground. When dealing with a manager from a collectivistic culture, relationships should be slowly and carefully cultured. On the other hand when dealing with a manager from an individualistic culture, one should be highly prepared and try to be as timely and quickly as possible in terms of decision making.

14.2.3.3 Neutral Versus Affective Cultures

A neutral culture can be described as always having their emotions in check. People in these countries will try not to show their feelings and maintain their composure. On the other hand, an affective culture consists of people who openly express their emotions. Emotional cultures are dominated by people who talk loudly when they are excited and greet each other with a great deal of enthusiasm.

Trompenaars recommends that people from affective cultures doing business in neutral cultures, should realize that a lack of emotion does not necessarily mean disinterest or boredom. Conversely, when people from neutral cultures doing business in affective cultures, Trompenaars recommends that they should respond warmly to the emotional affections of the other group.

Of the 10 investigated countries, Japan scores highest in this category (83 points); while Italy, France and the USA score lowest (Trompenaars 1994, p. 70). For managers doing business in Japan, it is recommended that one should not to overemphasize situations in which Japanese managers do not signal their feelings in public because it may be the case that the managers do not want to lose face.

14.2.3.4 Specific Versus Diffuse Cultures

In a specific culture, the professional life and private life of individuals is sharply separated. People in specific cultures tend to compartmentalize their relationships. This means that one's professional life and private life have no connection with each other. For example, in a specific culture, if a manager were to meet a subordinate for a game of golf, the manager's authority in the workplace would not carry over into the game of golf. In contrast to this, in a diffuse culture, the authority of a manager would carry over into the game of golf. Both dimensions can be described when comparing Japan and Austria. A Japanese Professor would generally be called "sensei" by students and office members in the university. However, when that same professor deals with other professors of a higher status, e.g. elderly and more experienced professors, he or she may only be called "san" (Mr. or Mrs.) or even "kun" (which is used when referring to boy). In contrast to this, an Austrian professor would be called "Herr Professor" no matter who he or she deals with (in case the professor is a man). Austria scores the highest in this category meaning that it is very specific, while Japan scores in the mid-range.

The next dimension Implies status. In this, all societies grant certain people a higher status. However, status can be received by achievement or also by ascription, by means of social connections, age, education, etc.

14.2.3.5 Achievement Versus Ascription

An achievement culture is a culture in which status is based on ones achievements and how well they perform their duties. On the other hand, an ascription culture status is based to some kind of attribute. For example, in an achievement culture, a sales team would recognize someone based on their achievements; while in ascription cultures, status is based on attributes such as age, gender, or social connections.

Trompenaars recommends that managers from achievement cultures doing business in ascription cultures, should not only direct their conversation to the "leaders" of a group in a negotiation but should also be careful to show proper respect to senior member on the other side of the table. Conversely, managers from ascription cultures doing business in achievement cultures, should make sure that their team has sufficient data and knowledge about people in order to convince the other group. A typical achievement culture is the US, again, Japan scores somewhere in the middle with 28 points (Trompenaars 1994, p. 103).

Apart from these five categories, Trompenaars introduced two other categories, time and environment.

14.2.3.6 Time

The time category is divided into two different subcategories: "sequential" and "synchronous." In sequential cultures, people tend to focus on activities one at a time. At the opposite, in synchronous cultures, people tend to do multiple activities at one time. In cultures where people use the synchronous approach there is much more flexibility. For example the US is a sequential culture; therefore, when a schedule is created people try to abide by it.

14.2.3.7 Environment

The environment category of Trompenaars refers to whether or not people believe that they can control their outcomes. This is referred to as the "inner-directed" environment. The opposite is to let things reach their own outcomes naturally. This is referred to as the "outer-directed" environment. To sum things up, managers either believe "they can and should control nature by imposing their will upon it… or they believe that man is part of nature and must go along with its laws, directions, and forces" (Trompenaars 1994, p. 137). In order to study this aspect of a culture, Trompenaars asked managers to choose one of the following statements, which best described their feelings:

1. "It is worthwhile trying to control important natural forces, like the weather".
2. "Nature should take its course, and we just have to accept it the way it comes and do the best we can".

Inner-directed managers, which believe in controlling their own environment, would opt for statement 1; while outer directed managers, would choose statement 2. For example, managers from Brazil and Portugal tended to vote for option 1; they think that the environment should be controlled. In contrast to this, Japanese managers believe that things move in waves and that this "flow has better to be followed." In other words, the Japanese have a flexible attitude, characterized by a willingness to compromise and maintain harmony in the environment. This statement is highlighted by the fact that 90 % of Japanese manager surveyed chose statement 2.

14.3 Conclusion

Culture is an important phenomenon to consider when discussing International Business. National cultures have to be separated from firm specific cultures because firm specific cultures may differ to a high degree even if the firms come from the same country.

Different methods exist to measure national cultural differences. This chapter focused on the three most important methods to measure cultural dimensions. The most widely cited is the Hofstede study; however the GLOBE project and Trompenaars undertook similar studies.

The study by Hofstede shows that Japan has an extremely masculine culture with a high avoidance to uncertainty. Japanese are also rather pragmatic in their behavior, which has a big impact on corporate Japan.

Questions

1. Where does the word culture come from and what does it originally mean?
2. Shortly describe the four original cultural dimensions by Hofstede
3. How does Japan score in the "uncertainty avoidance" dimension?
4. Is Japan a masculine or a feminine country according to the Hofstede study?
5. Can you give an example of how Japan is a highly masculine culture?
6. Describe how Japan scores for Hofstede's pragmatism dimension?
7. The GLOBE dimension of uncertainty avoidance scores are surprisingly lower for Japan than for the Netherlands. Do you have an explanation for this?
8. How does Japan score in the future orientation by the Globe study?
9. What is unique about Trompenaars research approach?
10. How does Japan score on neutral versus affective dimension?

Answers

1. The word culture comes from Latin language (cultura) and relates to worship or to a cult.
2. Power Distance Index (autocratic versus democratic management style), Uncertainty Avoidance Index (tolerance of uncertainty), Individuality (individualism versus collectivism) and Masculinity versus Femininity (degree of masculine assertiveness).
3. Japan scores very high on uncertainty avoidance with 92 points out of 100. It shows that Japanese people do not like uncertain situations and want to avoid them.

4. Japan is a rather masculine country, having the highest score out of all countries with 95 points.
5. An example of the high masculinity of Japanese culture is that hard work in general gets highly appreciated. Many employees work overtime not because they receive external pressure but because they want to give all their energy to the firm, or to a special project.
6. Japan scores high on pragmatism dimension, 88 out of 100. This means that Japanese do not tend to explain everything. People are mainly guided by example, like the Panasonic founder Konozuke Matsushita.
7. It is true that the GLOBE dimensions have a low score for Japan. It depends on the factors which were taken into this measure of uncertainty avoidance. Out of 14 years of Japan experience (personal note by the author), the Hofstede score seems to be the more reliable one.
8. Japan scores higher than the US. However, the difference of both countries at the Hofstede study results is low.
9. Trompenaars research is unique in that the questions are different than the other two studies. The questions are normally contrasting cases and managers have to decide which one to choose.
10. Japan scores high as a neutral culture. That means, open emotions and enthusiasm is hardly seen in Japan. Managers dealing with Japan are advised also not to show too much emotion.

References

Hofstede G (1980) Culture's consequences: international differences in work-related values. Sage Publications, Beverly Hills

Hofstede G (2001) Culture's consequences: comparing values, behaviors, institutions, and organizations across nations, 2nd edn. Sage Publications, Thousand Oaks

Hofstede G, Bond MH (1988) The confucius connection: from cultural roots to economic growth. Organ Dyn 16:4–21

Hofstede G, Hofstede GJ, Minkov M (2010) Cultures and organizations: software of the mind, 3rd edn. McGraw-Hill, New York

Hofstede Centre (2014) http://geert-hofstede.com/japan.html. Accessed 29 March 2014

House RJ, Hanges PJ, Javidan M, Dorfman PW, Gupta V (2004) Cultures, leadership, and organizations. GLOBE project

House R, Javidan M, Hanges P, Dorfman P (2002) Understanding cultures and implicit leadership theories across the globe: an introduction to project GLOBE. J World Bus 37:3–10

Javidan M, Dastmalchian A (2009) Managerial implications of the GLOBE project: a study of 62 societies. Asia Pac J Hum Resour 47:41–58

Joynt P, Warner M (1996) Managing across cultures. Thomson Business Press, London

Luthans F (1995) Organizational behavior, 7th edn. McGraw-Hill, New York, pp 534–535

Parsons T (1951) The social system. Free Press, New York

Robinson PA (2003) The embddedness of Japanese HRM practices: the case of recruiting. Hum Resour Manage Rev 13:439–465

Trompenaars F (1994) Riding the waves of culture: understanding cultural diversity in business. The Economist Press, London

Chapter 15
Expatriates and Other Choices

Abstract This chapter discusses human resource issues and expatriate staffing. Because a purely economic approach to M&A often fails to consider a key element—human resources, the people involved in the process. This chapter will focus on expatriates connected to Japan. It is also important to note that there are alternatives to sending expatriates to a foreign subsidiary; however, many firms still rely on expatriates despite the high costs. These expatriates are especially useful when it comes to communication with foreign-based offices. Because of this, Japanese firms rely more heavily on expatriates than e.g. foreign firms in Japan.

15.1 Introduction

Even if financially or strategically an acquisition is sound, if employees are ignored and not integrated correctly, the acquisition attempt will fail. Aurora et al. (2011, p. 279) states: "In most mergers, the human side is treated very lightly without realizing that such a move could be catastrophic. By focusing on the human aspect, the risk of failure of the proposed M&A can be reduced to a great extent." The new management has to "sell" a vision to all people involved, their regular employees and their non-regular employees consisting of dispatched and part time members. These latter mentioned group of employees may not think or feel the same way treated. Problems occur then especially at cross domestic acquisitions.

A very important question related to international business is; therefore, whether multinational companies (MNC) should send managers from headquarters to their foreign subsidiaries or simply rely on local managers from that subsidiary firm. The act of sending managers from the headquarters to a foreign subsidiary is called expatriation. To what extent the headquarters expatriate or rely on local managers in the host country will be a success factor at the foreign based subsidiary (Belderbos and Heijltjes 2005; Gong 2003; Harzing 1999; Tan and Mahoney 2006; Thompson and Keating 2004).

First, expatriation will be described in more detail. Then, the Agency Theory is discussed in regard to expatriations. After that, other types of assignments besides expatriation will be discussed. Finally, expatriates will be discussed in terms of Japan.

R. Bebenroth, *International Business Mergers and Acquisitions in Japan*,
DOI 10.1007/978-4-431-54989-5_15

15.2 Expatriates

Expatriates are employees sent from the headquarters to local foreign offices. This means that the expatriate is contracted to the headquarters, not to the local offices. Expatriates get appointed by the headquarters to stay abroad for anywhere between 2 and 5 years. Expatriates not only receive a high income but they also receive many high fringe benefits. Depending on the firm, expatriates, on average, cost about 3 times more than a local counterpart. Housing costs are also fully covered by the headquarters, which is why many expatriates tend to live in expensive houses that would not be affordable for locals. There is much discussion surrounding the topic of what expatriates do at foreign based subsidiaries, how they feel about other countries, and whether the costs of having them sent to foreign based offices is justified (Bebenroth et al. 2007). This topic becomes important especially after cross border M&A, when headquarters send expatriates to the new subsidiaries.

15.2.1 Reasons to Send Expatriates

The widely discussed classical framework of reasons for expatriations is based on the model proposed by Edstroem and Galbraith (1977). In their seminal work, they theorize three reasons why a firm sends managers from headquarters to their foreign based affiliates. The first reason is to simply fill positions; the second is to allow their younger managers to develop their management skills; and the third is to foster organizational development. In terms of the first reason, to simply fill positions, it is assumed that there is no local employee available to fill the position; therefore, headquarters sends appropriate skilled managers. This still may be the case when it comes to some developing countries whose employees lack certain technical knowledge; however, this problem is rare when it comes to Japan. Say for instance IT equipment developed by headquarters must be maintained, expatriated engineers would be needed since Japanese engineers may not be familiar with the technology. Also at a newly acquired firm, expatriates would be necessary. In terms of the second case, management development, MNC headquarters expatriate managers in order to help foster that manager's skills, which could be useful to the headquarters in the long run.

Finally, the third reason why a manger may be expatriated to a foreign affiliate is organizational development. Even if there is no pressing need to develop managers, headquarters may still expatriate managers to their foreign subsidiaries in order to help control the organization. This is especially true for startups and acquired firms, where expatriates tend to implement the first strategic moves (Bruning et al. 2011). One major reason to expatriate managers for organizational development is to help headquarters control foreign subsidiaries. One of the reasons to have expatriates for this would be that managers from headquarters may not have enough trust in the local managers; therefore, they decide to expatriate someone form the headquarters. There are advantages of having expatriates. In this vein, expatriates more openly point out problems and challenges facing the firm than local managers. This is especially true for Japan where (Japanese) managers are afraid to lose face, so they try and hide certain issues from those at headquarters.

Recent research argues that most expatriates are assigned for headquarter related reasons (Selmer and Lauring 2011). Expatriates maintain close links to the headquarters. What this means is that an expatriated manager differs from locally contracted even if both managers have the same citizenship status. While locally hired foreigners are familiar with subsidiary employees, expatriates are familiar with the headquarters and connect the top management of headquarters to foreign subsidiaries. Expatriates are able to communicate between the subsidiaries and the headquarters (Bruning et al. 2011).

However, there are also disadvantages reported when having expatriates at foreign subsidiaries. There is some evidence that shows expatriates consider themselves "as [simply] passing through their country of assignment rather than viewing themselves as a part of the local operation's long-term development" (Hechanova et al. 2003, p. 227). The number of expatriates has been declining due to the high costs of expatriating a manager. There is also a high risk that the expatriated managers would switch to another firm after the completion of the assignment

15.2.2 Expatriates from Agency Theory

The existence of expatriates can be discussed in the frame of the agency theory, where different interests exist between principals and agents. This deals with the issue of designing the optimal control mechanism that makes agents behave in the principles' interests (Jensen and Meckling 1976). The Agency Theory goes back to "The Modern Corporation and Private Property" with the seminal work of Berle and Means originally published in the year 1932 (Berle and Means 1967). In this work, the authors argue that the legal owners were less and less in control over the firm they invested their money in. This theory can be discussed at the field of human resource management to cover expatriate management. For example, the management of headquarters (the principal) wants their expatriates (the agents) to act on their behalf. Reasons for this could be to maintain the flow of information back and forth between a headquarters and its subsidiaries or to exercise control. The interest of headquarters may also be to use expatriates to have a closer connection to the subsidiary. However, expatriates may opt to act more independently. Also, because of their (with 2–5 years) rather short term assignments at the subsidiaries, expatriates are normally not willing to invest at the subsidiary. Instead of taking risky investments, expatriates rather want to squezze out profits while at the subsidiary. For this, managers succeeding expatriates are having difficulties to operate foreign subsidiaries successfully (Froese and Bebenroth 2012).

Based on this Agency Theory framework, Gong (2003) theorized and tested the effects of cultural distance from the expatriated parent country to the subsidiary at the workforce level. He found that cultural distance leads to a higher need of expatriates. However, as years of operation increase, the need for expatriates decreases over time (pp. 4–5).

15.3 Ethnocentric to Geocentric Phase

Several theoretical frameworks explain reasons for executive staffing at foreign based MNC subsidiaries. One of the classic frameworks is developed by Perlmutter (1969). He divided headquarter management policies into different behaviors according to the age of the firm. He started with three phases and later added a forth one. Out of simplicity, only the first three will be discussed, the *ethnocentric*, *polycentric*, and *geocentric* behavioral phases. Ethnocentric firms are small firms that have recently been established. In this vein, the management of an ethnocentric firm is handling all operation by themselves. Some of them however, may already have an international appearance, or may even be a foreign-based subsidiary out of a cross domestic acquisition. In that case, the management of the headquarters probably would not trust their foreign-based subsidiaries. In terms of expatriations, ethnocentric headquarters would prefer having managers sent from the headquarters to fill all top-level managerial positions in their foreign-based subsidiaries. In other words, headquarters would rather send expatriates to foreign based subsidiaries than to rely on local managers.

As firms age, their attitudes and behaviors change. According to the Perlmutter theory, firms would change from an ethnocentric to a polycentric behavior. As firms grow and become larger, polycentric firms would be more trustful towards local managers in foreign-based subsidiaries. In terms of human resources, a polycentric headquarters would preferably rely on local (foreign) managers. This means that headquarters would give locals more leeway to act as they see fit. The reason for this is that headquarters understand in order to grow even more it will be necessary to share trust with the partners. Besides an increased trust in relatively unknown business partners, firms also tend to deal more actively with consulting firms.

Again, after some time, according to Perlmutter, a multinational company would adopt a geocentric behavior. This means that the firm becomes a global player and would establish headquarters all over the world. In line with the strategic aim of the firm, the best employees regardless of nationality would be selected. There would no longer be a preference to hire local employees simply to reduce cost. Instead, the most appropriate manager would be sent to any given place regardless of one's citizenship or country of origin.

15.4 Alternatives to Expatriates

When discussing staffing decisions on the executive level in foreign subsidiaries, current HRM literature generally covers the distinction between expatriates versus locals. That means, a firm either expatriates or relies on locals in the foreign country (Harzing 1999; Belderbos and Heijltjes 2005; Thompson and Keating 2004). For example, if a German subsidiary operates in Japan, the German firm would have to choose whether to utilize German or Japanese managers. The view taken so far; however, has been overly simplistic because the situations facing firms these days is much more varied. The "expatriate versus local" discussion disregards several critical factors in making staffing decisions (Bebenroth and Pascha 2011). There are several other alternatives to the previously mentioned strategies.

It is also important to note that choosing the nationality of a manager may only be of ceremonial value. In reality, executive functions are shared by a team of managers with specialized competences and skill sets (Bebenroth and Pascha 2011). Furthermore; breakthroughs in telecommunication technology has made it possible for firms to cut back on transportation costs and on sending managers to other areas. Through methods such as telephone conferences, managers from headquarters are able to have a "virtual" presence in foreign subsidiaries.

Also, it is widely noted that Japan has recently opened up to foreign direct investment inflows much more than in the past, which includes structural changes in its labor market. This makes it easier for foreign companies to employ promising Japanese personnel of both genders and even managers in mid-career. A foreign firm is especially attractive to career driven Japanese women. Groznaya reports in her empirical study that English language skills is the main reason for Japanese women to work at foreign firms in Japan (2011). Additionally, Japanese women find better career opportunities at foreign firms and receive a higher payment for their performance.

Moreover, it is frequently argued that language has become less of a barrier in recent years, and cultural differences in general may have become less pronounced. This suggests the need for a fresh look at executive choices for foreign subsidiaries in the Japanese context. Three major options to executive staffing decisions will be discussed:

15.4.1 Locally Contracted Non-Japanese Managers

Locally contracted non-Japanese managers do not fit the classical distinction between host country nationals and parent country nationals (expatriates). Also, these managers seem to be available on the secondary labor market locally as well. Local contracted are likely to have different behaviorisms and attitudes towards the host country and the headquarters than expatriates. Locally hired foreigners, also known as self-initiated expatriates, (Peltokorpi and Froese 2009) may outperform expatriates in effective communication with locals in their offices. It is important to consider that local Japanese managers are less costly than expatriated ones. However, higher performance levels of expatriated managers could outweigh the higher costs associated with their position (Bebenroth and Pascha 2011). This is true despite the high failure rate of expatriates, defined as either premature return from assignment or as underperformance while on the assignment (Welch 2003). In this vein, local foreigners may better understand local employees than expatriates. However, locally contracted foreigners also face some challenges such as the so-called "glass ceiling". Expatriates receive much more favorable economic conditions and a higher status, but are often unable to contribute successfully to the local Japanese office. In many cases, locally contracted foreigners assist expatriates by relaying messages between headquarters and local Japanese managers. In the end, there are instances when locally hired get blamed by expatriates or by other local managers if projects do not meet expectations. Furthermore, a locally contracted may feel only partly committed to the local office, or to the headquarters. This means, that the headquarters may feel insecure about employing locally contracted managers because of their lower assumed commitment to the headquarters (Fayol-Song 2011).

15.4.2 Third-Country Nationals (TCN)

There may also be third-country nationals (TCNs) available to foreign based subsidiaries. This means that the manager is neither from the host country nor from the home country of the headquarters. The characteristics of such executives may differ from parent-country national executives and locally hired foreigners. The communication with headquarters should be less intensive for a third country national than that of an expatriated manager to a Japanese subsidiary. The presence of such individuals is not surprising considering the business environment of today's globalized business world.

15.4.3 Frequent Fliers

Frequent fliers are managers that frequently fly back and forth between headquarters and foreign-based subsidiaries. What makes them frequent fliers is the fact that they visit each subsidiary only for a short period of time. This is the most flexible way for firms to send managers to foreign-based subsidiaries. These managers either directly come from the headquarters, or they may visit several offices e.g. in Asia before they arrive to Japan. Some firms send their expatriates to several different Asian headquarters in order to establish their frequent fliers on the Asian market. For headquarters this can be beneficial because managers are "mentally" closer to several (often critical) Asian markets. Furthermore, expertise of frequent fliers can always be used at any given time. It is not necessary to wait for returnees (like in a case of expatriates to use their knowledge back at the headquarters). However, frequent fliers never stay longer at one single place; therefore, their knowledge about a foreign-based subsidiaries remains low compared to that of expatriated returnees.

15.5 Japan Connection

15.5.1 Japanese Expatriates Abroad

Japanese firms are well known for sending a relatively high number of headquarters based employees to foreign-based subsidiaries whether overtaken or established as a greenfield. The reason for this is that many decisions at Japanese foreign-based subsidiaries are made in Japanese. Even at foreign-based subsidiaries, it is vital for managers to speak the Japanese language. One of the downsides of this development is that local (non-Japanese) managers often face a "glass ceiling" when compared to expatriates (Japanese) coming from headquarters who implement decisions that have been prepared in Japan. Besides career issues of non-Japanese managers, simple decision making is a major challenge for many Japanese firms, which makes it difficult for Japanese subsidiaries abroad to find capable (local) managers. Exacerbating these issues is the fact that for many years the cost of living abroad was quite low compared to the cost of living in Japan. It was inexpensive to send Japanese managers abroad. Last but not least, communication between headquarters in Japan and Japanese subsidiaries in other countries is very intensive. The reason for this is that most Japanese headquarters rather make decisions by themselves concerning foreign-based businesses. In recent years, MNCs in all over the world realize that the increase of turnover is normally not at their home markets but abroad—in Emerging Market countries. In that, many MNCs have shifted power from the headquarters to the local offices. Researcher call this nowadays not anymore "multinational enterprises" (MNEs) but "globally integrated enterprises" (GIEs) with the advantage that managers at local offices receive more power and can help the whole group to reach their full potential. Japanese managers, however, are still rather traditional in their behavior and prefer to take all major decisions by themselves at their headquarters. Therefore, Japanese headquarters have a higher communication level to their foreign subsidiaries. This higher communication level is satisfied by transferring expatriates to subsidiaries. In other words, expatriates are appreciated to a higher extent at Japanese firms operating abroad than at headquarters in other countries.

15.5.2 Expatriates in Japan

In Japan there are about 3086 foreign affiliated firms represented (Chap. 3). However, the amount of expatriation differs based on the subsidiaries home country. For example, US-firms own around 40 % of all foreign affiliated investments in Japan. In other words, almost half of all investments in Japan comes from US affiliated firms. However, US firms hardly expatriate managers to their Japanese affiliates. Only 25 % of board members of US affiliated firms are from the US. Hofstede (Chap. 14) explains this fact that American culture has a relatively low avoidance of uncertainty. Therefore, managers at US firms tend to invest in Japan without being physically present or by sending managers from headquarters to the affiliate. Many US firms control their foreign affiliates by checking their quarterly figures.

In contrast to US firms, Asian firms own very few investments in Japan; however in recent years investment from Asian firms has been increasing. When an Asian firm invests into a Japanese firm, they will staff almost their entire management with headquarter send expatriates at the Japan based affiliate. A recent study by Bebenroth and Li shows that about 80 % of the mangers of Asian owned affiliates in Japan come from their headquarters (2010). European firms are indifferent about expatriating their managers. On average, European affiliated firms in Japan have about 40–50 % of their managers expatriated to their Japan based subsidiaries (Bebenroth and Li 2010).

There are high fringe benefits involved when being expatriated to Japan. For example, expatriates receive double salary when being sent to Japan. In fact, many foreign firms own houses (for their expatriates) in rather expensive areas in Japan. Many Kansai based expatriates live in luxury mansions in Ashiya while many Kanto based expatriates life in the prestigious location of Denenchofu.

Expatriates to Japan are normally able to save a high amount of money while in Japan due to the high salaries that they receive. Furthermore, if the expatriated has children, school fees are also covered by the firm. Some foreign firms in Japan even pay their expatriated for cars and cover a business class flight back home once a year—including their families. These are all very attractive benefits and incentives for expatiates in Japan.

Despite the luxurious life that many expatriates live, there are also some challenges reported. A leading manager of a pharmaceutical firm once stated that: "if you stay longer than 10 years in Japan doing business, you are not any more usable out there in the world." The reason for this is that the Japanese style of doing business is very different to that of other countries, especially compared to the style of doing business in the USA. In Japan, for example, decisions take unusually long time to be made. Before something is brought up in a meeting, the content has to be discussed personally with every member beforehand. This practice is called "nemawashi" in Japanese. This takes a lot of time and effort and is simply something that expatriated managers are not experienced with. Often time expatriated manner simply don't follow rules, which tends to result in tension between Japanese and expatriated managers.

Young managers who wish to climb the ranks in their home country headquarters, may also be unwilling to leave headquarters for such a long time. If expatriates stay out of their headquarter office for too many years, they will probably face many problems when trying to reintegrate to the headquarters. For example, in order to have a career at a European firm, managers need experience in dealing with the European region. Japan, is geographically far away (e.g. from European headquarters) and due to other booming economies in Asia, less attractive for expatriates. If young European or US managers want to leave for Asia, they are more willing to take assignments at subsidiaries in other Asian countries. In terms of Asia the emerging countries are very attractive. The reason for this is that many headquarters have fixed measures and definitions for performances. The performance of expatriates will also be measured using these definitions. One measure of performance is regularly the increase of turnover compared to a previous period. Subsidiaries in emergent market countries often grow by about 5–10 %; however, for a subsidiary in Japan, simply maintaining the same turnover from the past is already difficult to accomplish. This is due to the fact that competition is much fiercer than in other Asian Emerging Market countries. Therefore, why should a young and promising expatriate endanger his/her career by going to Japan and coming back with an unfavorable performance record? Furthermore, the cost for labor is much higher in Japan than in other Asian countries.

Despite all of these problems, some managers may want to stay in further contact with Japan so they can become a valuable liaison to Japan. In this case, expatriation to Japan could be a worthwhile investment, because a young manager may be able to become the person responsible for the Japan based office after return from expatriation assignment.

15.6 Conclusion

This chapter discussed the "human side" of M&A and specifically explored the case of expatriates and other ways a foreign firm can send employees to a foreign-based entity. It was shown that firms do have other choices than expatriations when it comes to staffing foreign subsidiaries. Despite the high costs associated with expatriates, many firms still continue to send them abroad. Japanese firms, tend to rely on expatriates more than headquarters at other countries. Also as expatriates to Japan are costly, foreign firms with a presence in Japan find recently other ways to staff their subsidiaries.

Questions Expatriates

1. What does it mean to be expatriated?
2. What are the differences between expatriated and locally hired foreigners?
3. What other types of non-local managers exist besides expatriates?
4. Apply the Perlmutter Theory to expatriates.
5. How do ethnocentric and geocentric strategies differ in regard to expatriates?

Answers

1. To get expatriated means to get sent to a foreign based office for normally 2–5 years. This stay will be financially attractive for the time being. Problems for expatriates arise when they return to headquarters. Because in the meantime other managers may move up in rank while expatriates may not because they stayed abroad for too long, "out of the race for the top" at the headquarters.
2. A locally hired foreigner (in the case for Japan) would be contracted to the Japanese local office (at a Japan based foreign affiliate). That means, the income conditions are normally much lower and there would be hardly any fringe benefits. A locally hired manager may; furthermore, find him or herself in a difficult situation when headquarters send managers come in to the office and lack understanding of how things are done in Japan. The locally hired would be in a sandwich position to serve the "customer from abroad" and his/her office at Japan

3. Locally hired foreigners, for example, an American citizen already living in Japan is hired at a Japan based US firm. Frequent fliers, managers who come in to the foreign based firm just for some days. They normally check the firm and deliver strategic content.
4. Perlmutter, researched about behavior of firms as they age. In the early stages, the managers would be ethnocentric, they want to do everything by themselves. After a while the firm ages and becomes polycentric. Managers would then prefer to outsource activities. The management would rely on locally hired people rather than send their expatriates from the headquarters any more. In the last stage, the firm is a global player. In that situation, a firm would try to recruit the best person available, no matter whether it is an expatriate, a local hired or even a third country national.
5. In the ethnocentric strategy, headquarters would send expatriates because they do not trust locals. In the geocentric stage, the best person would be taken to the subsidiaries no matter where they come from, from the host country, the parent country or even from a third country.

References

Aurora RS, Shetty K, Kalre SR (2011) Mergers and acquisitions. Oxford University Press, Oxford

Bebenroth R, Li D (2010) Expatriation and performance. In: Bebenroth R, Kanai T (eds) Challenges of human resource management in Japan. Routledge, London, pp 61–78

Bebenroth R, Pascha W (2011) Agency concerns and resource endowment issues of strategic management staffing decisions among German subsidiaries in Japan. In: IHRM in foreign subsidiaries in Japan. Z fuer Betriebswirtschaft (ZfB), special issue, (3):5–25

Bebenroth R, Pascha W, Schuermann M (2007) Expatriate versus local? Vor- und Nachteile von Expatriates in japanischen Tochtergesellschaften deutscher Unternehmen. Monograph, at DIHK, April

Belderbos RA, Heijltjes MG (2005) The determinants of expatriate staffing by Japanese multinationals in Asia: control, learning and vertical business groups. J Int Bus Stud 36:341–354

Berle AA, Means GC (1967) The modern corporation and private property, 2nd edn. Harcourt, Brace and World, New York

Bruning NS, Bebenroth R, Pascha W (2011) Valuing Japan-based German expatriate and local manager's functions: do subsidiary age and managerial perspectives matter? Int J Hum Resour Manage 22(4):778–806

Edstroem A, Galbraith JR (1977) Transfer of managers as a co-ordination and control strategy in multinational organizations. Adm Sci Q 22:248–263

Fayol-Song L (2011) Reasons behind management localization in MNCs in China. Asia Pac Bus Rev 17(4):455–471

Froese FJ, Bebenroth R (2012) Performance outcome of leadership succession at foreign subsidiaries in Japan. Does nationality matter? RIEB Discussion paper

Gong Y (2003) Subsidiary staffing in multinational enterprises: agency, resources, and performance. Acad Manage J 46:728–739

Groynaya E (2011) Foreign on national? What factors influence the choice of foreign companies by female employees in Japan? In: Bebenroth R, Pascha W (eds) IHRM in foreign subsidiaries in Japan. Z fuerBetriebswirtschaft (ZfB), special issue, (3):117–131

Harzing AW (1999) Managing the multinationals: an international study of control mechanisms. Edward Elgar, Cheltenham

Hechanova R, Beehr TA, Christiansen ND (2003) Antecedents and consequences of employees' adjustment to overseas assignment: a meta-analytic review. Appl Psychol Int Rev 52(2):213–236

Jensen MC, Meckling WH (1976) Theory of the firm: managerial behavior, agency costs and capital structure. J Financial Econ 3:305–360

Peltokorpi V, Froese FJ (2009) Organizational expatriates and self-initiated expatriates: who adjusts better to work and life in Japan? Int J Hum Resour Manage 20:1096–112

Perlmutter H (1969) HYPERLINK "http://cryobio.u-strasbg.fr/depotcel/DepotCel/274/Noel%20 Alain/4-Perlmutter.pdf" the tortuous evolution of the multinational corporation. Columbia World J Bus 9–18

Selmer J, Lauring J (2011) Expatriate academics: job factors and work outcomes. Int J Manpow 32(2):194–210

Tan D, Mahoney JT (2006) Why a multinational firm chooses expatriates: integrating resource-based, agency and transaction cost perspectives. J Manage Stud 43:457–484

Thompson K, Keating M (2004) An empirical study of executive nationality staffing practices in foreign-owned MNC subsidiaries in Ireland. Thunderbird Int Bus Rev 46(6):771–797

Welch DE (2003) Globalisation of staff movements: beyond cultural adjustments. Manage Int Rev 43:149–169

Index

R. Bebenroth, *International Business Mergers and Acquisitions in Japan*, DOI 10.1007/978-4-431-54989-5